Learn GameSalad for iOS: Game Development for iPhone, iPad, and HTML5

David Guerineau

Apress®

Learn GameSalad for iOS: Game Development for iPhone, iPad, and HTML5

Copyright © 2012 by David Guerineau

ISBN-13 (pbk): 978-1-4302-4356-4

ISBN-13 (electronic): 978-1-4302-4357-1

President and Publisher: Paul Manning
Lead Editor: Michelle Lowman and Douglas Pundick
Technical Reviewer: Henry Abrams
Editorial Board: Steve Anglin, Ewan Buckingham, Gary Cornell, Louise Corrigan, Morgan Ertel, Jonathan Gennick, Jonathan Hassell, Robert Hutchinson, Michelle Lowman, James Markham, Matthew Moodie, Jeff Olson, Jeffrey Pepper, Douglas Pundick, Ben Renow-Clarke, Dominic Shakeshaft, Gwenan Spearing, Matt Wade, Tom Welsh
Coordinating Editor: Anita Castro
Copy Editor: Mary Behr
Compositor: Bytheway Publishing Services
Indexer: SPi Global
Artist: SPi Global
Cover Designer: Anna Ishchenko

Distributed to the book trade worldwide by Springer Science+Business Media New York, 233 Spring Street, 6th Floor, New York, NY 10013. Phone 1-800-SPRINGER, fax (201) 348-4505, e-mail orders-ny@springer-sbm.com, or visit www.springeronline.com.

For information on translations, please e-mail rights@apress.com, or visit www.apress.com.

Apress and friends of ED books may be purchased in bulk for academic, corporate, or promotional use. eBook versions and licenses are also available for most titles. For more information, reference our Special Bulk Sales–eBook Licensing web page at www.apress.com/bulk-sales.

Any source code or other supplementary materials referenced by the author in this text is available to readers at www.apress.com. For detailed information about how to locate your book's source code, go to www.apress.com/source-code.

To Raphaelle, Chloe, and Noah.
–David Guerineau

Contents at a Glance

Contents

About the Author

**David Guerineau is a** hobbyist in development. This is his first book. He has a master's degree in engineering from the French National Institute of Telecommunications and a master's degree in finance and strategy from the Conservatoire National des Arts et Metiers. He is a Managing Director Asia Pacific for a telecom company based in Singapore. Although working in the field of computer science, his professional activity is in infrastructure. He worked with JavaScript, C, C++, and Visual Basic for 15 years. Then came the iPhone and all the revolutions around it, so he became interested in the iOS SDK and Objective-C (the Apple development language), finding it fairly easy coming from C; the complexity is in the incredible number of APIs in the iOS SDK. While looking for tools to simplify the development, he came across GameSalad and was immediately attracted to the concept: you focus on the game and its logic, and you design it in the interface without programming.

Guerineau is a 35 year old, a French-speaking native who has been living in Singapore for the last six years. He is married to the most fantastic woman on Earth and has two amazing kids that make life joyful every day.

About the Technical Reviewer

 **Henry Abrams** is one of the most experienced and knowledgeable GameSalad programmers. His apps have been seen on over 70 major web sites and have had thousands of downloads. He has also developed complete games for various clients. Before using GameSalad, Henry used Corona, Torque 2D, Unity, Xcode, and StencylWorks.

Acknowledgments

I would like to thank my wife, Raphaelle, and my two kids, Chloe and Noah, for their continued support and love during this incredible adventure.

I would also like to thank Michelle, Anita, Henry, Douglas, and the whole Apress family for their precious advice and patience.

–David Guerineau

Introduction

In 2007, Apple revolutionized our way of living by introducing the iPhone, but most important was the birth of iOS. Today, iOS is used in the iPhone, iPad, and iPod Touch. Via the App Store, a new business model has emerged that offers more than 500,000 applications and games, resulting in 25 billion downloads. This new business model is a huge opportunity for game entrepreneurs and hobbyists as there are more than 100,000 games in the App Store.

GameSalad is on a mission to help you to be an active actor in this revolution. GameSalad is a powerful, graphical 2D-game development engine for iOS. According to GameSalad, more than 3% of the games in the App Store are created with the GameSalad Creator, its development tool. The Creator has been downloaded more than 150,000 times since 2009.

The power of GameSalad comes from the fact that no programing knowledge is required. You read correctly: NO PROGRAMING at all! You focus on your game logic, and via an intuitive WYSIWYG interface you design your games with a few drag and drop actions. Forget the long learning curve of object-oriented programing (OOP) and Objective-C; this is no longer required with GameSalad.

However, this power does not come without a few constrains. For instance, you can only develop 2D games. Also, you are limited to a specified set of features—important ones but not complete compared to the iOS SDK. Don't worry—these constrains still leave you with an infinite number of games to create!

GameSalad comes in two versions: free and pro. The free version is obviously free of charge, whereas the pro version costs 299USD per year. I cover the differences between these two versions in Chapter 1.

The book is divided in three parts. Part 1 provides you with the fundamental skillset for GameSalad. Chapter 1 offers step-by-step tutorials for installing all the required tools on your computer to get you started with GameSalad. In Chapters 2 and 3, you design a fully functioning and classic game, Pong, and you get familiar with scenes, actors, attributes, and behaviors. You then create a new version of Arkanoid in Chapter 4, consolidating your skills and using the accelerometer for the first time. Chapter 5 concludes the first part of the book as you remake Space Invader and add new tools to your arsenal.

Part 2 spices things up with more complex features and projects in GameSalad. In Chapters 6 and 7, you create a fully functioning Angry Birds-like game, learning the required physics and creating a very advanced menu system. In Chapter 8, you add music and sounds to your project and implement a very powerful visual effect with a labyrinth game.

Part 3 completes the journey by bringing your game to the Apple Store. In Chapter 9, you finish the Arkanoid-like project started in Chapter 4 by polishing it in Game Center and adding features. Chapter 10 illustrates some non-game apps with GameSalad. You also learn about the device clock features. In Chapter 11, you publish your game on the App Store via a very detailed step-by-step tutorial. Chapter 12 offers a brief introduction to game promotion in Chapter 12. You learn the main tactics to get your game visibility so that it can potentially be the next big hitter!

Part 1

Learning the GameSalad Fundamentals

Preparing Your Design Environment

The work environment is a very important aspect for any game designer. Not only will you gain efficiency with a proper environment, but you will also gain pleasure. Imagine that you're about to finish your game and you want to test it immediately on your device, but then you realize that you haven't yet installed the testing environment. Although it may take only a few moments, isn't it frustrating? If this story resonates for you, take the proper time to follow the steps discussed in this chapter.

Before you start messing around with GameSalad, you need to prepare the design environment. This chapter will guide you in setting up the required tools.

GameSalad Requirements

These are the minimum hardware and software requirements for developing iOS games with GameSalad:

- Intel-based Mac computer with 1GB RAM
- Mac OS X 10.6 (Snow Leopard) or higher
- AniOS device (ideally a device per targeted platform)
- Xcode 4.2 or higher
- GameSalad Creator 0.9.91 or higher
- GameSalad Viewer 0.9.91 or higher

Although any Intel-based Mac running Snow Leopard will suffice, I strongly recommend that you to get a machine with a screen of 15"or larger and 2GB RAM. This will ease your life as the compiling time will get much shorter.

In this chapter, I will guide you in the following aspects:

- Registering in GameSalad
- Registering for the iOS Developer Program
- Installing Xcode
- Installing GameSalad Creator
- Installing GameSalad Viewer

Registering to GameSalad

To use GameSalad, you don't actually need to be registered on GameSalad.com but I strongly recommend doing it for several reasons. First, this will get you known by GameSalad as a user. As GameSalad is a very young startup company, it is important for them to know their developer community. The more users, the more attractive the platform. Second, this will allow you to post messages or questions on the forum. When you need support, being able to tap the community is an invaluable resource. Third, you'll be eligible for the standard technical support from GameSalad. Fourth, you need it to publish your games. It is not mandatory to register as a Promember to publish games and to reproduce most of the examples of this book, but to access Promember features, you must have a valid Pro account (299 US$ per year). I will cover some of the Promember features in Chapter 9. You may decide to register later when you feel more proficient.

To register, open your favorite web browser and go to http://gamesalad.com/download/getCreator.

You will need to:

- Provide a valid e-mail address.
- Choose a username.
- Select a password.
- Agree to the Terms of Use and Privacy Policy.

Figure 1-1 shows the very light registration form.

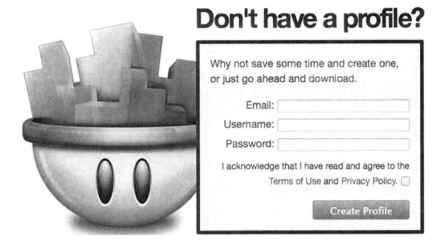

Figure 1-1. *GameSalad registration form*

You can review the Terms and Conditions at `http://gamesalad.com/terms`. You can review the Privacy Policy at `http://gamesalad.com/privacy`.

After filling the required information, you will be directed to the GameSalad Creator download and installation instruction page.

If you don't want to register yet, you can go directly to the download page at `http://gamesalad.com/download/latestCreator`.

You can continue to read this chapter while the file is downloading. I will provide installation instructions later in this chapter.

About GameSalad Pro

Going Pro has several advantages, especially if you intend to get a serious business out of game development.

A Pro account will enable you to publish on iOS without the GameSaladsplashscreen (put yours instead!), to put external links into your application (implement a "purchase full version" link in a lite version), to access GameCenter and iADs capabilities, to enable In-App Purchase and Kiip monetization, and to access priority technical support.

Also, although out of the scope of this book, a Pro membership will enable you to publish on the Android platform. Your potential market just widened instantly.

Figure 1-2 summarizes the features of a Promembership.

Features	Basic (Free!)	Pro ($299/year)
GameSalad Creator	✔	✔
GameSalad Viewer*	✔	✔
Web Publishing	✔	✔
Mac Publishing	✔	✔
iOS Publishing*	✔	✔
Custom Splash Screens	✔	✔
Android Publishing		✔
Twitter TweetSheet		✔
Game Center		✔
iOS In-App Purchase		✔
External Links		✔
iAds		✔
Innovative Monetization		✔
Standard Technical Support	✔	✔
Priority Technical Support		✔

* Requires iOS Developer Account for iOS

Figure 1-2. *Pro membership features*

Registering in the Pro program is very easy. Log into the GameSalad website with your free membership account. If you have skipped the registration part of this chapter, it is never to late to go back and register now. Then you need to go to http://gamesalad.com/membership/join. You will have to provide your password again. You can pay via via PayPal or Amazon.

Registering in the iOS Developer Program

If you are already registered in a paid version of the iOS Developer Program, you can skip this section and go directly to installing Xcode.

You don't need to be registered in any iOS Developer Program to use GameSalad, but this will become mandatory as soon as you want to publish apps in the Apps Store or access some of the GameCenter and iADs features. It is also a must in order to install GameSaladiOS Viewer on your devices and to test ad-hoc versions of your games.

In addition, the iOS Developer Program is very affordable. It costs only $99 US per year for individual access and you get access to thousands of tutorials and videos, registration access to WWDC, previews of future iOS releases, and publishing rights on the App Store.

Moreover, registeringin the Developer Program is mandatory in order to install any iOS application on an iOS device. To install the GameSalad Viewer, you need to install directly from Xcode to your iOS devices. This is called an ad-hoc installation. The Developer Program enables you to do that with up to 100 devices.

So let's get started. Open your web browser and go to http://developer.apple.com/programs/ios/.

Then click the Enroll now button.

Click the Continue button.

Select an option depending on your situation, as per Figure 1-3.

If you are a new Apple Developer,

   a) and you don't have an Apple ID yet (or you wish to create a specific one for development), then you need to select:

   I need to create a new account and Apple ID for an Apple Developer Program.

   b) and you have an Apple ID, then you need to select:

   I have an Apple ID I would like to use for my enrollment in an Apple Developer Program.

> **NOTE:** An Apple ID is your account that you may already use to purchase on iTunes, register Apple products, or access the Mac application store.

If you are an existing Apple Developer,

   a) but not registered in a Paid Program (iOS or Mac), then you need to select:

   I'm registered as a developer with Apple and would like to enroll in a paid Apple Developer Program.

b) and you are registered in a Paid Program, but you would like to add another subscription, then select:

I'm currently enrolled in iOS Developer Program or Mac Developer Program and want to add an additional program to my existing account.

The latter would be the case if you are registered on the Mac Developer program and would like to add the iOS Developer Program or if you are registered as an individual in the iOS Developer Program and would like to upgrade as an company registration.

Are you new or a registered Apple developer?

New Apple Developer

○ I need to create a new account and Apple ID for an Apple Developer Program.

○ I have an Apple ID I would like to use for my enrollment in an Apple Developer Program.

Existing Apple Developer

○ I'm registered as a developer with Apple and would like to enroll in a paid Apple Developer Program.

○ I'm currently enrolled in iOS Developer Program or Mac Developer Program and want to add an additional program to my existing account.

Note: If you intend to enroll in a paid Developer Program for business purposes, you may prefer to create a new Apple ID that is dedicated to your business transactions and used for accounting purposes with Apple. If your Apple ID is associated with an existing iTunes Connect account, please create a new Apple ID to avoid accounting and reporting issues.

Figure 1-3. *New or registered Apple developer page*

For the purpose of this book, I will show you the steps for the creation of a new Apple ID for the enrollment into the iOS Developer Program.

The next step is to choose between Individual and Company subscriptions. I strongly recommend you choose an Individual subscription. However, if you are a company, you should sign up as one. With an Individual subscription, the process is very quick and simple. You will be up and running in less than a day. A Company subscription requires that you send in many legal documents like company registration, proof that you are authorized to register the company, etc. to Apple, and the verification process takes several days.

Let's go with Individual, as shown in Figure 1-4.

Are you enrolling as an individual or company?

Individual
Enroll as an individual if you are a sole proprietor or if you develop under your own name.

Individual Development Only
You are the only one allowed access to Program resources.

App Store Distribution
Your name will appear as the "seller" for apps you distribute on the App Store.
View example

To enroll as an Individual you will need:

- Credit Card Billing information for identity verification.

- A valid credit card for purchase and identity verification. We may also require additional personal documentation to verify your identity.

Company
Enroll as a company if you are a company, government entity, or university.

Development Team
You can add additional developers to your team who can access Program resources.

App Store Distribution
Your company name will appear as the "seller" for apps you distribute on the App Store.
View example

To enroll on behalf of a Company you will need:

- A registered legal entity name.
  We do not accept DBAs, Fictitious Business or Trade names at this time.

- An address for the company's principle place of business or corporate headquarters.

- Legal authority to bind your company/organization to Apple Developer Program legal agreements and contracts.

- A valid credit card for purchase.
  We may also require additional business documentation to verify your identity.

Figure 1-4. *Individual or Company subscription*

The next step is to create an Apple ID. Use Table 1-1 to prepare the information you need to provide on the Apple Developer Program registration form.

Table 1-1. *List of Required Information*

Email address	
Password	
Birthday and birth month	
Security Question	
Answer to the security question	
First Name	
Last Name	

Company	
Country	
Address	
City	
State	
Postal Code	
Phone Number	

Next, you need to provide little additional information on your intended activities as an Apple developer. Apple wants to know on which platforms you develop: iOS, Mac OS X, or Safari.

This is not overyet; Apple is indeed very curious about your intentions. You need to select your primary target market as per the choices in Table 1-2.

Table 1-2. *Primary Target Market*

Business	Medical	Reference	Education
Music	Social Networking	Entertainment	Navigation
Sports	Finance	News	Travel
Games	Photography	Utilities	Health & Fitness
Productivity	Weather	Lifestyle	

Then Apple requests the area of application you intend to develop, offering the same choices as per Table 1-2 (but you can choose more than one).

You must then indicate the primary category for your applications.

- Free Applications
- Commercial Applications
- Enterprise (In-house) Applications
- Web Applications

You must also provide information about your developer experience in years and development experience on other platforms (Figure 1-5).

How many years have you been developing on Apple platforms?

○ New to Apple platforms

○ < 1 year

○ 1 to 3 years

○ 3 to 5 years

◉ 5+ years

Do you develop on other mobile platforms?

◉ Yes

○ No

Which other mobile platforms do you develop on? Select all that apply.

☐ Android   ☐ BREW

☐ Symbian   ☐ BlackBerry

☐ Palm   ☐ Windows Mobile

☐ Other

Figure 1-5. *Developer experience questions*

As you just experienced, Apple likes to know a lot about their developer community.

The next page requires you to agree with the Registered Apple Developer Agreement. You can see the agreement (valid at the time of the writing) as a PDF file at the following address:

http://developer.apple.com/programs/terms/registered_apple_developer_201
00301.pdf

Read the agreement and agree to it by checking the box at the bottom of the page. The next step is to enter the verification code that was just sent to the e-mail address you previously provided, as shown in Figure 1-6.

Enter the verification code sent to your email

Figure 1-6. *Verification code page*

Once the verification code is entered, you will be directed to the billing information page. You will need to enter the exact information on your credit card.

Select the iOS Developer Program at $99 USD (or 128 SGD, if you live in Singapore, as I do).

Figure 1-7. *iOS Developer Program fee*

You have the opportunity to review your enrollment information one last time before submitting. Carefully review the information.

Next, accept the iOS Developer Program License Agreement (so many agreements to read). You can access the agreement (as of the October, 2011) at the following address:

`http://developer.apple.com/programs/terms/ios/standard/ios_program_stand ard_agreement_20111004.pdf`

Confirm your acceptance by checking the Agreement box at the bottom of the page and clicking "I Agree."

You're almost finished! This is the last mile. You must add the iOS Developer Program to the cart, as per Figure 1-8.

Figure1-8. *Adding the iOS Developer Program to the cart*

Checkout of the store and make the actual payment. This part I'll leave it to you and your credit card. Make sure that the name on the credit card is the same name that was used to create the developer account. If you have selected company registration, you will need to fax many legal papers to Apple.

The final step is the activation of your account. It could take from a few minutes to a few days. Once this is complete, Apple will send you an e-mail informing you that your iOS Developer Program account is ready.

These steps are summarized in Figure 1-9.

Figure 1-9. *iOS registration workflow*

Installing Xcode

Xcode is the development environment from Apple. The installation of Xcode is fairly simple and can be done in a few steps.

1. Installing Xcode requires you to go to the Mac Application Store.

2. Type "Xcode" in the search area of the App Store application. Figure 1-10 shows the Xcode page.

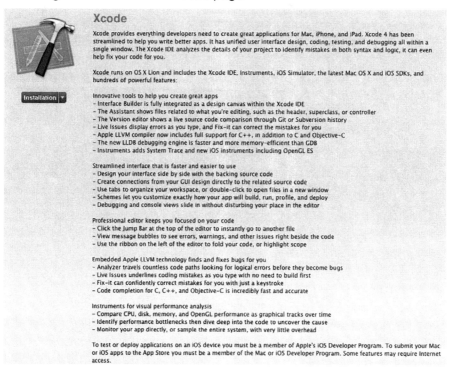

Figure 1-10. *Xcode App Store page*

3. Click the button below the Xcode icon. This will start the download of the Xcode installation file.

This may take a little bit of time, as the file is 1.68GB. Be patient.

4. Once the download is completed, open `Install Xcode.app`, as shown in Figure 1-11. It's located in the Application folder. This will start the installation process. You must quit all other applications before starting the installation of Xcode.

Install Xcode

Figure 1-11. *Install Xcode icon*

5. Confirm that you want to install Xcode by clicking the Install button, as per Figure 1-12.

Figure 1-12.Xcode Installer page

6. Read and accept the Xcode License Agreements as per Figure 1-13.

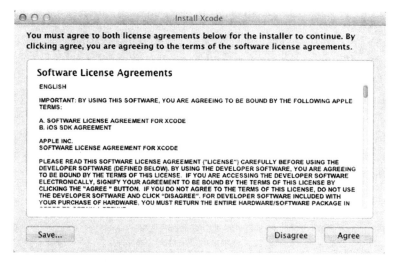

Figure 1-13. *Xcode License Agreements*

Once you agree on the Agreements, the Xcode installation process will start, as per Figure 1-14. It may take between 10 to 20 minutes depending on your machine. Closing down other applications will speed up the installation.

Figure 1-14. *Xcode Installer at work*

Once the installation is complete, the Xcode Welcome page will display, as shown in Figure 1-14. An Xcode icon will be added automatically to the dock.

Figure 1-15. *Xcode Welcome page*

Installing GameSalad Creator

Installing GameSalad Creator is very easy. If you have not registered and downloaded the installation file yet, go to http://gamesalad.com/download/latestCreator.

1. Double-click the .dmg file that you downloaded.

2. Read and agree to the GameSalad.com Terms of Service, as per Figure 1-16.

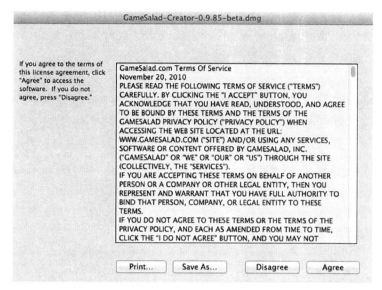

If you agree to the terms of this license agreement, click "Agree" to access the software. If you do not agree, press "Disagree."

GameSalad.com Terms Of Service
November 20, 2010
PLEASE READ THE FOLLOWING TERMS OF SERVICE ("TERMS") CAREFULLY. BY CLICKING THE "I ACCEPT" BUTTON, YOU ACKNOWLEDGE THAT YOU HAVE READ, UNDERSTOOD, AND AGREE TO BE BOUND BY THESE TERMS AND THE TERMS OF THE GAMESALAD PRIVACY POLICY ("PRIVACY POLICY") WHEN ACCESSING THE WEB SITE LOCATED AT THE URL: WWW.GAMESALAD.COM ("SITE") AND/OR USING ANY SERVICES, SOFTWARE OR CONTENT OFFERED BY GAMESALAD, INC. ("GAMESALAD" OR "WE" OR "OUR" OR "US") THROUGH THE SITE (COLLECTIVELY, THE "SERVICES").
IF YOU ARE ACCEPTING THESE TERMS ON BEHALF OF ANOTHER PERSON OR A COMPANY OR OTHER LEGAL ENTITY, THEN YOU REPRESENT AND WARRANT THAT YOU HAVE FULL AUTHORITY TO BIND THAT PERSON, COMPANY, OR LEGAL ENTITY TO THESE TERMS.
IF YOU DO NOT AGREE TO THESE TERMS OR THE TERMS OF THE PRIVACY POLICY, AND EACH AS AMENDED FROM TIME TO TIME, CLICK THE "I DO NOT AGREE" BUTTON, AND YOU MAY NOT

Print...   Save As...   Disagree   Agree

Figure 1-16. Terms of Service

3. Drag the GameSalad icon into the Application folder, as per Figure 1-17.

Figure 1-17. *nstall Screen*

4. Open GameSalad.app in the Application folder and you are ready (see Figure 1-18).

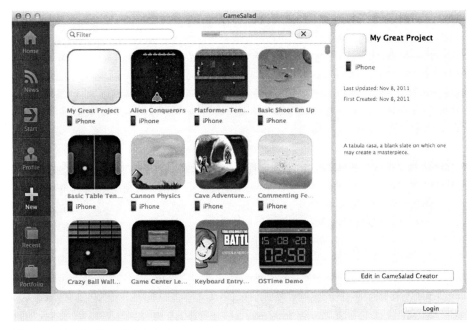

Figure 1-18. *The GameSalad start page*

This was much easier than registering to the Apple Developer Program!

Installing GameSalad iOS Viewer

The GameSalad Viewer is an Xcode project. This means that you download a piece of code that you will compile and install on your iPhone or any other iOS device. This is one of the main reasons you installed Xcode previously.

Why is GameSalad iOS Viewer a piece of code?

Well, this way GameSalad enables the installation of a viewer without going through the App Store distribution. GameSalad Creator will send your project to the viewer via Wi-Fi without the possibility of getting the code generated from GameSalad. This protects the GameSalad business model.

Getting the GameSalad iOS Viewer

You can download the GameSalad iOS Viewer from
http://gamesalad.com/download/getViewer.

You will download a .zip file with the last version of iOS Viewer. But before rushing to unzip the file, let's go through the creation of a provisioning profile on your iOS device.

Installing the Developer Certificate in Your Keychain

The developer certificate is a key element for installing the iOS Viewer or any other ad-hoc games. It is used to sign your applications so that you can install them on your iOS devices.

First, you need to find your keychain. The keychain is located in Utilities.

1. Open a Finder window and navigate to your Utilities folder (within your Application folder).

2. Double-click the Keychain Access application.

From Keychain Access, you will use the assistant to request a developer certificate from Apple.

3. Navigate to Keychain Access ➤ Certificate Assistant ➤ Request a certificate from a certificate authority.

A window form will open, as shown in Figure 1-19.

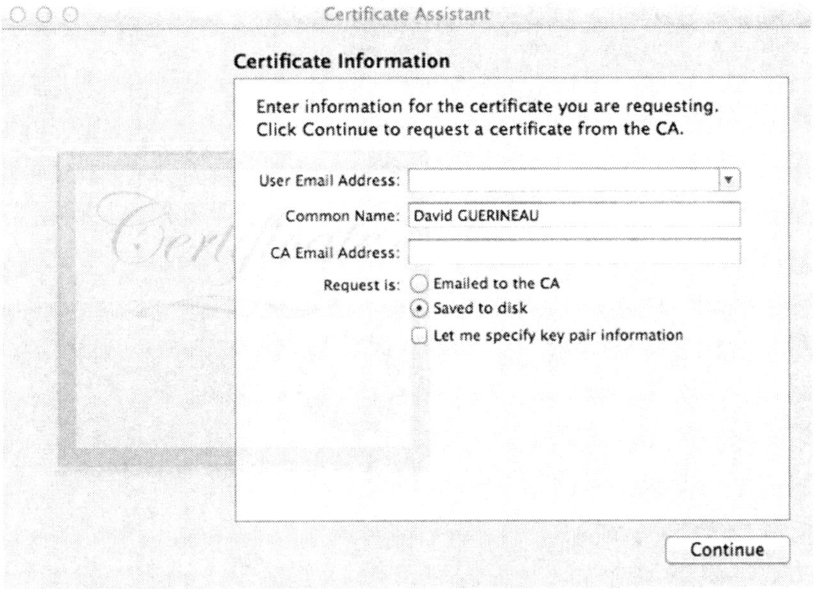

Figure 1-19. *Request a certificate*

Fill in the e-mail address using the e-mail address you used to register in the iOS Developer Program and select "Saved to disk."

Click the Continue button.

Select the location to save your certificate. You may choose to save it on your desktop so you can find it easily. The file that you just downloaded is a Certificate Signing Request (CSR) that you will use to generate the certificate.

4. Close the Keychain Access application by going to Keychain Access ➤ Quit Keychain Access.

Quitting the Keychain Access application helps to reduce the potential errors when installing the certificate.

5. Open your web browser and go to the Developer Member Center (http://developer.apple.com/membercenter/) and then click the iOS Provisioning Portal.

At this stage, you should have not have any certificates. Check this by clicking the Certificate menu on the left side and verifying that there is no Development or Distribution certificate.

Download the WWDR intermediate certificate, as this certificate is required to be installed in your keychain, by clicking on the link shown in Figure 1-20.

*If you do not have the WWDR intermediate certificate installed, click here to download now.

Figure 1-20. *Link to download WWDR intermediate certificate*

6. Under the Development tab in Certificate, click the Request a Certificate option.

You will be directed to a page titled Create iPhone Development Certificate (Figure 1-21). Select the Certificate Signing Request (CSR) that you created in step 3.

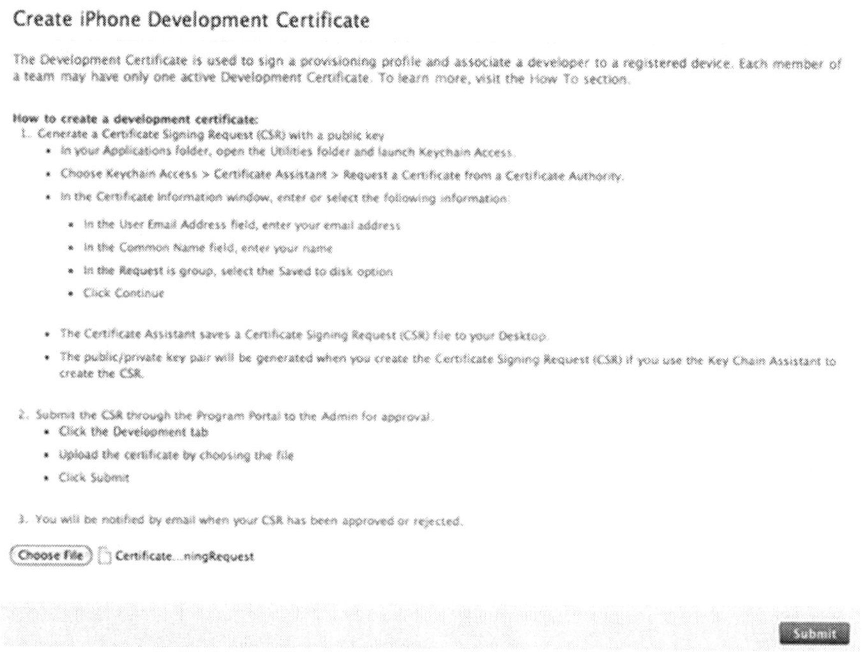

Create iPhone Development Certificate

The Development Certificate is used to sign a provisioning profile and associate a developer to a registered device. Each member of a team may have only one active Development Certificate. To learn more, visit the How To section.

How to create a development certificate:

1. Generate a Certificate Signing Request (CSR) with a public key
    *   In your Applications folder, open the Utilities folder and launch Keychain Access.
    *   Choose Keychain Access > Certificate Assistant > Request a Certificate from a Certificate Authority.
    *   In the Certificate Information window, enter or select the following information:
        *   In the User Email Address field, enter your email address
        *   In the Common Name field, enter your name
        *   In the Request is group, select the Saved to disk option
        *   Click Continue

    *   The Certificate Assistant saves a Certificate Signing Request (CSR) file to your Desktop.
    *   The public/private key pair will be generated when you create the Certificate Signing Request (CSR) if you use the Key Chain Assistant to create the CSR.

2. Submit the CSR through the Program Portal to the Admin for approval.
    *   Click the Development tab
    *   Upload the certificate by choosing the file
    *   Click Submit

3. You will be notified by email when your CSR has been approved or rejected.

(Choose File) Certificate...ningRequest

Submit

Figure 1-21. *Create iPhone Development Certificate*

Once you have selected the file, click the Submit button.

7. Go to the Distribution tab and do the exact same thing.

Wait 1 to 2 minutes, then refresh the page. Your development and distribution certificates should be ready for download.

8. Download both the Development and Distribution certificates respectively located under the Development and Distribution tabs by clicking the Download button next to the certificates.

You should have now three files in your download folder:

  ▓ AppleWWDRCA.cer

  ▒ iOS_development.cer

  ▒ iOS_distribution.cer

9. Install the certificates in your keychain.

You need to install those three certificates, starting with the AppleWWDRCA.cer. To install each of them, simply double-click each file. This will open Keychain Access. Verify that the certificate is correctly installed by checking its presence in the My Certificates window. Then completely quit KeychainAccess before repeating the operation with the next certificate.

You now have the certificates installed on your machine.

Creating a Provisioning Profile for iOS Viewer

Before installing the iOS Viewer, you first need to create a provisioning profile for GameSalad iOS Viewer.

Open your web browser and go to the Developer Member Center (http://developer.apple.com/membercenter/) and then click the iOS Provisioning Portal.

1. Register your device in your Provisioning Portal.

Go to Devices ➤ Add Devices. Type a name and the Device ID, as per Figure 1-22, and click the Submit button.

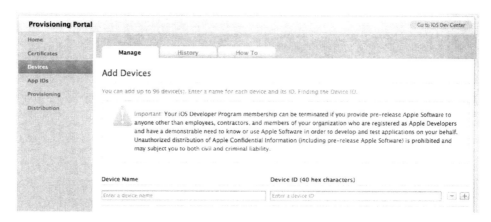

Figure 1-22. *Adding an iOS device to the Provisioning Portal*

To get your device ID, connect your iOS device via the USB cable to your Mac computer and open Xcode. In Xcode, navigate to Window ➤ Organizer. The 40-hex character string in the Identifier field is your device's ID.If this is the first time you're using your device for development, click "Use for development" on this page.

2.   Create an AppID for the iOS Viewer.

Click App IDs and select New App ID. For the description, use an all-attached string like iOSViewer. Don't modify the Team ID option. And select a unique bundle identifier. This identifier is something that must be unique in the world. Apple recommends that you use your web domain name backward and add a unique application name. Click the Submit button (Figure 1-23).

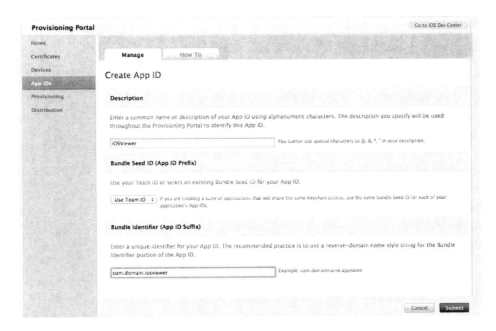

Figure 1-23. New App ID

3. Create a provisioning profile for the iOS Viewer.

Click Provisioning ➤ Development ➤ New Profile.You will create a new Development provisioning profile that will let you install the GameSalad Viewer on your iOS device.

Provide a profile name like "iOSViewer." Check the box with your certificate. Select the App ID you just created and select the device(s) you previously registered, as per Figure 1-24.

Figure 1-24. *New provisioning profile*

> 4. Download the provisioning profile.

Download your newly created provisioning profile by clicking Download. If the status is still Pending, hit the Refresh button, and it should be OK within a few seconds.

> 5. Install the provisioning profile.

Double-click your provisioning profile in the Download folder. This will automatically install it on your machine. To confirm the correct installation of the profile, open Xcode and launch the Organizer by navigating to Window ➤ Organizer. On the left side of the Organizer, select Provisioning Profiles and check that your profile appears in the list on the main window. If this is not the case, repeat the installation by double-clicking your provisioning profile file.

Installing iOS Viewer

It's now time to go back to the iOS Viewer `.zip`file. After such a long wait, your patience is rewarded. You can now unzip it.

Double-click the `iOSViewer<version>.xcodeproj` file (where <version>is be the version number of your iOS Viewer).This will automatically launch Xcode.

> 1. Change the bundle identifier.

Click the GameSalad Viewer on the left pane of Xcode. This will display the project summary information, as shown in Figure 1-25.

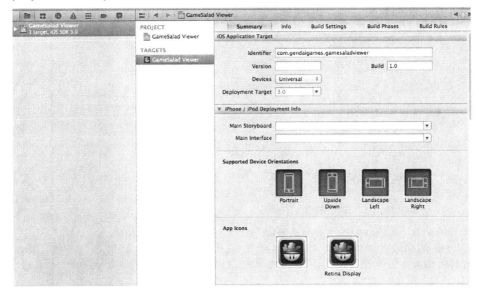

Figure 1-25. *GameSalad Viewer info*

Change the Identifier field to the value that you used in step 3 as your unique bundle identifier.

2.   Change the code signing.

In the GameSalad viewer project page, go into Build Settings and change the Code Signing as per your new provisioning profile "iOSViewer," like Figure 1-26.

Figure 1-26. *Changing code signing*

Are you ready to run iOSGameviewer?

Connect your iOS device to your Mac, select the target platform to your iOS, make sure that your device is selected from the drop-down bar next to the Stop button, count to three, and press the Run button.

It may take 1 to 2 minutes to compile and install. Xcode will display the progress in the status dashboard

Then you will see the screen in Figure 1-27 on your iOS device.

Figure 1-27. *GameSalad Viewer*

You can test the viewer by opening one of the GameSalad templates like "Basic Shoot Them Up," and click "Preview on iPhone" or "Preview on iPad" depending on your iOS device (see Figure 1-28).

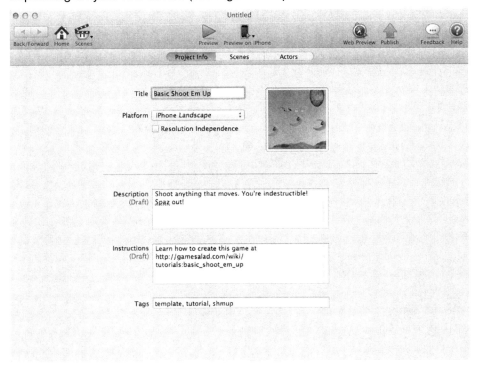

Figure 1-28. *GameSalad viewer enabled*

Congratulations! You've set up your design environment. You can now move on to the fun of GameSalad. Let's create some games!

Summary

Well, the most boring part is done. GameSalad development required this small sacrifice. From here on, things will be much more fun.

This chapter covered:

- The registration and installation of GameSalad
- The registration on iOS Developer Program
- The installation of Xcode

■   The installation of GameSalad Viewer

In the coming chapters, you will create some really fun games as you learn the basics of GameSalad.

Your First Game from Scratch: The Pong Game

Now that you have properly set up your environment, let's use GameSalad to create a real game. In this chapter, I will guide you through the creation of a complete game: Pong. This chapter covers the basics of GameSalad; the next chapter covers a few more features of the game.

This chapter specifically covers:

- GameSalad project creation

- Creating scenes, actors, attributes, and behaviors

- An introduction to collision

To have a look at what you will achieve in this chapter, you can open the file MyFirstPong_step6.gameproj, which is located in the Chapter_1_File folder at www.apress.com. Opening this file will launch GameSalad. Then you simply need to hit the Preview button in GameSalad.

A Little Bit of History About Pong

The seventies saw the birth of the video game industry. Pong showed the path to many other game developers. Of course, the technology was not advanced as it is today so games were quite limited. One of the most important limitations was the graphics. As one of the very first arcade games, Pong was no exception. The user interface was very simple, as you can see in Figure 2-1. Still, it was so revolutionary that the public massively adopted it.

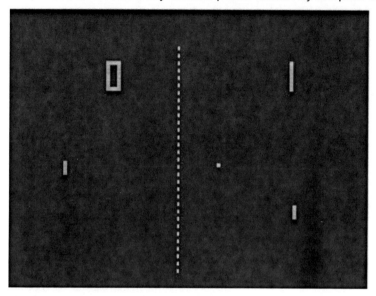

Figure 2-1. *A screenshot of the original Pong game*

Allan Alcorn created Pong in 1972 while working at Atari. But the world almost didn't get to know this game. As a trainee, Allan was assigned the exercise of creating a game in order to develop his skills. He came back with Pong. The Atari management team was so completely bluffed by the end result that they decided to go commercial with the game. It was probably one of their best decisions. The first release of Pong as an arcade game was a huge success and it gave birth to the video game industry. Figure 2-2 shows the arcade version of Pong.

Figure 2-2. *The original Pong arcade machine*

Pong was later developed in several versions, including a home game. The
home version of Pong, shown in Figure 2-3, was created in 1974 but was only
released in 1975 due to difficulty in finding a distribution channel. Several
versions (and clones) have been released over time.

Figure 2-3. *Mass production of the Pong game*

I remember playing Pong on my Atari home game device for hours. Originally, my father bought an Atari 2600 for himself. It was the special "Darth Vader" Edition, an all-black model with four switches, released in 1982. This was one of the first video game consoles. With a console, you had a device capable of running several games (via a cartridge system)—not just a single game, as was the case with Home Pong. I was only five at that time but I clearly remember playing like crazy, making my father angry because after a few days I was unbeatable.

Specifying the Game Concept and Rules

When you begin a new game project, it's a good practice to start by specifying the game concept and writing the rules of the game down on paper. This provides structure to your work.

The Game Concept

The purpose of this game is to defeat your opponent in a simulated table tennis (ping-pong) game by being the first to reach a score of 11. It is a two-dimension game where players vertically control a paddle (ping-pong racket).

The Game Rules

Human player 1 plays on the left side of the screen against human player 2. (The CPU player is covered in the next chapter.) Players use the racket to hit the ball back and forth.

Creating a New GameSalad Project

Are you ready to play pong?

First, let's create a new GameSalad Project. Click on the GameSalad icon, as shown in Figure 2-4, in Applications to open GameSalad Creator.

Figure 2-4. *The GameSalad app logo*

Select the Plus button (New), select "My Great Project," and click "Edit in GameSalad." This will open a new project in GameSalad (Figure 2-5).

Figure 2-5. *The GameSalad launch screen*

You will arrive to the page shown in Figure 2-6.

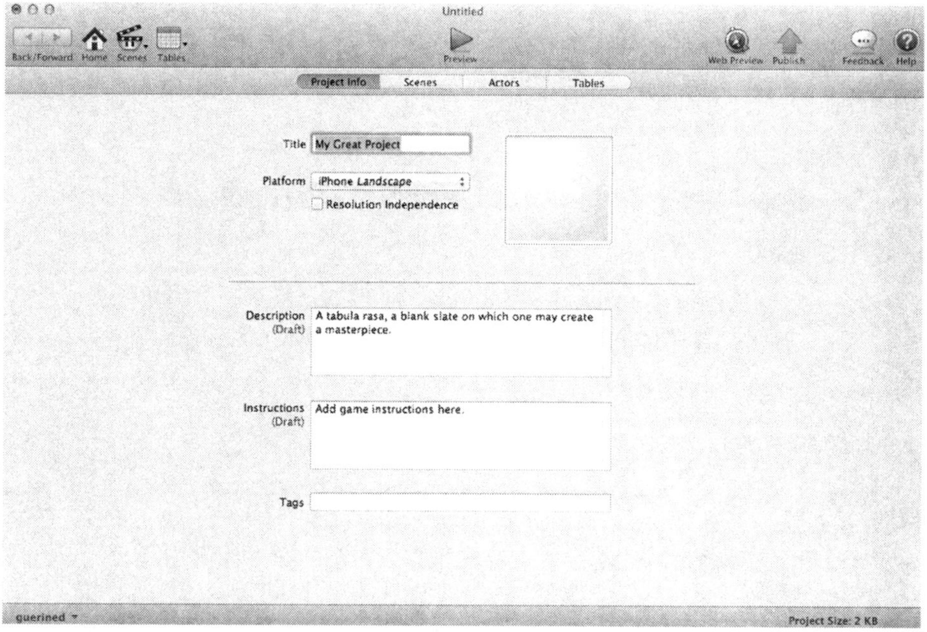

Figure 2-6. *The Project Info page*

This page is the project information page. It contains general information about the project, such as the title of the project, the game's platform, a description, and instructions. Enter the information shown in Table 2-1.

Table 2-1. *Game Creation Information*

Title	My First Pong Game
Platform	iPhone Landscape
Resolution Independence	Checked
Description	This is a remake of the famous Pong game by Atari
Instructions	Use your finger to move the racket or tilt the phone
Tags	Pong

Your screen should look like Figure 2-7.

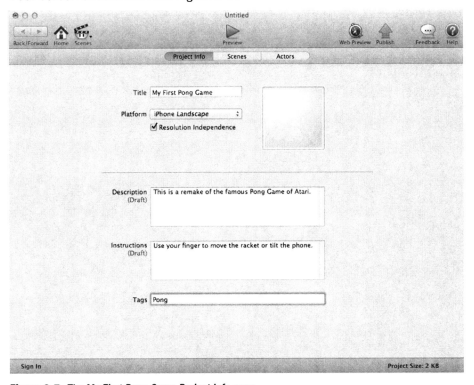

Figure 2-7. *The My First Pong Game Project Info page*

All of this information is draft only. You will have opportunities to review it before you submit your work for App Store validation.

Save the project. Create a folder in your documents and name it LearnGameSalad_chap2.

Save a copy of your project now. This way you can frequently save your progress. Click File ➤ Save As, name the file MyFirstPong.gameproj, and save it in the newly created folder (Figure 2-8).

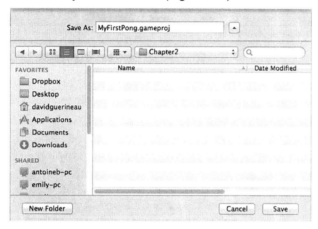

Figure 2-8._Saving the game_

You are all set to start your project.

About Resolution Independence:

Resolution independence is a great feature of GameSalad. In short, it lets you design a high resolution version of the game that can adapt to the various resolutions of iOS devices. This increases the number of potential targets for your games.

How does it work? GameSalad will automatically adjust the size of all your artwork to fit the iOS device resolution by creating lower resolution copies of your artwork.

To enjoy this feature, select resolution independence and design your game artwork for retina display resolution.

There's a little secret to make it work nicely. All you artwork must have a pixel size that you can divide by 4. Why 4? Because, to nicely display your artwork, it must be an even number (like 20x20). GameSalad will adjust automatically to lower resolution (i.e. divide by 2), so it needs to be an even number! Thus the 4!

Word of caution: there is a size limit of 1024x1024 for images.

If you are planning a low-resolution game (480 x320), there's no need to check resolution independence. Another good reason to deselect this option and plan for a low-resolution game is that older devices (like the first generation of the iPod touch) will have difficulties to handling those graphics. As ever, the best advice: test, test, and test again.

The pages you have read thus far mention actors, scenes, and projects. So you may naturally ask yourself, "Am I reading the right book? I thought I was reading about game creation and everything looks like movie production. I don't have the money to hire Bruce Willis for my production!"

Yes, you are reading a book about game design. But isn't it easier to think about game creation like a movie production where you have a plot (game mechanics), some actors (characters or objects), and a direction (behaviors and attributes)?

GameSalad allows you to design your game like a movie. You will use scenes (splash screen, menu, level, gameplays) and actors to interact in these scenes.

Adding Actors

Ready to play the movie director…er…the game director role? Let's fabricate some actors!

What is an actor?

An actor is an object with specific behaviors and attributes that you will place in the scene. Typically, in the Pong game, the ball is an actor. As for specific behaviors, you will tell the ball how to react when colliding with some rackets and with walls. The ball will also have some attributes that will define the ball itself; for example, it will be moveable.

A view of the Actor Editor is shown in Figure 2-9.

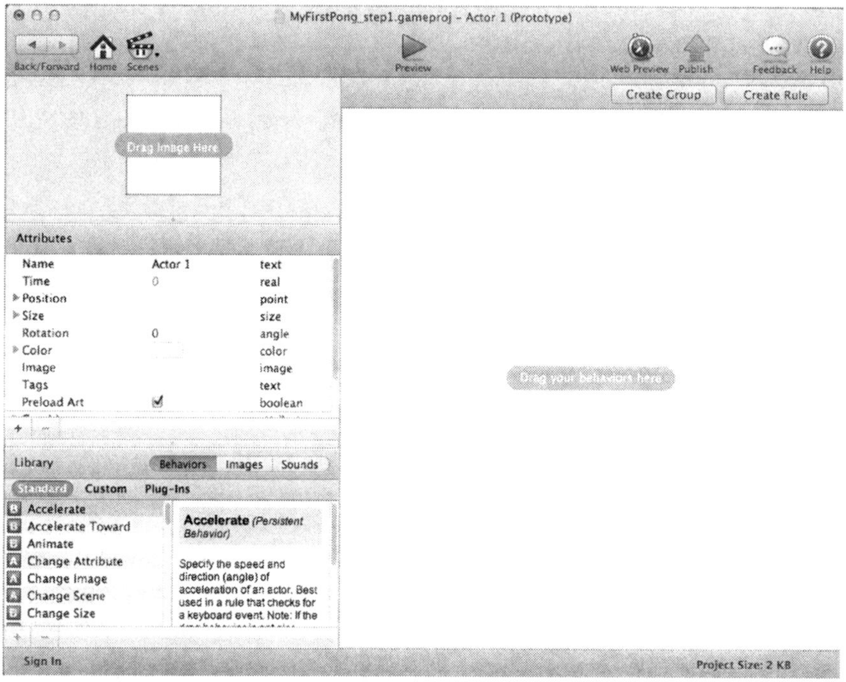

Figure 2-9. *The ActorEditor*

Creating actors

There are two ways to create actors:

- Via the Project Editor
- Via the Scene Editor

Personally I mostly use the Scene Editor to create new actors as I create my scene, but if you are a very good planner, you may use the Project Editor to create most (if not all) of them when you create your project. I will cover the creation of an actor with the Scene Editor here.

Click the Scenes icon shown in Figure 2-10.

Figure 2-10. *Scenes icon*

Select "Initial Scene." The Scene Editor opens. Locate the Actor Inspector window on the left side, as per Figure 2-11. Click the + sign below the Actor Inspector window.

Figure 2-11. *Actor Inspector window*

That's it! You have just created your first actor!

Modifying Actors Attributes

An actor's attributes can be modified by behaviors. But first you need to understand a crucial concept.

Instance or Prototype

Before you go any further, I need to introduce the Very Important Concept (VIC) of actor prototype versus actor instance.

The actor prototype is where you define the master actor. You will define the actor, its attributes, and its behaviors.

Then every time you place this actor in one of the scenes of the game, you automatically create an instance of this actor. The instance will automatically inherit from the properties (attributes and behaviors) of the prototype.

About Object-Oriented Programming:

Object-oriented programming (OOP) is a programming concept centered on objects. An object is a data structure that contains descriptive information about the object as well as actions (called methods). OOP is out of the scope of this book, but perhaps you've noticed the resemblance between OOP and GameSalad. Actors are the objects, attributes are the descriptive information, and behaviors are the methods. In reality, this is no surprise. GameSalad only hides the programming aspects of iOS development! The iOS development language is Objective-C, and guess what? Objective-C is an object-oriented programming language.

If you need to modify some attributes or a behavior of a specific instance, you must unlock the instance to access its attributes and behaviors. Scene attributes, such as camera or orientation attributes, can only be accessed from actors located on the scene. As such, you will need to edit the actor instances.

Actor Attributes

To best understand the concept of actor attributes, you need to think about attributes as items that describe the actor. For example, to describe a human actor, you would mention hair color (blond, brown, grey, dark, or none), eye color (blue, brown, green), etc. Thus an attribute is a characteristic of the item and its value.

So what does this mean in GameSalad? Let's say that you have an actor called Ball. It can be moveable (yes or no), it has a height and width, a color, etc.

Commonly Used Attributes

Let's quickly review the most important attributes of an actor. Those attributes are accessible from the Actor Editor shown in Figure 2-9.

Name

This field contains the name of the actor. Use specific names; this is especially important if you will have many actors in your project.

Size

You can specify the size of the actor. If you are planning to use an image, key in the size of the image.

Don't forget about the tip regarding the size (make it divisible by 4!)

Color

You can fill a color in your actor if you are not using an image.

Tags

Tags are a way to group actors and to have them to behave in a similar way. For example, you can group some actors to be collidable. Then you can define a rule that a special object (a ball, for example) collides with all collidable-tagged objects.

Physics/Density

Located under Physics, density represents the heaviness of an actor. The way GameSalad implements density is very close to real life. According to the GameSalad support, the units in GameSalad equal standard density in kilograms per cubic meter.

Physics/Friction

Located under Physics, this attribute is used to simulate friction, which is the force resulting from the contact of two materials. The lower the value of friction, the softer it will simulate the reaction. A value of 0 will simulate ice.

Physics/Moveable

Located under Physics, this attribute lets you decide if the object can move or not. If not moveable, the object will be in a fixed position. However, the actor will be able to be moved through Change Attribute and Interpolate behaviors.

This list is not exhaustive. Many more attributes will be covered in the coming chapters and you will learn how to create some custom attributes.

Modifying Attributes

To modify an actor, double-click the actor in the Actor window in the Scene Editor. This will open the actor prototype in the Actor Editor. Then you simply need to access each of the attributes in the Actor Editor. Let's practice.

Double-click the actor you previously created (Actor 1), as shown in Figure 2-12.

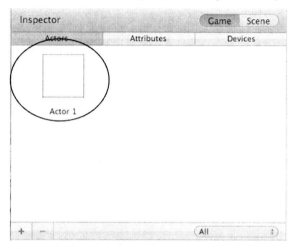

Figure 2-12. *Actor 1 in the Inspector*

Double-clicking Actor 1 opens to the Actor Editor, as shown in Figure 2-13.

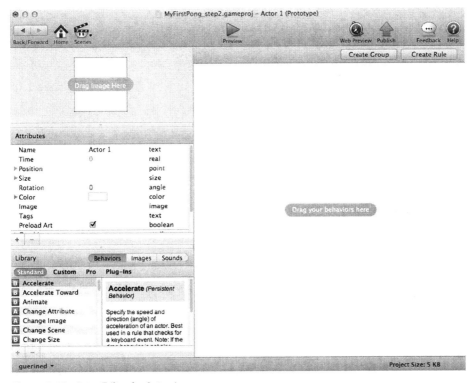

Figure 2-13. *Actor Editor for Actor 1*

Now let's change the following attributes:

- Name: Rack Player 1

- Size/Width: 16

- Size/Height: 120

- Color: White

- Physics/Density: 500

- Physics/Friction: 3

- Physics/Restitution: 0

- Physics/Fixed Rotation: Checked (This will avoid the actor rotating after a collision with the ball.)

Now save your project.

About the Restitution Attribute:

The restitution attribute defines the bounciness. Zero means no bounce! Confused? Why not use bounciness? How will the ball go back if it can't bounce? Well, the ball will bounce, not the racket! (Imagine the racket bouncing out of the wall. Not very playable.) A value of 1 in restitution means that no energy is lost out of the collision (so it's perfectly elastic).

Adding Behaviors

You can open `MyFirstPong_step2.gameproj` to start from this point.

In order to add actions to your actors, you need to add behaviors. With behaviors, you can change the actors' appearance, put some conditions to some specific actions, or have them perform actions based on a timer. Thus you use behaviors to add logic to your game.

What are behaviors?

To understand behavior in GameSalad, let's continue the analogy of a human actor. As a movie director, you direct your actors to perform certain tasks (like when the cop sees the bad guys, the cop will shoot at them).

In GameSalad, behaviors direct your actors. You may instruct an actor that if a condition is met, it will auto-destroy itself. This is an example of a behavior.

You can have behaviors for actions (such as how to react when colliding) or behaviors that check on specific conditions (if the score is below 11, continue to play).

There are three types of behaviors:

1. Behaviors that occur once (these have an "A" letter in a red box next to their name).

2. Persistent behaviors that act continuously (these have a "B" letter in a green box to their name).

3. Rules that use conditions to perform other behaviors (these have a "G" letter in a blue box next to their name).

Adding Behaviors

Adding a behavior is fairly easy from the Actor Editor. On the bottom left, you have access to the library of behaviors. You select the targeted behavior by dragging and dropping it into the behavior area.

If you need to create a Rule behavior, you can either drag and drop the Rule behavior from the list of behaviors or click the Create Rule button located in the top right corner of the Actor Editor, as shown in Figure 2-14.

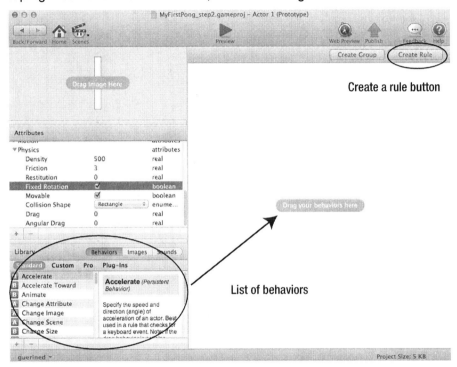

Figure 2-14. *Actor Editor*

> About Rule Behaviors:
>
> A rule behavior is used to define a condition to a behavior. It could be a condition on the actor or on an attribute. It could be one condition, several conditions at the same time, or any of several conditions at a given time.

Now let's practice. Start with the up and down movement. To do so, create a rule that when a key is pressed a behavior (movement) is triggered.

1. Click on the New Rule button.

2. Rename the rule as "Down" by clicking "Rule" next to the On button

A rule has three parts, as shown in Figure 2-15.

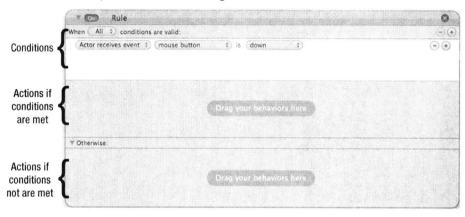

Figure 2-15. *The three parts of a rule*

Rule conditions are located at the top part of the rule. As you may have several conditions, you can choose to have either all of the conditions be met in order to trigger the behaviors or to have any of the conditions be met in order to trigger the actions.

3. Modify the condition to "Actor receives event." Also, choose "down" for the key, as shown in Figure 2-16.

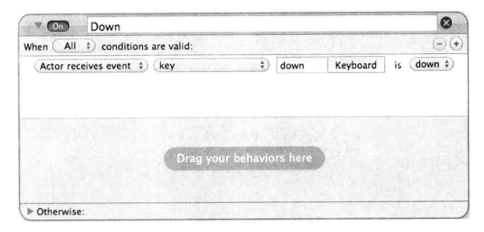

Figure 2-16. *Conditions of Downrule*

4. From the behaviors library, drag a Move behavior (not the Move To behavior) and drop it into the behavior area of the rule if the condition is met. Modify the Move behavior with a direction of 270.

The completed rule is shown in Figure 2-17.

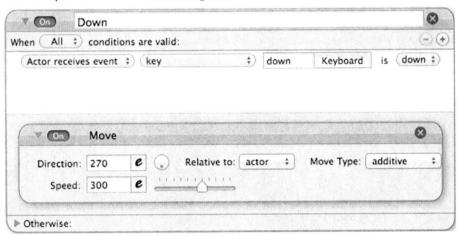

Figure 2-17. *Behavior of Downrule*

About the Move Behavior:

There are several perimeters to the Move behavior.

Direction: You can either enter a value in degrees or a mathematical equation to define the direction that the actor will take. For example, 0 will have an actor move to the East of his point of reference for the movement (see below).

Relative to: This defines the point of reference for the movement. You have two choices: the actor itself or the scene. Relative to the scene is a movement in the absolute referential of the scene. If you put 0 relative to the scene, the actor will move to the right of the scene. If you put 0 relative to the actor, the actor will move to his right, which could be the left of the scene if the actor is upside down.

Move type: You can choose between additive or stacked. Additive will sum up the speed and direction of other Move or Move To behaviors, while stacked will only apply the speed and direction of the most recent Move or Move To behaviors.

Speed: You can either put a value or open the Equation Editor by clicking the little box with the "e" on it to the right of the value box and entering a mathematical equation to define the speed of the movement

Try to create the Up rule on your own. Here are a few hints:

- You can duplicate the Down rule by holding option and dragging the rule down, renaming it, and changing the settings. Alternatively, you can select the Down rule, copy (Command + C), and then paste (Command + V). Another approach is to create a new rule, as you did for the Down rule.

- The name of this rule is Up.

- The condition of the rule is "Actor receives event" and the key is "up."

- Drag and drop a Move behavior and change the settings as per the Down rule but with direction set to 90.

You can open `MyFirstPong_step3.gameproj` file to follow up from this point.

Before placing this actor on the scene, add one more behavior for each rack. Constrain its positions on the horizontal axis. This means that the racket will move up and down but will be on a fixed horizontal position (constant value on the X axis). To do so, use the Constraint Attribute behavior.

In the behavior library (Figure 2-14), locate the Constrain Attribute behavior and drop it into the Actor Behavior pane below the Up rule you just created. To select the attribute to constrain, use the Attribute Browser. Click the button with the three dots located to the right of the value input field. Browse to Rack Player 1 ➤ Position ➤ X, as shown in Figure 2-18.

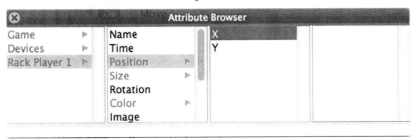

Figure 2-18. *Attribute Browser*

Double-click the X attribute to validate it. Assign a value of 20 for this constraint, which will constrain the racket on a vertical axis located 20 pixels from the left of the screen. The completed behavior is shown in Figure 2-19.

Figure 2-19. *Constrain Attribute*

And now you are ready to position the actor on the scene.

Adding an Actor to the Scene

So you have created the racket for player 1. Now let's position it on the scene.

Go back to the Scene Editor, and drop the actor into the scene. The location only needs to be approximate because you have constrained the racket on the x-axis, as shown in Figure 2-20.

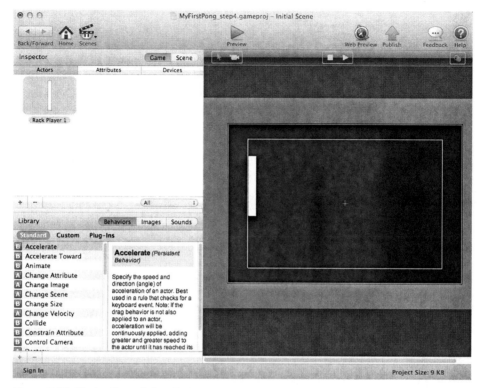

Figure 2-20. *Placing the racket on the scene*

Hit Preview! You have a racket on the scene that you can move up and down with the arrow keys of your keyboard.

You can access this stage by opening file`MyFirstPong_step3.gameproj`.

Creating Other Actors

I have taken you through a very detailed approach to creating the racket for Player 1. You will now create some of the remaining actors. You will define the racket for the Player 2, the ball, and walls to get a defined playing area. You will also add a little bit of dynamics so that you can have fast play.

I will guide you more quickly but I will highlight some new items as they appear.

Racket Player 2

To create the racket for Player 2, create a new actor. Double-click this new actor to edit it in the Actor Editor. Change the attributes as per the following:

- Name: Rack Player 2
- Size/Width: 16
- Size/Height: 120
- Color: White
- Physics/Density: 500
- Physics/Friction: 3
- Physics/Restitution: 0
- Physics/Fixed Rotation: Checked

Then create the two following rules:

1. A rule named Down. It will be triggered when the "A" key is down (the condition). The behavior will be a Move with a direction of 270.

2. A rule named Up. It will be triggered when the "Q" key is down (the condition). The behavior will be a Move with a direction of 90.

Last, add a behavior called Constrain Attribute, with actor X constrained to 460.

Now, place your racket on the scene. You can place it approximately as the position constrain will automatically position it correctly. Your Rack Player 2 editor screen should look like Figure 2-21.

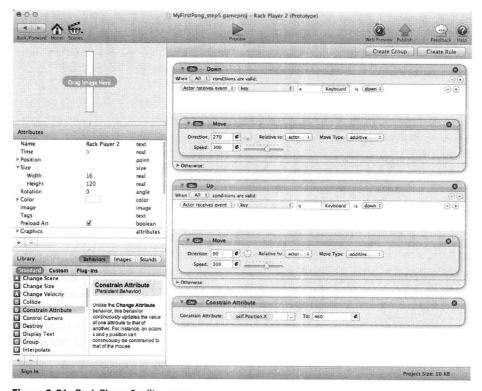

Figure 2-21. *Rack Player 2 editor screen*

The Ball

You will now create the ball. For reason of simplicity, you will create a square ball of 16 x 16 pixels. This actor will be generated from another actor: either Rack Player 1 or Rack Player 2. In the GameSalad vocabulary, we say that this actor is *spawned*.

As usual, create a new actor and change the following attributes in the Actor Editor:

- Name: Ball
- Size/Width: 16
- Size/Height: 16
- Color: Red
- Physics/Restitution: 1

- Physics/Fixed Rotation: Checked

- Physics/Collision Shape: Circle

You have two options to define how the actors will collide. The shape will be either rectangle or circle.

The ball will be spawned from either Rack Player 1 or Rack Player 2, depending on which player is serving for the game. By default, Player 1 will start the game by serving first. The winner of the point will serve the next ball. To define which player will serve, use a Boolean attribute on whether Player 1 will serve. If true, Player 1 will serve; if false, Player 2 will serve.

In the Scene Editor, select the Attributes Inspector window and create a new Boolean attribute by clicking the + sign, as per Figure 2-22.

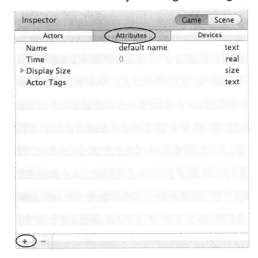

Figure 2-22. *Attributes Inspector window*

Name this attribute `P1Serving` and check it.

Back in the Actor Editor for the Ball actor, create a new rule. The rule will check which player is serving and, based on the result, will change the direction. To do so, use the Otherwise part of the rule.

Create a new rule and call it Ball Direction. The condition is if the attribute of game. P1Serving is true. Drag in a Change Velocity behavior.

Change the direction using the Expression Editor. Click the small "e" at the right of the direction field, as shown in Figure 2-23.

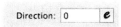

Figure 2-23. *The Expression Editor icon*

This will open the Expression Editor shown in Figure 2-24.

Figure 2-24. *Expression Editor*

Select the Random (min, max) function by clicking on the insert function drop-down menu and replacing the min with -45 and the max with 45. By doing so, the ball will go in a direction between -45 degrees and +45 degrees. Then, click the green check mark to actually insert the function. Figure 2-27 provides a visual representation of the angles.

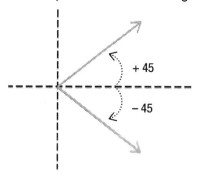

Figure 2-25. *Ball direction (-45, +45)*

Drag another Change Velocity behavior in the Otherwise section, which can be accessed by clicking the arrow in front of the Otherwise text on the bottom of the rule, and change the direction value to Random (135,225) and click the green check mark. Figure 2-26 provides a visual representation of the angles.

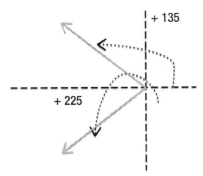

Figure 2-26. *Ball direction (135, 225)*

You should end up with a rule that looks similar to Figure 2-27.

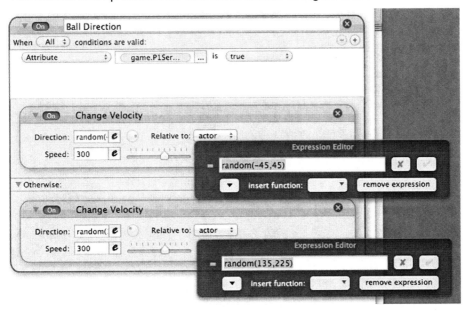

Figure 2-27. *The Ball Direction rule*

About the Expression Editor:

The Expression Editor is the advanced editor where you can use advanced mathematical formulas to define complex actions and movements. I will cover more mathematical aspects later.

There are a few tips you need to know about the Expression Editor:

1.   .. is used to show more than one attribute.

Example: (actor.position.X)..(actor.position.Y)

2.   "text" is used to display text.

Example: "X Position: "..(actor.position.X)

3.   \" is used to insert a double quote in the text within a double
       quoted text.

Example: "This is a quote \" in a text"

4.   \32 is used to insert a space in the text within a double quoted
       text.

Example: "This\32is\32a\32space"

5.   \n is used to start a new line in the text within a double quoted
       text.

Example: "This add \n a new line"

Let's go back to the rackets to enable them to spawn the ball. The ball will be spawned when the space bar is pressed. And guess what? You'll use a rule.

Open the Rack Player 1 in the Actor Editor. Create a new rule and name it Serving. The condition is when the Actor receives event and when the space key is down.

You also need to check if it is Player 1's turn to serve. To do so, use the attribute that you previously created, P1Serving. If P1Serving is true and the space bar is pressed, then Rack Player 1 will spawn the ball.

Add a new condition in the Serving rule by clicking the + sign. The condition will be if attribute game.P1Serving is true.

Now, add a Spawn Actor behavior in the behavior area of the Serving rule. Change the actor to Ball and the horizontal position to 16. This will spawn the ball just in front of the racket.

The Serving rule should look similar to Figure 2-28.

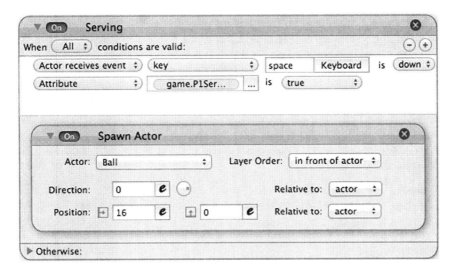

Figure 2-28. *Serving rule*

Now you can do the same for Rack Player 2 with the following modification:

▨ In the condition of Attribute game. P1Serving is false.

▨ Spawn Actor is the ball and the position is -16 (to spawn the ball on the left side of the racket).

Figure 2-29 shows the Serving rule for Rack Player 2.

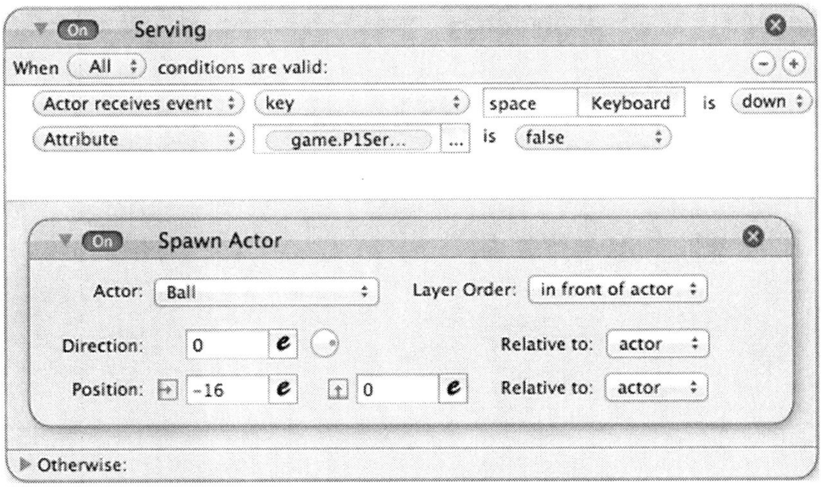

Figure 2-29. *Serving Rule for Rack Player 2*

You can open the MyFirstPong_step5.gameproj file to see the results at this stage. By changing the value of P1Serving from true to false in the Attribute Editor, you can serve from either Racket 1 or Racket 2 in the Preview mode.

Let's put some walls around this game now!

Walls

The next step is to create some walls around the playing area and implement some bounciness.

As usual, create a new actor. Double-click this new actor to edit it in the Actor Editor. Change the attributes as per the following:

- Name: Bouncing Wall
- Size/Width: 480
- Size/Height: 10
- Physics/Density: 500
- Physics/Restitution: 0
- Physics/Fixed Rotation: Checked
- Physics/Moveable: Unchecked

Go back to the Scene Editor. Drag the Bouncing Wall into the scene and position it just above the visible scene. Drag another Bouncing Wall into the scene and position it just below the visible scene. Refer to Figure 2-30 to see the result.

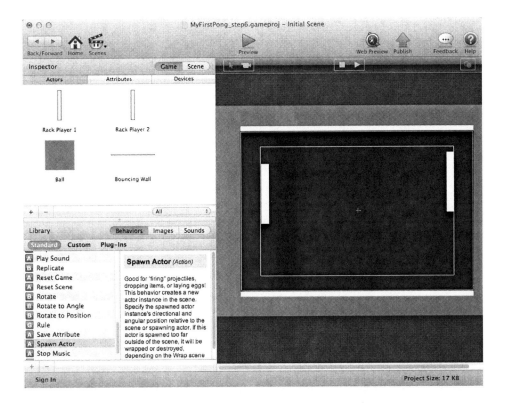

Figure 2-30. *Scene with walls*

By dragging the Bouncing Wall into the scene twice, you just created two instances of the same actor. If you double-click the actor in the Actor Editor, you can modify the prototype and all instances will reflect the modification. But if you double-click one of the instances, you will edit just that instance and not the others.

Does this ring a bell? This was the VIC (Very Important Concept) that was introduced before.

Tags

Tags are very useful tools. They are a way to group actors together and then have a behavior that applies to the tag (i.e. the group of actors). The group of actors that you will create now is the Collidable group of actors.

To create a new tag, click the Home icon as per Figure 2-31.

Figure 2-31. *Home icon*

Click the + button on the left button side of the home screen, as per Figure 2-32.

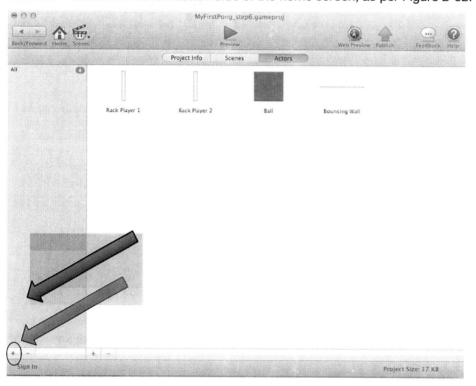

Figure 2-32. *Home Screen*

Name the tag Collidable.

Drag each of the four objects on the right side of the tag you just created.

Double-click Rack Player 1 to edit it. Add a Collide behavior. Configure the behavior for Bounce when colliding with actor with tag and "Collidable," as per Figure 2-33.

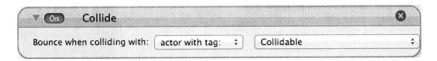

Figure 2-33. *Collide behavior*

Repeat the same for Rack Player 2, the Ball, and the Bouncing Wall.

Let's Play

You can open the file MyFirstPong_step6.gameproj to get to the current stage.

Are you ready for your first Pong game? Hit the Preview button. You can now play Pong. Use the Up and Down keys to control Player 1 and the Q and A keys to control Player 2. Press the space bar to serve a ball.

Summary

Congratulations! You have created your first playable game. But this is not your only achievement. In this chapter:

- You learned the basic concepts of GameSalad.
- You created your first project.
- You created your first actors.
- You implemented some player controls.
- You used the collision concept.

Are you enjoying this process? Good! But you have still a lot to fix. In the next chapter, you will do the following:

- Design a scoring system.
- Manage which player will serve.
- Implement touch detection for Player 1 racket.
- Implement CPU to control Player 2.
- Manage the display.

Chapter

3

Finishing Pong: Scoring and Game Interaction

In the previous chapter, you created a pretty cool game in just a few minutes. You now have a grasp of the capabilities of GameSalad, but your project is far from being perfect. In this chapter, you will continue learning GameSalad by implementing some add-ons and fine-tuning the Pong game.

Let's Keep Score

Who's winning the game? When playing table tennis, isn't one of the top goals to win or achieve a high score? But to do so, a game needs a scoring system. So what are you waiting for?

For the Pong game, you will create a scoring system based on the following rule: if you miss the ball, your opponent scores a point. The first player to reach 11 wins the game.

You can open the file `MyFirstPong_step6.gameproj` to follow the next steps.

The trick to knowing if one player has missed the ball is to create an invisible actor that will detect when the ball touches it—but one that is not collidable so the ball goes through it. This actor will cover the complete height of the gamefield. You will also take the opportunity to destroy the current ball instance. This will free up some memory resources.

About Memory:

Memory is a precious resource in an iOS device. Although iPhone 4S can have up to 64GB, the dynamic memory allocated for your runtime is much more limited (a few MB only). It is an excellent practice to destroy an actor as soon as it becomes useless for the rest of the game. If your actor will be needed later, an advance technique for performance optimization is recycling. Recycling is covered in Chapter 7.

To keep score, create two attributes to store the scores of each player.

In the Scene Editor, select the Attributes Inspector window and create a new Integer attribute by clicking the + sign. Name it P1 Score. Repeat the operations but name the attribute P2 Score.

In the Scene view, create a new actor and change the following attributes:

- Name: Left Winning Zone
- Size/Width: 10
- Size/Height: 320
- Color/Alpha: 0
- Physics/Density: 0
- Physics/Moveable: Unchecked

As you may have noticed, fixed rotation is left unchecked here. Fixed rotation is to prevent an actor from spinning around when it collides with another actor. As this actor will not collide with any other actors, it is unnecessary to check fixed rotation.

You should end up with the same attributes as Figure 3-1.

Attributes		
Name	**Left Winning Zone**	**text**
Time	0	real
▼ Position		point
X	0	real
Y	0	real
▼ Size		size
Width	10	real
Height	320	real
Rotation	0	angle
▼ Color		color
Red	1	real
Green	1	real
Blue	1	real
Alpha	0	real
Image		image
Tags		text
Preload Art	✓	boolean
▶ Graphics		attributes
▶ Motion		attributes
▼ Physics		attributes
Density	0	real
Friction	3	real
Restitution	1	real
Fixed Rotation	☐	boolean
Movable	☐	boolean
Collision Shape	Rectangle ⇕	enumera…
Drag	0	real
Angular Drag	0	real

Figure 3-1. *Left Winning Zone attributes*

Now add some rules and behaviors to that actor.

The first rule will detect the overlap between this zone and the ball. Create a rule and name it Ball Detection rule. The rule is "Actor receives event" and "overlaps or collides" withactor of type"ball."

Drag the Change Attribute behavior into the rule. Change the settings to Change Attribute: game. P2 Score. Then, use the Expression Editor (the little icon located to the right of To:) to self-increment by 1 the P2 score attribute. You expression must look like Figure 3-2.

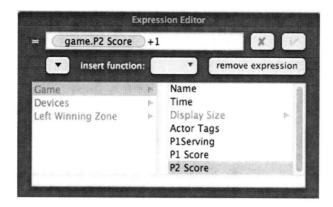

Figure 3-2. *Self-increment of P2 score*

Now you can keep track of the Player 2 score. Repeat the same steps to keep track of the Player 1 score.

Create a new actor and change the following attributes:

- Name: Right Winning Zone
- Size/Width: 10
- Size/Height: 320
- Color/Alpha: 0
- Physics/Density: 0
- Physics/Moveable: Unchecked

Next, add a rule to detect the overlap between this zone and the ball. Create a rule and name it Ball Detection rule. The rule is "Actor receives event" and "overlaps or collides" with actor of type "ball."

Drag the Change Attribute behavior into the rule. The behavior is Change Attribute: game.P1 Score. Use the Expression Editor to self-increment by 1 the Player 1 score.

Go back to the Scene View Editor. Drag and place the Left Winning Zone on the complete left side of the visible zone, as shown in Figure 3-3.

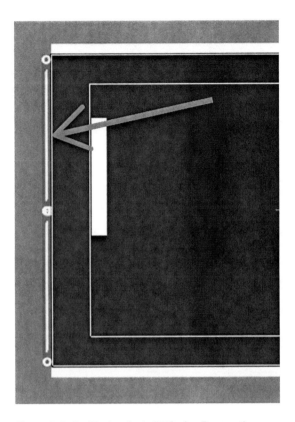

Figure 3-3. *Positioning the Left Winning Zone on the scene*

Repeat a similar action with the Right Winning Zone on the complete right side of the visible zone, as per Figure 3-4.

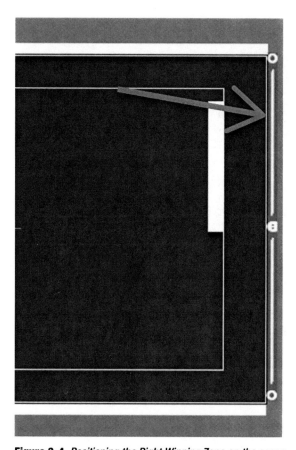

Figure 3-4. *Positioning the Right Winning Zone on the scene*

It's great to keep score for each player but it would be greater to see the scores! To display text on the scene, you will use an actor as a recipient holder. You will introduce a new behavior called Display Text. This behavior is used to display text into an actor.

In the Scene Editor, create a new actor and change the following attributes:

- Name: P1 Score
- Size/Width: 50
- Size/Height: 50
- Color/Alpha: 0
- Physics/Moveable: Unchecked

Setting Alpha to 0 will make the actor transparent but the display text will remain visible. This is how you achieve the best result.

In order to perfectly position the score display on the scene, use a Change Attribute behavior to constrain its position. Drag and drop a Change Attribute behavior into the behavior area of the P1 Score actor. Then select the P1 Score.Position.X attribute and change it to 215. Once selected, it will display as self.Position.X. Repeat the operation with P1 Score.Position.Y with a change to 295.

Last but not least, drag a Display Text behavior. The Display Text behavior is shown in Figure 3-5.

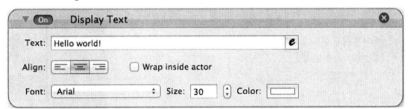

Figure 3-5. *The Display Text behavior*

In the Display Text behavior box, you can either enter your own text or access the Expression Editor. You have several options to format your text, such as choosing the alignment, the font, the size, and the color. The "Wrap inside actor" option creates line breaks so that your text fits inside the actor.

In the Display Text behavior box that you just dropped, open the Expression Editor and select the following attribute: game.P1 Score. Set the size as 20 and choose an orange color so it is clearly visible on the scene.

Figure 3-6 shows the final result.

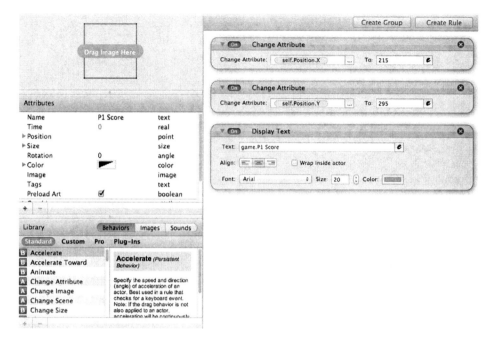

Figure 3-6. *P1 Score actor*

Repeat the same sequence of action to create the P2 score actor, display the game.P2 score, and constrain the actor to the position (265,295). Figure 3-7 shows the final result.

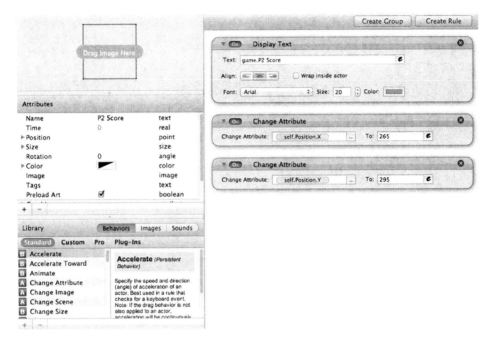

Figure 3-7. *P2 score*

Go back to the Scene Editor and drop P1 Score and P2 Score on the scene.

Before jumping to the next paragraph, you need to free up the memory once the point is made. To do so, use the Destroy behavior on the ball itself.

Open the Ball in the Actor Editor and create a new rule. Name the new rule Destroy. This rule will have two conditions but with an "Any" of those conditions. To have the Any option, click the "All" in "When 'All' conditions are valid" and select "Any."

The first condition is "Actor receives event" and "overlaps or collides" with actor of type "Left Winning Zone."

The second condition is very similar: "Actor receives event"and "overlaps or collides" with actor of type "Right Winning Zone."

Then, drag and drop a Destroy behavior. There is no option setting for this behavior. When any of the conditions you previously made are valid, it will destroy the instance of the actor. Your rule should look like Figure 3-8.

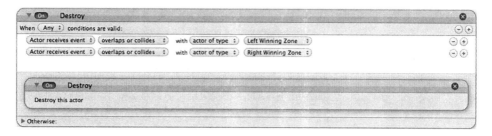

Figure 3-8. *Destroying the ball*

You can open the file MyFirstPong_step7.gameproj to access to the current stage of the design.

It's All About the Ace!

Are you ready to ace the game? Before starting the competition, you need to create two additional features of the game: winning points and serving the next ball.

At this point, not only can Player 1 serve but he can serve an infinite number of balls into the game at the same time. Press the space bar multiple times if you don't believe me.

Serving Feature: The Winner of the Point Serves the Next Ball

Implementing the function "the one who makes the point will serve the next ball" is fairly easy, especially because you have set up almost everything already. As you only have two players in the game, it can only be Player 1 or Player 2 who is serving. Another way of saying this is that Player 1 is serving or not (if not, then Player 2 is serving).

In the previous chapter, you created an attribute for serving that you will reuse now. The attribute P1Serving will get modified according to which player makes the points.

Open the Left Winning Zone actor in the Actor Editor by double-clicking it. You already have a rule that makes the scoring point. Add a Change Attribute to this existing rule to modify the P1Serving attributes in addition to the score. The rule detects when Player 2 makes the point. In that case, it's Player 2's turn to serve. Thus, P1Serving should be set to false.

Drag a Change Attributebehavior into the Ball Detection rule. Set
game.P1Serving to 0, as in Figure 3-9.

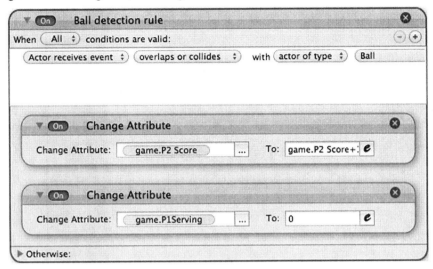

Figure 3-9. *Change P1Serving to false*

About Boolean:

Boolean attributes are true/false attributes. To save a little bit of time,
you can substitute true and false with 0 and 1, respectively.
GameSalad will automatically associate 0 to false and 1 to true

Repeat the operation with the Right Winning Zone; this time game.P1Serving
must be set to 1, as in Figure 3-10.

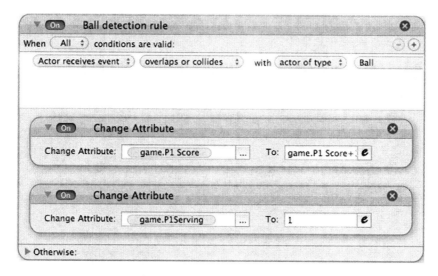

Figure 3-10. *Changing P1Serving to true*

Keeping One Ball in the Game at a Time

Now, let's limit the number of balls in the game to one. (You can decide otherwise later and adapt it to your own game's rules.)

You will use a Boolean attribute that will be changed to true as soon as a ball actor is spawned and to false when the ball is destroyed. Then you will modify the spawn behavior to check if this new attribute is false before spawning the ball.

In the Scene Editor, select the Attribute Inspector pane. Create a new Boolean attribute as per Figure 3-11.

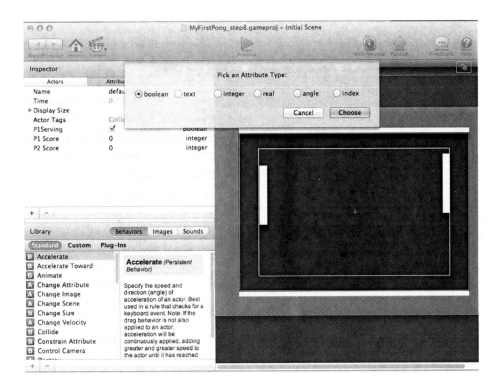

Figure 3-11. *A new Boolean attribute*

Name this attribute ActiveBall and leave it unchecked, as initially there will be no ball in the game.

Let's go back to the spawning behavior. Remember, the ball is spawned but the rackets are spawning. So you need to modify the behavior of the racket actors.

Open Rack Player 1 and add a new condition in the Serving rule. The condition is if game.ActiveBall is false. Then you need to add a Change Attribute behavior that will occur at the same time as the ball spawning. Drag a Change Attribute below the Spawn actor and implement game. ActiveBall to 1. This will change the attribute to true, preventing a new ball from being spawned when the space bar is down. Figure 3-12 shows the modified Serving rule.

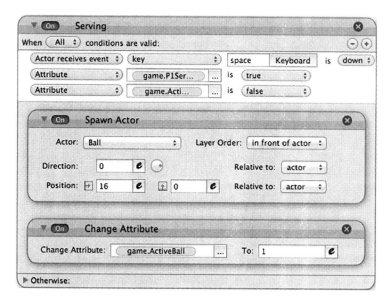

Figure 3-12. *Modified Rack Player 1 Serving rule*

Repeat the operation for Rack Player 2.

Last but not least, you need to modify the Destroy behavior of the Ball actor to indicate that there is no longer an active ball in the game. Double-click the Ball actor. Drag a Change Attribute behavior above the Destroy behavior and change the ActiveBall attribute to false. Your rule should look similar to Figure 3-13.

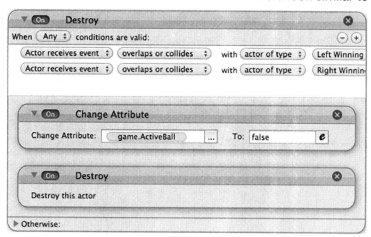

Figure 3-13. *Modified Destroy behavior*

Launch the game in Preview and check the appropriate behavior.

You can open the file MyFirstPong_step8.gameproj to reach this step.

Do You Have the Touch?

The real fun begins now! You will start using some of hardware functions of the iOS device. The first one is the touch interface of your device. You will implement two functions. The first one will spawn a ball when you tap the screen. The second one will move the Rack Player 1 with your finger.

Serving with a Pinch of Touch

You will implement touch serving for Player 1 only. The idea is that by the end of the chapter you will be able to play Player 1 against the computer!

To do so will take you about 5 seconds. Yes, you read correctly! Only 5 seconds.

Double-click Rack Player 1 to open the actor in editor mode. Modify the Serving rule's first condition: replace "key" with "touch." Then select "outside." So instead of having the player press the space bar down to spawn a ball, the player will touch the screen and the racket will spawn a ball. Your Serving rule should look like Figure 3-14.

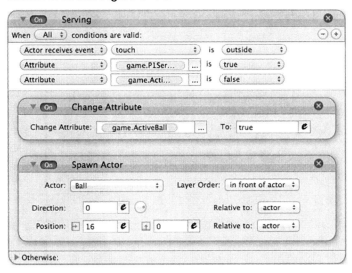

Figure 3-14. *Serving with a touch*

Now you want to be able to move Player 1's racket with a finger. Remember that the racket is constrained on a specific horizontal value. It can only move up or down. So you only have to work on the y-axis.

The trick is to detect the touch, to collect the value of the y-axis of the touch, and to constrain the Racket actor to this value. To collect the value of the touch position, you are going to use the mouse device.

The Mouse Device

The mouse special object is an object inside GameSalad in the Devices category. The Devices category helps you to take advantage of the hardware functionalities of iOS devices. Here you have access to the accelerometer, screen, audio, clock, touch, and mouse features. The mouse feature represents where you touch the screen and you collect this information through the position attributes.

Still, there is something very important to do to make it work. The racket shall not move outside of the visible area. You manage this point by only taking into account the touch within the range of 60 and 260.

1. Create a new rule and name it Touch Detection.

2. Add the following condition: Actor receives event of touch inside (you could replace "inside" with "pressed").

3. Add the two additional conditions:

   ▪ Attribute, game.Mouse.Position.Y,>, 60

   ▪ Attribute, game.Mouse.Position.Y, <, 260

4. Add a Constrain Attribute of Rack Player 1.Position.Y to game.Mouse.Position.Y.

The completed rule should look like Figure 3-15.

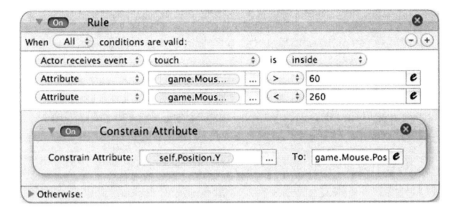

Figure 3-15. *Touch rule*

You can access to this stage by opening the file `MyFirstPong_step10.gameproj`.

Giving Your Game a Brain

iOS devices are powerful but implementing artificial intelligence with GameSalad is not possible. However, with a little bit of imagination, you can implement a few rules and behaviors that can do the trick.

You will proceed in a two-stage implementation. You will detect when the ball is coming to the Player 2 racket; when it passes half the screen, you will collect the y-value of the ball and store the value into an attribute. You will use a second attribute to limit the racket movement. The second stage will be to move the racket to this value.

Detecting the Direction and Getting the Y Value

1. Create a real attribute and name it "predict."

2. Create a Boolean attribute and name it "positionyourself" with a default value of false (leave it unchecked).

3. Open the Ball actor in the Actor Editor.

4. Create a new rule and add these conditions:

    - Attribute, Ball.Motion.Linear.Velocity.X, ≥,0: This will detect the movement direction of the ball. If the value is positive, the x-value will increase. So the movement will be from left to right, going into the Player 2 racket.

    - Attribute, Ball.Position.X, ≥, 240: This is when the ball passes over the half of the screen.

    - Attribute, Ball.Position.X, ≤, 300: This is before the ball bounces back on the racket.

5. Add a Constrain Attribute behavior and configure game.predict to ball.Position.Y

6. Add a Change Attribute behavior and configure game.positionyourself to 1.

7. Add a last Change Attribute behavior but in the Otherwise section, and configure game.positionyourselfto 0.

The finished rule is as per Figure 3-16.

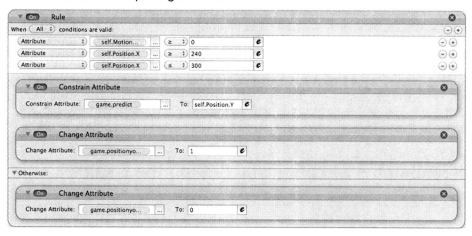

Figure 3-16. *Movement detection and position*

Moving Player 2 Racket to the Stored Value

1. Open the Rack Player 2 actor in the Actor Editor.

2. Create a new rule and add the following condition:

   Attribute game.positionyourself is true.

This detects the allowed period to move itself to move to the stored position.

3. Drag a Move To behavior.

4. Configure the Constrain Attribute as per Figure 3-17.

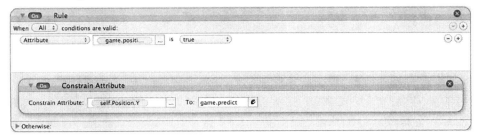

Figure 3-17. *Constrain Attribute*

You also need to do a modification on the Serving function so that Player 2 can serve automatically after winning a point. To do so, just remove the condition that the space key is pressed by scrolling over and clicking the - sign next to the condition.

The modified rule is shown in Figure 3-18.

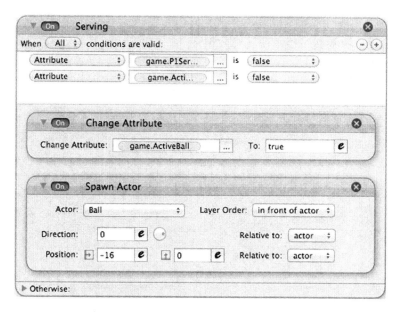

Figure 3-18. *Modified Serving rule*

You can directly reach this step by opening MyFirstPong_step11.gameproj.

Pong, Talk to Me

A final touch-up to the Pong project is to add some key messages that interact with the player. GameSalad has no speech capability but it can display text messages on the iOS device screen. As you did before with the score, you will use an actor to display some key interaction messages to the user.

In the Scene view, create a new actor and change the following attributes:

- Name: Display
- Size/Width: 360
- Size/Height: 100
- Color/Alpha: 0
- Physics/Moveable: Unchecked

In order to perfectly position the score display on the scene, you will use a Constrain Attribute behavior to constrain this position.

Drag and drop a Constrain Attribute into the behavior area of the Display actor. Then select Display.Position.X and constrain it to 240. Repeat the operation with Display.Position.Y and a constraint of 160.

Create a new rule with the following conditions:

- Attribute game.ActiveBall is false
- Attribute game.P1Serving is true

Drag a Display Textbehavior and configure it as per Figure 3-19.

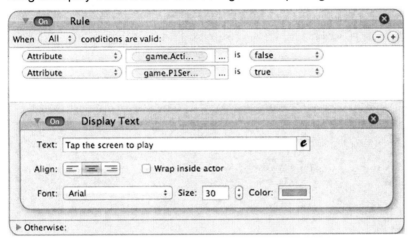

Figure 3-19. *Display key message*

Last but not least, drag and drop the actor on the scene.

You can reach this step directly by opening `MyFirstPong_step12.gameproj`.

Let's Play on Your Device

It's time to use the GameSaladiOS viewer.

Start the GameSaladiOS viewer on your iOS device and hit the Preview on iPhone button orthe Preview on iPad button. Your GameSalad will look like Figure 3-20.

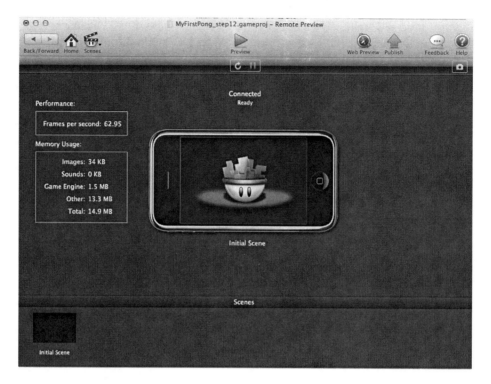

Figure 3-20. *Pong in iOS viewer*

Summary

You've come a long way since the beginning of Chapter 2. You now have a fully functional game that was built in two chapters.

In this chapter, you learned about:

- Scoring management
- Serving the ball
- Implementing artificial intelligence so Player 2 is controlled by the CPU
- Adding game/player interaction

I hope you enjoyed developing and playing the Pong game!

Break A Wall: Implementing Comments, Accelerometer Movements, LifeManagement, and Pause

This chapter will cover the first part of the creation of Break a Wall, a remake of the famous Breakout. Before you jump into the design of the game, I would like to cover a little bit of the game's history.

Atari developed Breakout (Figure 4-1) in 1976. Released four years after the Pong, Breakout became an arcade game immediately. Later, Atari released video game console version of Breakout.

Figure 4-1. *Breakout original poster*

Nolan Bushnell and Steve Bristow developed the game from an idea of having a one-player Pong game. The player uses racket to hit a ball to destroy bricks in a wall. If the player misses the return of the ball, he loses.

The original Breakout features a prisoner trying to escape using his ball and chain to break the bricks. There are two levels. Level 1 is made of eight rows of bricks of four different colors (two rows per color, shown in Figure 4-2). With the ball and the racket, the player must destroy all the bricks. The player can make up to 448 points per level.

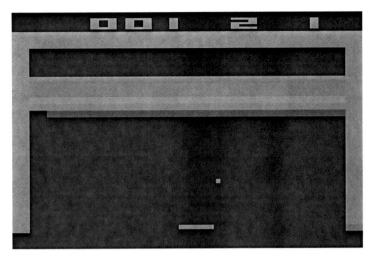

Figure 4-2. *Atari 2600 home version of Breakout*

A little note:

The original arcade version of Breakout was manufactured with black and white screens. Atari used some colored scotch strips on the screen itself to give the appearance of colors.

A little note:

Steve Jobs and Steve Wozniak were involved in the development of Breakout. They worked on the optimization of the circuitry boards in the game to reduce the number of transistors.

This chapter will cover the following subjects:

- Reinforcing your basic GameSalad skills
- Adding comments to your work
- Using the Accelerometer to control your game
- Managing lives and the Game Over process
- Adding a Pause feature to your game

Laying Down the Basics

In this section, you will quickly create the basic elements of the game. You will start by creating the actors and then you'll define the rules and behaviors for each of them. Lastly, you will position the actors on the scene.

You can jump-start this section by directly opening the file BreakaWall-step1.gameproj.

Defining the New Project

Start by opening the GameSalad creator. Under New Project, select My Great Project template and click Edit in GameSalad Creator.

Configure the project info as per Table 4-1.

Table 4-1. *Project Info*

Title	Break a Wall
Platform	iPad Portrait
Description	This is a remake of the famous Breakout game from Atari, originally released in 1972 as an arcade game.
Instructions	Tilt your iPad left and right to move the racket.
Tags	Breakout

Click File ➤ Save As to save your project. Name it BreakaWall.gameproj.

Defining the Actors

For this game you will create the following actors:

- Racket
- Brick
- Ball
- Vertical Wall
- Horizontal Wall

- Losing Zone
- Display

Racket

The racket is controlled by the player to bounce the ball back to the brick.

Create a new actor and double-click it to open the Actor Editor.

Edit the actor attributes with the parameters in Table 4-2.

Table 4-2. *Racket Actor Attributes*

Name	Racket
Size/Width	200
Size/Height	20
Color/Red	0
Color/Green	0
Color/Blue	1
Density	500
Friction	0
Restitution	1
Fixed Rotation	Checked

Brick

Bricks constitute the unitary elements of the wall to destroy. Create a new actor and double-click it to open the Actor Editor. Edit the actor attributes with the parameters in Table 4-3.

Table 4-3. *Brick Actor Attributes*

Name	Brick
Size/Width	128
Size/Height	20
Color/Red	0
Color/Green	1
Color/Blue	0
Density	500
Friction	0
Restitution	1
Fixed Rotation	Checked
Moveable	Unchecked

Ball

The ball is the moving element bouncing inside the playing area. Create a new actor and double-click it to open the Actor Editor. Edit the actor attributes with the parameters in Table 4-4.

Table 4-4. *Ball Actor Attributes*

Name	Ball
Size/Width	20
Size/Height	20
Color/Red	1
Color/Green	1
Color/Blue	1
Density	1
Friction	0
Restitution	1
Fixed Rotation	Checked
Collision shape	Circle

Vertical Wall

Walls are used to define the game area. Create a new actor and double-click it to open the Actor Editor. Edit the actor attributes with the parameters in Table 4-5.

Table 4-5. *Wall Actor Attributes*

Name	Vertical Wall
Size/Width	20
Size/Height	1048
Color/Red	1
Color/Green	1
Color/Blue	1
Density	500
Friction	0
Restitution	1
Fixed Rotation	Checked
Moveable	Unchecked

Horizontal Wall

Create a new actor and double-click it to open the Actor Editor. Edit the actor attributes with the parameters in Table 4-6.

Table 4-6.*Horizontal Wall Actor Attributes*

Name	Horizontal Wall
Size/Width	792
Size/Height	20
Color/Red	1
Color/Green	1
Color/Blue	1
Density	500
Friction	0
Restitution	1
Fixed Rotation	Checked
Moveable	Unchecked

Losing Zone

Similar to the Winning Zone in the Pong game, you will create a Losing Zone below the racket to detect when the player has missed a ball. Create a new actor and double-click it to open the Actor Editor. Edit the actor attributes with the parameters in Table 4-7.

Table 4-7. *Losing Zone Actor Attributes*

Name	Losing Zone
Size/Width	792
Size/Height	20
Color/Red	1
Color/Green	1
Color/Blue	1
Color/Alpha	0
Density	1
Restitution	1
Fixed Rotation	Unchecked
Moveable	Unchecked

Display

The display actor is used to display information on the screen. Create a new actor and double-click it to open the Actor Editor. Edit the actor attributes with the parameters in Table 4-8.

Table 4-8. *Display Actor Attributes*

Name	Display
Size/Width	700
Size/Height	300
Color/Red	1
Color/Green	1
Color/Blue	1
Color/Alpha	0
Density	1
Restitution	1
Fixed Rotation	Unchecked
Moveable	Unchecked

Creating the Collidable Tag

You will repeat the approach you took for Pong to create a Collidable tag for all the actors that will collide.

Create a new actor tag and name it "Collidable."

Drag and drop the following actors over the Collidable tag:

- Brick
- Racket
- Ball
- Horizontal Wall
- Vertical Wall

Defining the Attributes

As in the previous chapters, attributes will play a great deal in your game engineering.

ActiveBall attribute will be used to know if a ball is already active on the screen and if so, prevents the user from spawning another ball in the game. To do this, you will use a Boolean.

BrickCount will be used to know when the ball destroys the last brick. You will set this integer attribute with the initial number of bricks on the screen. Then everytime a brick is destroyed, you will decrement this integer.

TextToDisplay will be used to communication game information with the player.

Create the attributes as per Table 4-9.

Table 4-9. *Attribute List*

Attribute Name	Type	Initial Value
ActiveBall	Boolean	False
BrickCount	Integer	6
TextToDisplay	Text	

Implementing the Rules and Behaviors

Actors, attributes, and tags are now all set. But no logic and interaction has been implemented yet. The next steps will add the rules and behaviors that will define the game logic for each of actors.

Ball Rules and Behaviors

In order to give the ball an initial movement when it is spawned you will use a Change Velocity behavior.

Drag and drop a Change Velocity behavior into the actor and change the setting to direction of random (70,110) relative to the scene at a speed of 300, as per Figure 4-3.

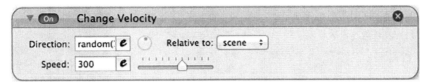

Figure 4-3. *Initial velocity of the ball*

Next, you need to ensure that the ball will collide with all collidable actors, so use a Collide behavior.

Drag and drop a Collide behavior into the actor and change the setting to "actor with tag:" and "collidable" as per Figure 4-4.

Figure 4-4. *Collide behavior of the ball*

Let's create the rule when the player misses the ball. You will use the same logic as per the Pong game. An actor will be positioned below the racket and when the ball overlaps it, it will destroy the ball and change the attribute ActiveBall to false.

ClickCreate Rule and add the condition "Actor receives event" "overlaps or collides" with "actor of type" "loosing zone." Drag and drop a Change Attribute behavior and change game.ActiveBall to 0. Then, drag and drop a Destroy behavior just below the Change Attribute behavior. Your rule should be similar to Figure 4-5.

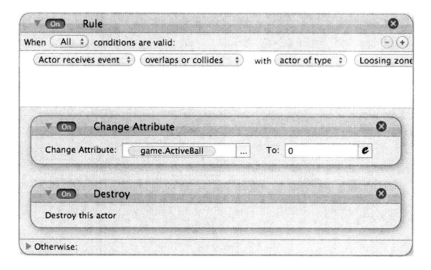

Figure 4-5. *Loosing rule*

Next, create a rule that will destroy the ball when the last brick has been destroyed and will also display the text "You Win!" Click Create Rule and add the condition "Attribute""game.BrickCount""=""0." Drag and drop a Change Attribute behavior and change game.TextToDisplayto "You Win!" Then, drag and drop a Destroy behavior just below the Change Attribute behavior. Your rule should be similar to Figure 4-6.

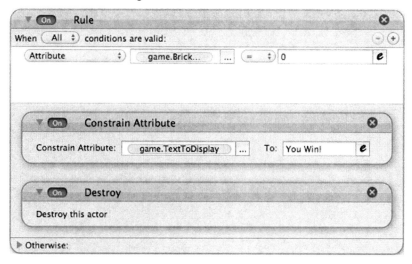

Figure 4-6. *Finishing the game*

If you have played a significant number of Pong games, you may have noticed that the ball sometimes gets stuck horizontally; this is very boring. In order to avoid this, let's introduce a disturbance. You will monitor the ball, and as soon as it is stuck horizontally or vertically, you will add a random effect to change the next bounce. To achieve this objective, you must monitor the linear velocity of the ball. The linear velocity is the motion among the axis of the 2-D plan. If the linear velocity of the Y is 0, this means that the ball keeps a constant Y position. In other words, your ball is moving at a perfect horizontal movement (the ball is stuck between the left and right wall). If the linear velocity of the X is 0, this means that the ball keeps a constant X position. In other words, your ball is moving at a perfect vertical movement.

Click Create Rule and add the condition "Attribute""ball.Motion.Linear Velocity.Y""="""0". Drag and drop a Rule behavior and add the condition "Actor receives event""overlaps or collides" with "actor with tag""collidable." Then drag and drop a Change Attribute behavior and change ball.Motion.Linear Velocity.Y to random (70,120). Your rule should be similar to Figure 4-7.

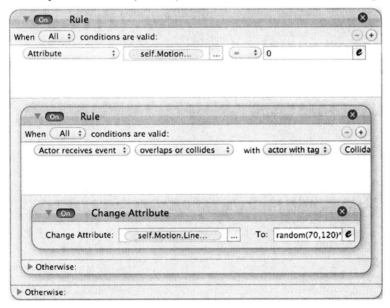

Figure 4-7. *Preventing horizontal jam*

Click Create Rule and add the condition "Attribute""ball.Motion.Linear Velocity.X""="""0". Drag and drop a Rule behavior and add the condition "Actor receives event""overlaps or collides" with "actor with tag""collidable." Then drag and drop a Change Attribute behavior and change ball.Motion.Linear Velocity.X to random (70,120). Your rule should be similar to Figure 4-8.

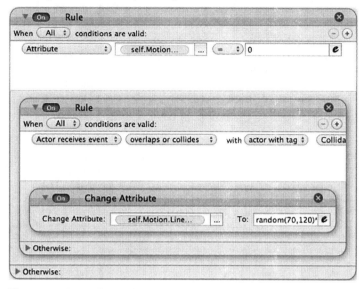

Figure 4-8. *Preventing vertical jam*

Racket Rules and Behaviors

Drag and drop a Collide behavior into the actor and change the setting to "actor with tag:""Collidable" as per Figure 4-9.

Figure 4-9. *Collide behavior of the ball*

Drag and drop a Constrain Attribute behavior into the actor and change the setting of Racket.Position.Y to 40 as per Figure 4-10. This will constrain the racket to its position vertically.

Figure 4-10. *Constrain attribute for racket*

Now create two rules to implement the movement of the racket. As you did previously, you will use the keys to move the racket left and right.

Click Create Rule and add the condition "Actor receives event""key" "left" keyboard is "down." Drag and drop a Move behavior and change the settings to:

  ▨ Direction: 180

  ▨ Relative to: actor

  ▨ Move Type: additive

  ▨ Speed: 300

Your rule should be similar to Figure 4-11.

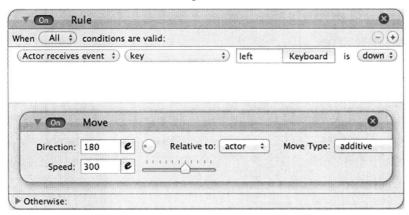

Figure 4-11. *Left movement rule*

Click Create Rule and add the condition "Actor receives event" "key" "right" keyboard is "down." Drag and drop a Move behavior and change the settings to:

  ▨ Direction: 0

  ▨ Relative to: actor

  ▨ Move Type: additive

  ▨ Speed: 300

Your rule should be similar to Figure 4-12.

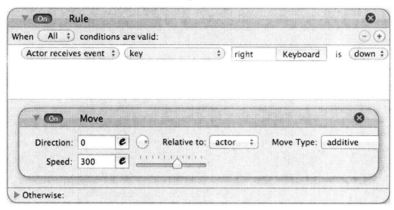

Figure 4-12. *Right movement rule*

Lastly, create a rule to spawn a ball actor when the screen is touched outside of the actor and when there is no active ball.

Click Create Rule and add the condition "Actor receives event" "touch" is "outside." Add a second condition to check the game.ActiveBall attribute. The condition will be "Attribute" "game.ActiveBall" is "false." Drag and drop a Spawn Actor behavior and change the settings to:

- Actor: Ball
- Layer Order:in front of actor
- Direction: random(75,135)
- Relative to: actor
- Position: 0, 10
- Relative to: actor

Drag and drop a Change Attribute behavior and change game.ActiveBall to 1. Your rule should be similar to Figure 4-13.

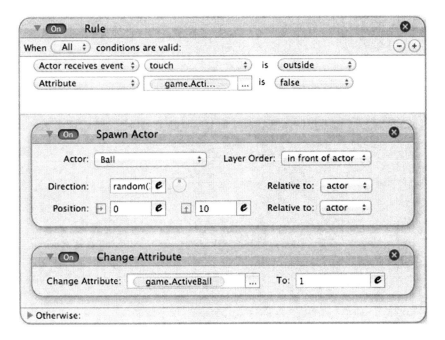

Figure 4-13. *Spawning the Ball actor rule*

Brick Rules and Behaviors

There will be only one rule for the brick actor. The rule will detect a collision with the ball and then destroy the actor and decrement the brickCount attribute.

Click Create Rule and add the condition "Actor receives event" "overlaps or collides" with "actor of type" "Ball." Drag and drop a Destroy behavior. Drag and drop a Change Attribute behavior and change game.BrickCount to game.BrickCount-1. Your rule should be similar to Figure 4-14.

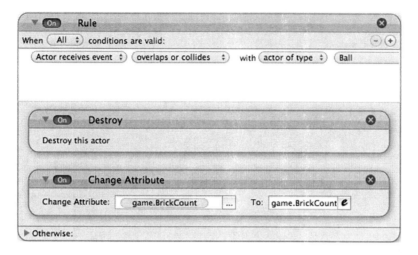

Figure 4-14. *The Brick rule*

Display Text Rules and Behaviors

The last actor that needs a behavior at this stage is the display text. It will permanently display the content of a text attribute on the scene. The trick is that the attribute will be empty until the game is won.

Drag and drop a Display Text attribute and change the setting of Text to "game.TextToDisplay." You can leave all the rest as per default. Your behavior should be similar to Figure 4-15.

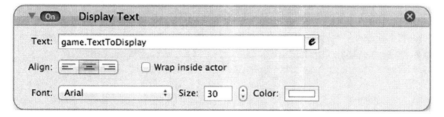

Figure 4-15. *Displaying the winning text*

Layout of the Scene

The next step is to position the actors on the scene. Drag your actors onto the scene and try to match Figure 4-16. You will need to drag the Brick into the scene six times in order to create six instances of this actor.

Figure 1-16. *Step 1 scene*

Although invisible, drag the Display actor at the center of the scene.

Commenting Your Work

If you skipped the previous part, you can directly open the file BreakaWall-step1.gameproj to continue from this point.

Should you write comments? What is a good comment? I must admit that I used to hate to write comments. I thought it was useless and diverted me from the objective: coding! But this is wrong! First and foremost, comments make your game design clearer. By commenting, you can describe the responsibilities of the actor or the intent of the rule. Next, it makes your game projects easier to understand for others. When you work on a team, you will save your colleagues a tremendous amount of time if you include the right comments. A good comment provides useful information about your design strategy and any tricky arrangements in your rules.

To add a comment, use the Note behavior of GameSalad. It can be placed as any behavior in the Actor Behavior pane or within a rule. Let's practice a little bit.

Open the Racket actor in the Actor Editor. Drag and drop a Note behavior at the top of the pile of the behaviors. Type the following comment:

```
The Racket is the paddle to be controlled by the player.
       The racket will collide and bounce with collidable objects.
       The racket will be constrained on the Y=40 axis.
```

Your comment should be similar to Figure 1-17.

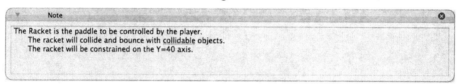

Figure 1-17. *General comment for the racket*

Now, drag and drop a Note behavior above the Left Movement rule. Type the following comment:

```
When the left key is pressed, the actor will move to the left direction.

When the right key is pressed, the actor will move to the right direction.
```

Your comment should be similar to Figure 1-18.

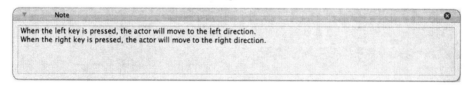

Figure 4-18. *Comments on racket movement rules*

From this step forward, I will not tell you which comment to write but the project files will contain some of my comments. Feel free to read them.

Moving the Paddle with the Accelerometer

To follow from this point, you can simply open the file BreakaWall-step2.gameproj.

Let's have some fun! In order to move the racket, you will use the built-in accelerometer of the iOS device. In order to create such a feature, you will again use the device attributes, especially the accelerometer. In fact, you will need to use detection on the X-axis of the accelerometer.

Open the Racket actor in the Actor Editor. In the left movement rule, add a new condition. The condition is "Attribute""game.accelerometer.X""<""-0.05". You also need to change from "All" to "Any" in "When 'Any' conditions are valid." That's it! Your new rule will be similar to Figure 4-19.

This implementation of the movement based on the accelerometer is rough at this stage and does not take into consideration any amount of tilt in the movement. It is only a first approach. You will learn a more advanced approach in Chapter 8.

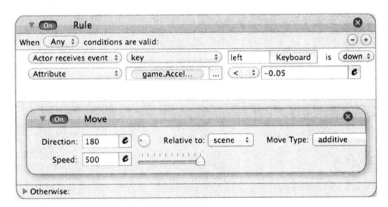

Figure 4-19. *Left Movement rule with the accelerometer*

The Accelerometer

The accelerometer is measuring the device's own acceleration in the 3-D space. Sensors in your iOS device capture every movement and tilt so it can calculate the orientation of the device and many other usages (such as which direction the device is moving).

When you put the iPad in a Portrait mode, as per Figure 4-20, the X-axis will be pointing to you.

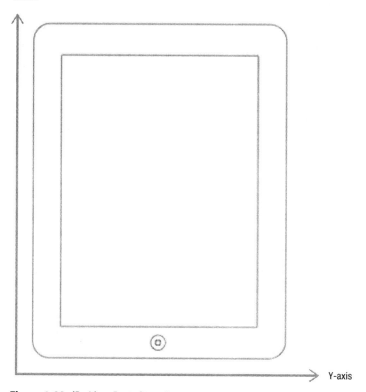

Figure 4-20. *iPad in a Portrait mode*

Negative acceleration is a counterclockwise rotation around the x-axis, as per Figure 4-21.

Figure 4-21. *Counterclockwise rotation*

Positive acceleration is a clockwise rotation around the x-axis, as per Figure 4-22.

Figure 4-22. *Clockwise rotation*

As you want to capture intended movement and not vibration, you select the trigger value of 0.05. You may play around this value to find the one you feel most comfortable with.

Let's modify the Right Movement rule to include the accelerometer condition. In the Right Movement rule, add a new condition: "Attribute""game.accelerometer.X"">" "0.05". You also need to change from "All" to "Any"as in "When 'Any' conditions are valid." That's it! Your new rule will be similar to Figure 4-23.

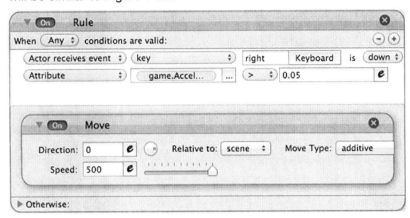

Figure 4-23. *Right Movement rule with accelerometer*

If you change from Portrait to Landscape orientation or to support both orientations, you will need to change your accelerometer rules.

Create a group of behaviors for the racket by clicking Create Group in the Actor Editor for the Racket. Drag and drop the two rules into the group.

The rules that you just created work well for Portrait orientation. You need to inverse them for the Portrait Upside Down orientation. Doing so is very easy with GameSalad. Create a rule that will detect the screen orientation and enable the correct rules accordingly.

Create a new rule with the conditions of "Attribute""game.Screen.Device Orientation" "is" "Portrait." Then drag and drop the newly created group. The new rule should be as in Figure 4-24.

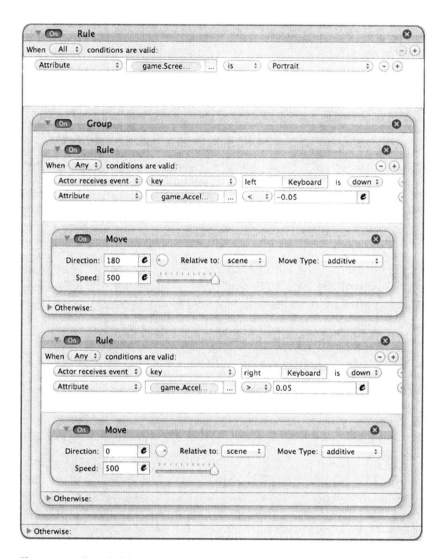

Figure 4-24. *Portrait Orientation rule*

Select the rule you just created and press Command + C to copy the rule. Press Command + V to paste the rule and change the following settings: "Portrait" to "Portrait Upside Down", and then the first sub-rule for the left movement will change its condition to ">""0.05" and the second sub-rule for the right movement will change its condition to "<""-0.05". Your rule will be similar to Figure 4-25.

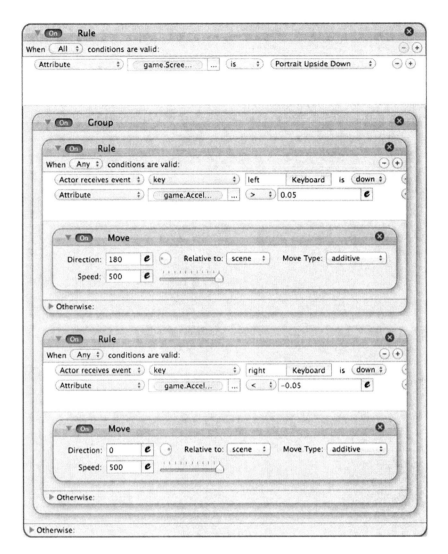

Figure 4-25. *Portrait Upside Down Orientation rule*

You now manage the orientation of your device!

EXERCISE

Test this project in the iOS viewer. Follow the instruction from the previous chapter. You will also change the Autorotate attribute to enable Portrait Upside Down. To do so, in the Scene Editor, click the Scene button as per Figure 4-26 and expand the Autorotate attribute. Tick the box next to Portrait Upside Down.

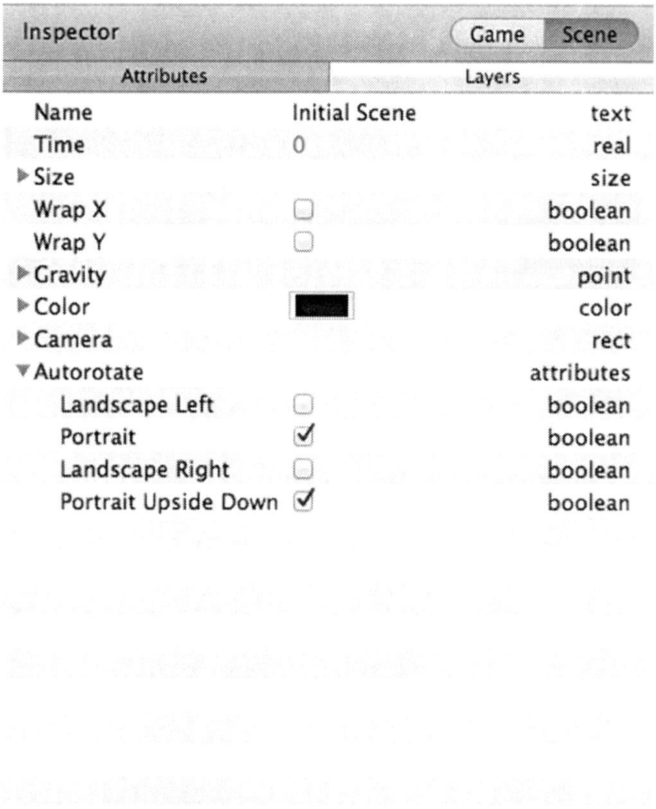

Inspector		Game	Scene
Attributes		**Layers**	
Name	Initial Scene		text
Time	0		real
▶ Size			size
Wrap X	☐		boolean
Wrap Y	☐		boolean
▶ Gravity			point
▶ Color	■		color
▶ Camera			rect
▼ Autorotate			attributes
Landscape Left	☐		boolean
Portrait	☑		boolean
Landscape Right	☐		boolean
Portrait Upside Down	☑		boolean

Figure 4-26. *Scene Attribute Inspector*

Managing Lives and the GameOver process

To follow from this point, you can simply open the file BreakaWall-step3.gameproj.

To make the game more realistic, you can give the player three lives. This means that the third time the ball is missed, you will display a Game Over message and the player will not be able to spawn a new actor. You will also display a Retry button that will reset the scene and let the player attempt to win again.

As you may have guessed already, you will use an attribute to manage the lives. Every time the ball is missed, you will decrement the attribute by 1. You will add a condition to check that the number of lives is strictly superior to 0 before spawning a new ball. In the display text, you will have a rule to display the Game Over message when the lives attribute is equal to 0.

Time to GameSalad design! Create a new integer attribute, rename it "lives", and set the default value to 3. Your attribute will look like Figure 4-27.

| lives | 3 | integer |

Figure 4-27. *Lives attribute*

Open the Ball actor in the Actor Editor by double-clicking it. In the Losing Zone rule, drag and drop a Change Attribute behavior and position it between the game.ActiveBall Change Attribute behavior and the Destroy behavior. Modify game.lives to game.lives-1.

The Losing Zone rule will be as in Figure 4-28.

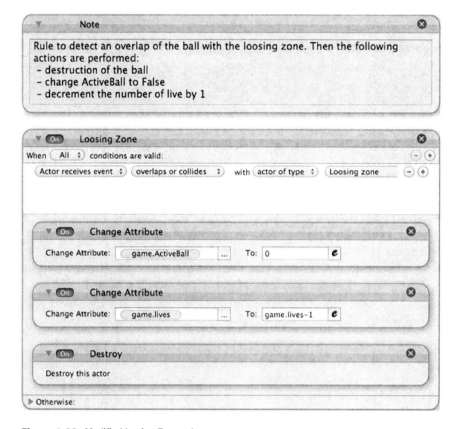

Figure 4-28. *Modified Losing Zone rule*

Next, create a new rule and change the condition to "Attribute""game.lives""="
"0". This will detect when there are no more lives available. Drag and drop a
Change Attribute behavior and change game.TextToDisplay to "Game Over! –
Tap here to retry" as per Figure 4-29.

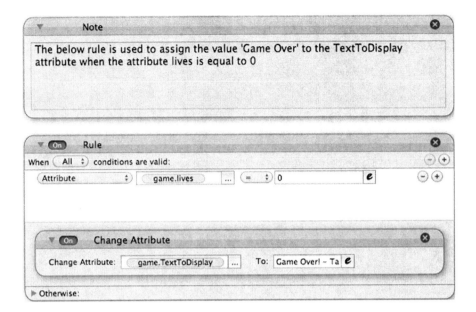

Figure 4-29. *Game Over display rule*

You need to modify the Ball Spawning rule attached to the Racket actor in order to add a condition on the number of lives (>0).

Open the Racket actor in the Actor Editor. Select the Ball Spawning rule and add the following condition: "Attribute""game.lives"">""0" as per Figure 4-30.

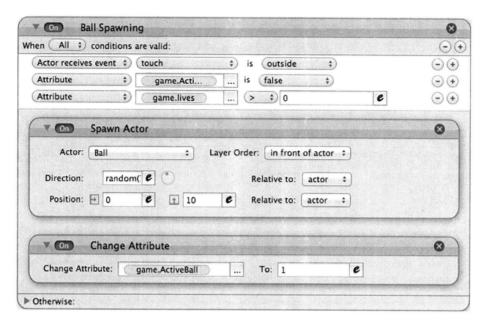

Figure 4-30. *Modified Ball Spawning rule*

You're almost there but you need to implement the Retry feature when the game is over. This is fairly easy. You will use the Reset Game behavior.

About Reset Game and Reset Scene:

Although it may sound obvious, Reset Scene will only reset the scene and not the game. This is very useful when you have a multiple-level game and you want to give more tries to the players, but keep in mind that resetting the scene will <u>only</u> reset the scene, and as such, the game attributes will not be reset. So when you design your game, take the time to think about which attributes should be game or scene attributes.

Open the Display actor in the Actor Editor and create a new rule as per Figure 4-31.

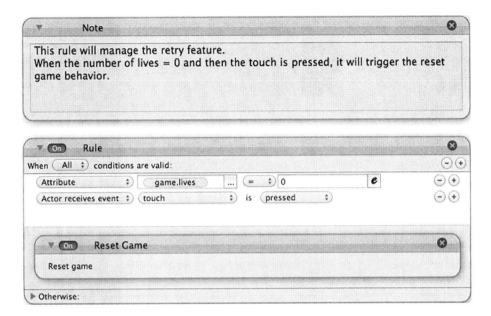

Figure 4-31. *Retry feature*

Adding a Pause Feature

To follow from this point, you can simply open the file BreakaWall-
step4.gameproj.

Pausing in GameSalad is extremely easy, but you need to understand the
concept in order to use it efficiently.

The Pause behavior will overlay a new scene on the top of your current scene
and suspend all the physics of the current scene. It does not pause music,
sound, nor timers. To efficiently build a Pause function, you need:

- An actor that can trigger the Pause behavior.
- A scene to use as a Pause screen.
- A button on the Pause screen to resume the game.

Let's put all this into practice.

Create a new scene. Click the Home button and select the Scene tab. Then click
on the + sign at the bottom left. Rename the scene by clicking on the name.
Type "Pause" as the scene name.

As per Figure 3-32, you now have two scenes in your project.

Initial Scene   Pause

Figure 3-32. *Scene view*

Create a new actor. Edit the actor attributes with the parameters in Table 4-10.

Table 4-10. *Pause actor attributes*

Name	Pause
Size/Width	200
Size/Height	100
Color/Alpha	0

Drag and drop a Display Text attribute and change the setting as per Figure 4-33.

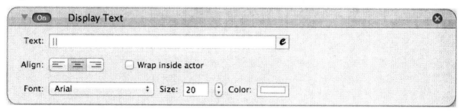

Figure 4-33. *Pause display*

Create a new rule and add the following conditions:

- "Actor receives event" "touch" is "pressed"
- "Attribute" "game.lives" ">""0"

Then drag and drop a Pause Game attribute and select the Pause scene that you previously created. The complete rule is shown in Figure 4-34.

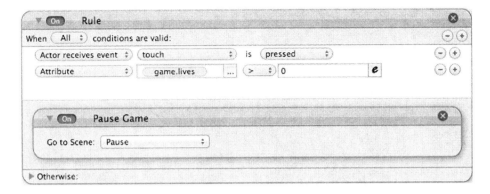

Figure 4-34. *Pause rule*

Now position the Pause actor on the screen at the top left corner as per Figure 3-35.

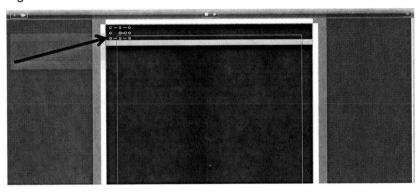

Figure 3-35. *Positioning the Pause actor*

By clicking the Scenes button, select the newly created scene named Pause.

Create a new actor called ResumeGame. Edit the actor attributes with the parameters in Table 4-11.

Table 4-11. *Resume Game Actor Attributes*

Name	Resume Game
Size/Width	600
Size/Height	300
Color/Alpha	0

Drag and drop a Display Text attribute and change the setting as per Figure 4-36.

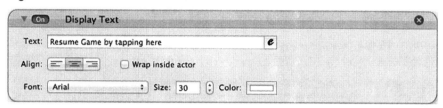

Figure 4-36. *Resume Game display*

Create a new rule and add the following conditions:

- "Actor receives event" "touch" is "pressed"

Then drag and drop an Unpause Game attribute. The complete rule is shown in Figure 4-37.

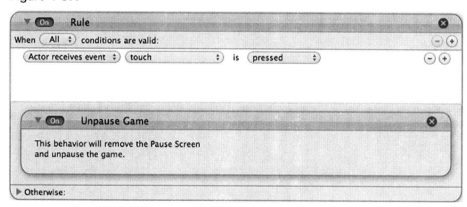

Figure 4-37. *Unpause Game rule*

Last, you need to position the ResumeGame actor in the center of the screen. And that's it! You have a Pause feature in your game!

You can open the file `Breakawall-step5.gameproj` to reach this point.

You will continue to work on this game in Chapter 9. In the meantime, you will develop skills in physics, gravity, audio, and graphics effects.

Summary

You are on the verge of creating a new Arkanoid! You have a second game in your portfolio.

In this chapter, you have:

- Reinforced your basic GameSalad skills.

- Added comments to your work.

- Used the Accelerometer to control your game.

- Managed lives and the Game Over process.

- Added a pause feature to your game.

Making a Shoot 'Em Up Game: Carrot Invader

When I was a kid, I remember in a bad way my parents trying to get me to finish my mashed carrots. "Eat this, you will have nice skin!" Arhh!!! I still have nightmares about carrots! This is why, in order to pay a tribute to one of the most famous video games, you will remake Space Invaders with carrots instead of aliens.

Space Invaders is a Japanese game that was released in 1978 by Taito Corporation. Taito was originally an import/export company that traded vending machines in Japan. They moved into the gaming industry in the 60s. More recently, Square Enix acquired Taito in 2005. Square Enix is famous in the gaming industry for the Final Fantasy games.

Space Invaders was inspired by a previous electro-mechanical game from Taito called Space Monsters. Space Invaders has been a colossal success for Taito. The arcade version of the game is shown in Figure 5-1.

Figure 5-1. *A Space Invaders arcade cabinet.*

Space Invaders is a shoot 'em up game. You control a spaceship that shoots at its enemies with a cannon. The enemies are aliens that move from left to right in rows (and from time to time move down by a few pixels). The purpose is to shoot at all the enemies before they touch down on the Earth and start the invasion.

In this chapter, you will practice the basics of GameSalad by creating another new project that contains actors, rules, and behaviors. You will also learn about the management of images and how to use images with actors. This chapter will also cover the following:

- A basic introduction to mathematics to create complex movements

- Visual effects of spaceship movement without moving

- The Interpolate behavior to manage the energy bar

- The Change Scene behavior to transition scenes

Preparing the Basic Elements of the Scene

As per the previous chapter, you may jump-start this section by directly opening the file CarrotInvaders-step1.gameproj.

In this section, you will create a new project for your Carrot Invader project. Then you will focus on the actors of the project. You will reinforce your skills in actor creation, rules, and attributes design. You will also learn something new: the image features, such as importing images, the inspector, and adding a picture to an actor.

Creating the Carrot Invader Game Project

Open the Game Salad Creator and create a new project. Configure the project info as per Table 5-1.

Table 5-1. *Project Info for Carrot Invaders*

Title	Carrot Invaders
Platform	iPhone Portrait
Description	Carrot Invader is a remake of Space Invaders, an arcade video game created in 1978 by Tomohiro Nishikado for Taito.
	Defeat Carrot Invasion by shooting at them
Instructions	Automatic shooting
	Tilt the device to move left and right (or use the arrows)
Tags	Carrot Invaders

Name and save your file as Carrot_Invaders.gameproj.

Artist Entrance: Creating the Actors

Carrot Invaders requires the following actors:

- Carrots: Used as enemies
- Spaceship: Used as the hero
- Background: Used to create the context

- Bullet: Used to destroy the enemies
- Wall: To define the scene

Before creating the actors, you will do something new. You will prepare some costumes for your actors. Yes, you will put some clothes on them (by clothes, I mean you will use pictures). I will provide you later with more information about graphics and graphic optimization in GameSalad; this chapter focuses on how to import and use an image in GameSalad.

To display an image on the screen, you need an actor. But for actor to access the image, the image must be first imported into GameSalad.

Importing images in GameSalad is easy. In the Scene Editor, select the Images tab next to the Behavior tab, as per Figure 5-2.

Figure 5-2. *Scene Editor with Images tab selected*

Click the + sign at the bottom corner to open a system selection window and select the file you want to import.

NOTE: Images can be imported in a few other ways. They can be dragged into the Images section directly from the desktop or a folder. They can be dragged onto an actor from the desktop or folder. They can also be added by right-clicking the .gameproj file and selecting "Show package contents and images" and dragging it into there, but this is not recommended.

Import the following files into the Images Resources located in the chapter 5 folder: carrot.png, background.png, spaceship.png, tomato.png, and explosion.png (as per Figure 5-3).

Figure 5-3. *Imported images*

As you create the actors, note that if the attributes are not specifically mentioned, the value is left by default.

Creating the Enemies: Carrots

Create a new actor and double-click it to open the Actor Editor.

Edit the actor attributes with the parameters in Table 5-2.

Table 5-2. *Carrots Actor*

Name	Carrots
Size/Width	12
Size/Height	42

Click the Images tab to display the images that you just imported. Drag and drop `carrot.png` to the Actor view as per Figure 5-4.

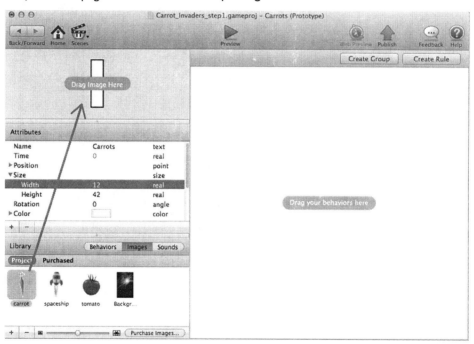

Figure 5-4. *Moving a picture to the actor*

Traveling through Space: The Spaceship

Create a new actor and double-click it to open the Actor Editor.

Edit the actor attributes with the parameters in Table 5-3.

Table 5-3. *Spaceship Actor*

Name	Spaceship
Size/Width	20
Size/Height	40
Physics/Fixed Rotation	Checked
Physics/Restitution	0

Click the Images tab to display the images that you just imported, and drag and drop spaceship.png to the actor.

In a Far, Far, Far away Galaxy: Creating the Background

Create a new actor and double-click it to open the Actor Editor.

Edit the actor attributes with the parameters in Table 5-4.

Table 5-4. *Background Actor*

Name	Background
Size/Width	320
Size/Height	480
Physics/Moveable	unchecked

Click the Images tab to display the images that you just imported, and drag and drop background.png to the actor.

Load Your Guns: Defining the Bullets

Create a new actor and double-click it to open the Actor Editor.

Edit the actor attributes with the parameters in Table 5-5.

Table 5-5. *Bullet Actor*

Name	Bullet
Size/Width	2
Size/Height	20
Color/Red	1
Color/Green	1
Color/Blue	0

Boundaries In Deep Space: The Wall

Create a new actor and double-click it to open the Actor Editor.

Edit the actor attributes with the parameters in Table 5-6.

Table 5-6. *Wall Actor*

Name	Wall
Size/Width	10
Size/Height	480
Physics/Restitution	0
Physics/Moveable	unchecked

Your actor inventory should match Figure 5-5.

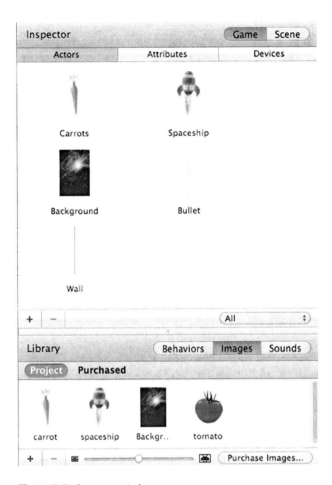

Figure 5-5. *Actors created*

Controlling the Number of Enemies with Game Attributes

At first, you will only create one attribute that will be used to contain the number of carrots remaining on screen. As such, it will be an integer attribute that you will call NumberCarrots.

At the start of the game, this attribute will contain the number of carrots on the screen and it will be decremented by 1 each time a carrot is smashed by the bullet beam.

Click the Attribute tab in the inspector in Scene Editor mode. Then click the + sign to create a new attribute and select integer. The initial value should be 0 and the type should be integer as per Figure 5-6.

NumberCarrots   0   integer

Figure 5-6. *NumberCarrots attribute*

Setting the Screenplay: Implementing Rules and Behaviors

You need to define the logic of your game and you will use rules and behaviors to accomplish this task. You will use the Timer and Accelerator behaviors to create controls and the auto firing.

Carrots: The Ultimate Enemy Role

Drag and drop a Change Attribute behavior into the Carrots actor and change game.NumberCarrots to game.NumberCarrots+1 as per Figure 5-7. Every time you position a Carrots actor on the scene, this will increment by 1 the attribute NumberCarrots. So when you start the scene, you will have the number of carrots on the screen contained in the game attribute NumberCarrots.

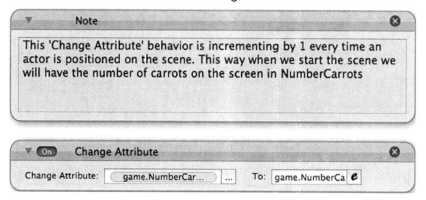

Figure 5-7. *Change Attribute NumberCarrots*

Now create a rule that will detect when a collision occurs between a bullet and a carrot, trigger a decrement of the number of enemies, and then destroy the enemy.

Click Create Rule and name the rule "Destroy the Carrot." Add the following conditions: "Actor receives event" "overlaps or collides" with "actor of type" "Bullet." Drag and drop a Timer behavior and change the setting to "After" "0.4" seconds. Check the box for "Run to Completion." Then drag and drop a Change Attribute behavior and change game.NumberCarrots to game.NumberCarrots-1. Lastly, drag and drop a Destroy behavior as per Figure 5-8.

Why are you using a Timer? Later in this chapter you will implement an explosion effect with a duration of 0.4 seconds. Thus the timer is to give you the time to display this effect before destroying the actor.

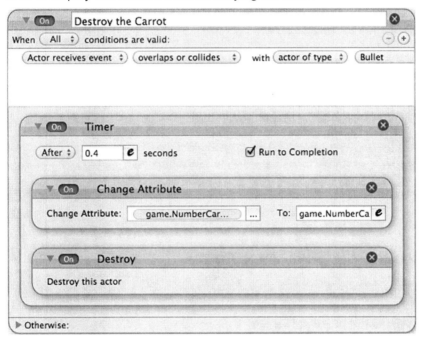

Figure 5-8. *Destroy the Carrot rule*

Flying the Spaceship

First, you will ensure that the spaceship stays on a horizontal axis at Y=25 by using a Constrain Attribute behavior.

Drag and drop a Constrain Attribute behavior into the Spaceship actor and configure spaceship.position.Y to 25 as per Figure 5-9.

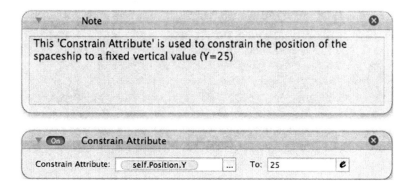

Figure 5-9. *Constraining the spaceship at Y=25*

Next, use the collision with the walls to create some boundaries for the spaceship.

Drag and drop a Collide behavior and change the settings to Bounce when colliding with "actor of type""wall" as per Figure 5-10.

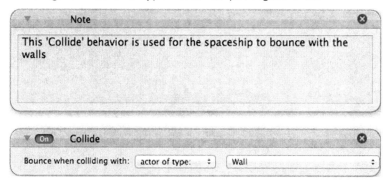

Figure 5-10. *Colliding with the wall*

Group the Movement rules together to increase readability. You will use rules to detect the accelerometer movements and make the spaceship move accordingly.

Click Create Group and name it "Movement." Click Create Rule to create a rule inside the group. Name the rule "Right Movement" and configure to "Any" the following conditions:

- "Actor receives event""key""right" keyboard is "down"
- "Attribute""game.Accelerometer"">""0.2"

Then drag and drop a Move behavior and configure the following settings:

- Direction: 0
- Relative to: Scene
- Move Type: additive
- Speed: 300

Your rule should be similar to Figure 5-11.

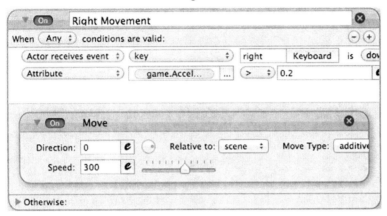

Figure 5-11. *Right Movement rule*

Create a new rule in the Movement group. Name it "Left Movement" and configure to "Any" the following conditions:

- "Actor receives event""key""left" keyboard is "down"
- "Attribute""game.Accelerometer""<""-0.2"

Then drag and drop a Move behavior and configure the following settings:

- Direction: 180
- Relative to: Scene
- Move Type: additive
- Speed: 300

Your rule should be similar to Figure 5-12.

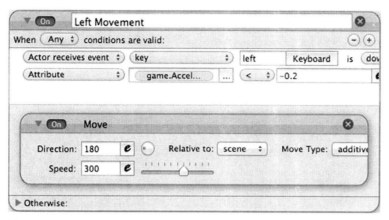

Figure 5-12. *Left Movement rule*

Now implement an auto-fire of the bullets by the spaceship. To do so, create a rule that states that as long as the number of carrots on the screen is strictly larger than 0, a bullet is fired every 0.5 seconds.

Create a new rule and name it "Auto Fire" with the condition "Attribute""game.NumberCarrots"">""0". Then drag and drop a Timer behavior and change the settings to "Every""0.5" seconds with "Run to completion" unchecked. Lastly, drag and drop a Spawn Actor behavior and change the settings to:

- Actor: Bullet

- Layer Order: in back of actor

- Direction: 0

- Relative to: actor

- Position: X: 0 Y: 0

- Relative to: actor

The Auto Fire rule will be the same as Figure 5-13.

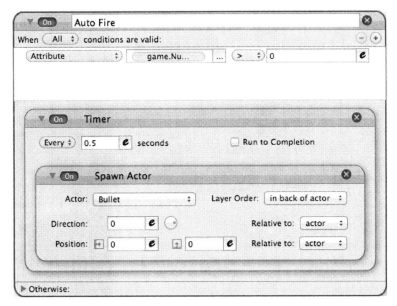

Figure 5-13. *Auto Fire rule*

Firing at Full Force: Bullet

First, you will change the velocity of the bullet in order for the bullet to move as soon as it is spawned.

Drag and drop a Change Velocity behavior on the Bullet actor and configure these settings (also shown in Figure 5-14):

- Direction: 90
- Relative to: scene
- Speed: 300

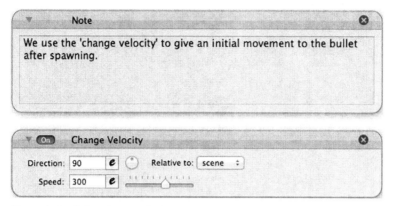

Figure 5-14. *Bullet change velocity*

The next step is to destroy the actor when it collides with an enemy or as soon as it is no longer visible on the screen. You will know that the bullet is not visible by detecting its Y-axis value.

Create a new rule and name it "Destroy." Configure the conditions to "Any" of the following conditions:

- "Actor receives event""overlaps or collides" with "actor of type""Carrots"

- "Attribute""bullet.Position.Y"">""560"

Then drag and drop a Destroy behavioras per Figure 5-15.

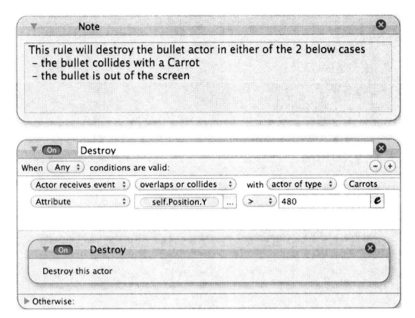

Figure 5-15. *Bullet Destroy rule*

The Invasion is Starting: Creating the Scene Layout

The next step is to position the actors on the scene. Try to match Figure 5-16.

Figure 5-16. *Carrot Invaders Step 1*

Adding Advanced Features

It's now time to add a few advanced features to your game. You will learn some mathematic aspects to create complex movements and movement visual effects, manage an energy bar with the Interpolate behavior, and transition the scene with the Change Scene behavior.

Complex Movements

You can open the file `Carrot_Invaders_step1.gameproj` to follow the steps from this point.

Mathematics is fun! I am pretty sure that most of you won't believe me, but I can assure you that the math required for game development is really basic and it lets you make fun games!

By now you must have hit the Preview button and destroyed the carrots. And you manage to destroy them quite easily: still, defenseless targets! But what if the carrots could move? They would be less easy to kill. As you have guessed by now, you will use mathematics to define their movements.

Before you jump into the movement definition in GameSalad, I would like to clarify what I mean by "complex movement." A complex movement is not a random movement. A random movement is chaotic by its very nature. A complex movement has a very pre-determined pattern but is different from a simple linear movement.

Parametric Equations Are Fun

So fasten your seatbelt and jump into the world of parametric equations. Basically a parametric equation is a way to draw a graph with an equation where both the X and Y position depend on a specific parameter. It means that every point in the drawing of the graph is a couple of coordinates (X,Y). At this point, you should say "ah ha!" Yes, GameSalad represents the location of the actors with X and Y coordinates. For example, Actor1's position on the screen is X=0 and Y=0. This is the bottom left corner of the screen.

Let's go one step further. Imagine that instead of having a fixed value (0,0) you have a parameter that varies over time. Let's call this parameter "t." Now you can define the position by X=t and Y=t. The result is that your actor will move in a linear movement in the top right direction. The t parameter could be, for example, a number incremented by 1 every seconds or maybe a clock.

Basically, that's it. A parametric equation defines the X and Y based on a t parameter. In GameSalad, you will define complex movement by constraining the position.X and position.Y attributes to a formula based on the t parameter where t is the Time attribute of the actor.

The next step is to develop your Google search skills to find a parametric equation describing the complex movement you want to implement.

> **NOTE:** The Time attribute is the internal clock of every implementation of an actor on the scene. The clock will start from the moment the actor appears on the scene or at the same time the scene is displayed if the actor is initially on the screen. It is sensitive up to five digits after the second. It will increase itself continuously with time.

Let's put into practice what you just learned.

Creating Movement with Parametric Equations

A quick search on Google gave me the following parametric equation for a heart shape:

- $X = \sin^3(t)$
- $Y = \cos(t) - \sin^4(t)$

The graph of this equation is shown in Figure 5-17.

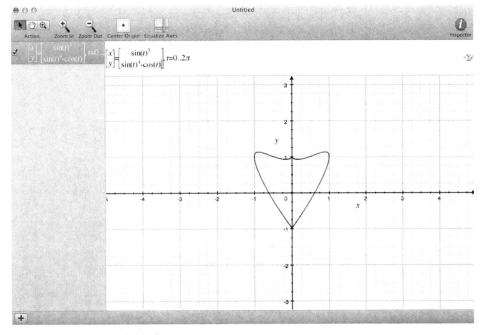

Figure 5-17. *Heart drawing in Grapher*

To draw this equation, I used Grapher with a Mac OS utility provided by default. MacRumors.com hosts a very simple but efficient guide on the Mac Grapher tool. In the Chapter5_Files folder, you will find the Grapher file for this equation.

Back to GameSalad: open the Carrots actor in the Actor Editor. Create two actors attributes of type "real" by clicking the + sign at the bottom left of the Actor Attribute window, as shown in Figure 5-18. Name them "InitX" and "InitY." You will use these two attributes to store the initial location of each implementation of the Carrots actor.

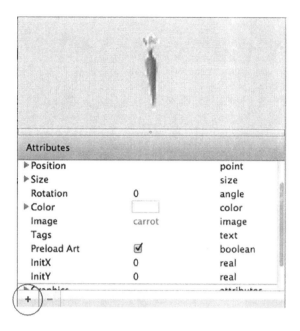

Figure 5-18. *Actor Attribute creation*

> **NOTE:** When you create actor attributes, each implementation of the actor will have their own values in the actor attribute. Thus, if you plan to have carrots, you don't have to create 10 game attributes. Or if you have a dynamic number of actors (if they are spawned, for example) you can store values specific to each actor implementation on the scene.

Create a new group and name it "Movements."You will use this group as a container for all the behaviors that define the movement.

Drag and drop a Change Attribute behavior into the group and change Carrots.InitXtoCarrots.Position.X. Drag and drop a second Change Attribute behavior into the group and change Carrots.InitY to Carrots.Position.Y. The initial position is now stored in two attributes.

> **NOTE:** The Change Attribute behavior only happens once. In contrast, theConstrain Attribute updates the attribute value on a real-time basis.

Drag and drop a Constrain Attribute behavior into the group. Select Carrots.Position.X as the attribute to constrain and open the Formula Editor. Set the following formula (also shown in Figure 5-19):

```
Carrots.InitX+20*sin(Carrots.Time*100)^3
```

Let me explain this formula. You want to have a movement from the initial position, so you start by defining the starting point as InitX. Then you move around InitX by 20*sin (Carrots.Time*100)^3. Sin and Cos will only return value between -1 and 1. You multiply by 20 to give amplitude to the movement. Also, Sin and Cos will vary from -1 to 1 with t varying from 0 to 360, from 361 to 720, and from -1 to 1. So to have a full heart movement, you need to go from 0 to 360, which is basically 6 minutes (1 degree per second, so 60 degrees per minute and then 6 minutes for 360 degres). Thus multiplying by 100 accelerates the movement. You can play with these values if you want to vary the amplitude and the speed.

Figure 5-19. *X formula in Formula Editor*

Drag and drop a second Constrain Attribute behavior into the group. Select Carrots.Position.Y as the attribute to constrain and open the Formula Editor. Set the following formula (also shown in Figure 5-20):

```
Carrots.InitY+20*(sin(Carrots.Time*100)^4-cos(Carrots.Time))
```

Figure 5-20. *Y formula in Formula Editor*

Hit the Preview button to give it a try. Isn't it fun!

Your Movements group should match Figure 5-21.

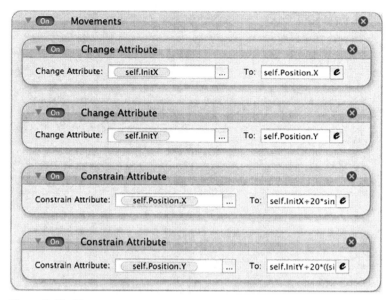

Figure 5-21. *Movements group*

Now because this is all about the invasion, you need the carrots to go down. Configure it so that the carrots go down by 15 pixels every 10 seconds.

Drag and drop a Timer into the group.Change InitY attribute every 10 seconds as per Figure 5-22.

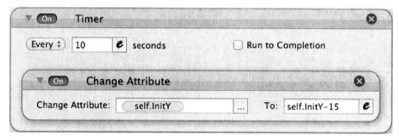

Figure 5-22. *The invasion*

Giving the Impression of Spaceship Movement

Movement is relative. What do I mean by this? Well, you don't need to have the Spaceship actor move to give an impression of movement. You just need to have other actors move!

In order to provide more dynamism in the game, you will add some asteroids in the spaceship trajectory, but instead of moving the spaceship, the asteroids will move.

Follow the steps described in the "Artist Entrance: Creating the Actors" section to import the image file named `asteroid.jpg` located into the Chapter5_Files folder.

Create a new actor and double-click it to open the Actor Editor.

Edit the actor attributes with the parameters in Table 5-7.

Table 5-7. *Asteroid Attributes*

Name	Asteroid
Size/Width	64
Size/Height	64
Physics/Fixed Rotation	Checked
Physics/Restitution	0

Click the Images tab to display the image that you just imported, and drag and drop `asteroid.png`into the actor.

Make the Asteroids Move

Drag and drop a Change Velocity behavior and change the settings to:

- Direction: 270
- Relative to: scene
- Speed: random(100,300)

Create a new rule with the condition "attribute""asteroid.Position.Y""<""-60". Then drag and drop a Change Attribute behavior in the rule and change Asteroid.Position.Y to 530. This will reposition the asteroid at the top of the screen. But it would be boring to have the asteroid always on a same line at the same speed. Drag and drop a second Change Attribute behavior and change Asteroid.Position.X to random (0,320). Now the asteroid will appear at any place on the X-axis. Now give the asteroid a variable speed. Select the Change Velocity behavior that you just implemented by clicking once next to the behavior name. Copy the behavior by pressing Command + C or by dragging the behavior while pressing the Alt key. Your rule should match Figure 5-23.

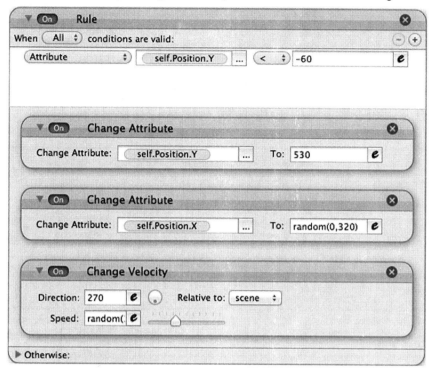

Figure 5-23. *Asteroid Movement rule*

Go back to the Scene Editor and position two asteroids just above the visible area of the scene as per Figure 5-24.

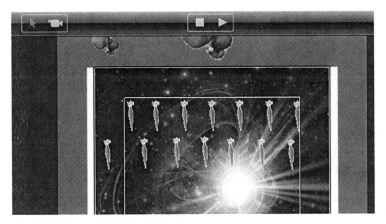

Figure 5-24. *Positioning the asteroids*

EXERCISE 5.1

Implement a rule that when there are no more carrots on the screen, the actor is destroyed.

EXERCISE 5.2

Implement a rule that when the asteroid collides with the spaceship, the game is reset.

EXERCISE 5.3

Implement a rule that when the asteroid collides with a bullet, it disappears from the screen and comes back again from the top in a random X-axis position.

To see the answers to these three exercises, open the file named
`Carrot_Invaders_step3.gameproj`.

Managing the Energy Bar

Every hero needs an energy bar! No, I am not talking about a chocolate caramel snack. I am referring to the life bar for your main characters. There are many ways to manage this in GameSalad. You can use attributes, actors, or any combination of them with rules. I won't cover all of the possibilities; rather, I want to show you a new behavior called "Interpolate," which I will illustrate through the energy bar.

The Interpolate Behavior

The Interpolate behavior is a very powerful behavior. In simple terms, it will calculate all the values between a starting point and a finishing point in a given period of time with a specific method. Imagine your actor is at point A (the starting point) and the actor needs to go to point B. If you apply a Change Attribute to the position, your actor will make a quantum jump from A to B. That's not the effect you want.

If you have read the previous chapters or if you are proficient with GameSalad, you will think to yourself, "No need to use Interpolate, just use Move to." You are almost correct! Move to is a linear implementation of Interpolate, but Interpolate provides one more option: not being linear. This applies to any attribute. I repeat: any attribute. This gives you a lot of possibilities to introduce some very cool features in your game.

In this section, you will use the Interpolate behavior on the color of an actor. Your energy bar will be green when 100% but will change from green to orange (and all the colors between green and orange) when it is at 50% and then from orange to red when it is at 25%. Every hit of an Asteroid will remove 25% of the energy bar. You will also make a second use of the Interpolate behavior by decreasing the size of the energy bar after each collision with an asteroid.

Enough talking. Let's practice now.

Interpolate In Action

You can continue from your existing `Carrot_Invaders` file or open `Carrot_Invaders_step3.gameproj`.

Create two game attributes of type integer and name them respectively "EnergyBar" and "EnergyBarInit." Set both to a default value of 100. The names are quite implicit on the purpose of those attributes, but why do you need two?

You will use decrementation, so you need a buffer attribute in order to avoid a recursive endless loop (I will show this later in the implementation).

Create a new actor and double-click it to open the Actor Editor.

Edit the actor attributes with the parameters in Table 5-8.

Table 5-8. *Energy Bar Attributes*

Name	EnergyBar
Size/Width	100
Size/Height	10
Color/Red	0
Color/Green	1
Color/Blue	0
Physics/Moveable	unchecked

In order to have perfect positioning on the screen, change the position attributes of the actor with some Change Attributes behaviors.

> **NOTE:** about positioning the actor
>
> You will have notice that I often use Change Attribute behaviors to position the actors. It gives an impeccable result. It consumes a very little bit of memory but the impact is very negligible. You may want to use another approach, which is to change the position attribute of the actor instance by double-clicking the actor instance on the scene.

Drag and drop a Change Attribute behavior into the actor and change energy bar.Position.X to 0. Drag and drop a second Change Attribute behavior and change energy bar.position.Y to 20.

Positioning the actor to X=0 will only display half of the actor on the screen. This is done intentionally. As you modify the size of the actor, it will keep its center position but reduce from both left and right side. By creating an actor double of the required size and making only half visible, you will create a visual effect that only one side is shrinking. Alternatively, you may constrain the position at the same time the size decrease, but this would consume many more resources.

The next step is to constrain the width of the Energy Bar to the EnergyBar attribute. This way, the Energy Bar actor width will be the real-time value of the EnergyBar attribute. If the EnergyBar attribute goes from 100 to 75 by interpolation, then you will have a visual effect of the Energy Bar actor shrinking.

Drag and drop a Constrain Attribute into the Energy Bar actor and change the settings of Energy bar.size.width to game.EnergyBar.

The behaviors you just implemented should be as per Figure 5-25.

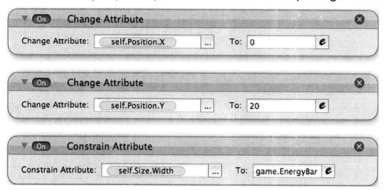

Figure 5-25. *The Energy Bar behaviors*

Now let's create the color changes.

From Green to Orange to Red: Managing Energy Bar Color

Create a new rule named "Orange" with the following condition: "attribute""game.EnergyBar""<""75.""Then drag and drop an Interpolate behavior and change the settings to:

- Interpolate attribute: Energy bar.Color.Red
- To: 1
- Duration: 1
- Function: Linear

Drag and drop a second Interpolate behavior and change the settings to:

- Interpolate attribute: Energy bar.Color.Green
- To: 0.5

- Duration: 1
- Function: Linear

The rule is show in Figure 5-26.

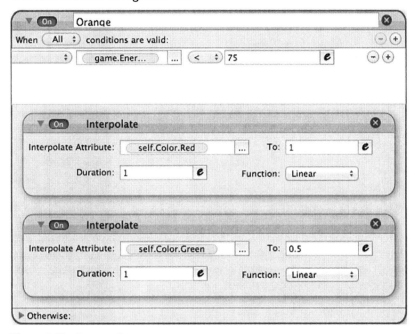

Figure 5-26. *Orange rule*

Let's do the red warning now. Create a new rule in the actor named "Red" with the following condition: "attribute""game.EnergyBar""<""50." Then drag and drop an Interpolate behavior and change the settings to:

- Interpolate attribute: Energy bar.Color.Green
- To: 0
- Duration: 1
- Function: Linear

The rule is show in Figure 5-27.

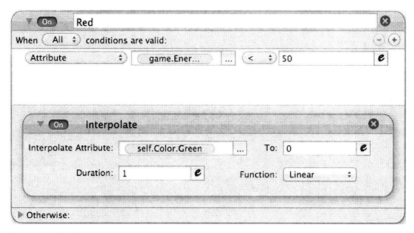

Figure 5-27. *Red rule*

Updating the Asteroid

Open the Asteroid actor in the Actor Editor by double-clicking it. In the rule that detects the collision with the Spaceship actor, remove the Reset Game behavior by clicking the circled cross or by selecting and pressing Delete. Drag and drop an Interpolate behavior and change the settings to:

- Interpolate Attribute: game.EnergyBar

- To: game.EnergyBarInit-25

- Duration: 1

- Function: Linear

This is where you use the buffer attribute called EnergyBarInit. If you were to write EnergyBar-25, then you would go into an end-less recursive loop. Not sure? Then let's put it on the iteration, like so:

- Interpolation 0: EnergyBar = 100, to EnergyBar-25 = 100-25=75

- Interpolation 1: EnergyBar= 99, to EnergyBar-25=99-25=74

- And so on, because every time GameSalad interpolates, the target is also moving.

To finish the buffer trick, drag and drop a Time into the Spaceship Collision rule and change the setting to "After" "1.1" seconds with "Run to completion"checked. Then drag and drop a Change Attribute into the timer and change game.EnergyBarInit to game.EnergyBar. The rule is shown in Figure 5-28. The last behavior will ensure that the new value after completion of the interpolation is stored into the buffer to be used for the next collision.

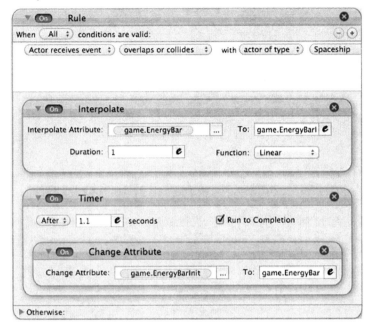

Figure 5-28. *Collision detection*

EXERCISE 5.4

Using Interpolate, Timer, and Alpha, make the Energy Bar blink when it is in the red color zone.

Scene Management

Last but not least, let's look at the Change Scene behavior. This behavior is very simple to use, and it changes your action to another scene. The scene could be the next in order or a specific scene that you have chosen, such as back to the menu.

Basically, you want to change the scene when there are no more carrots on the screen. This means that the attribute number Carrots is equal to 0. You already have a rule in the game that detects when the condition numberCarrots equals 0.

The first step is to create a new scene. Click the Home button and then click the + sign at the bottom left of the screen to create a new scene. Change the name of the scene to "New" by simply clicking in the name area and typing the new name.

Open the Asteroid actor in the Actor Editor. Drag and drop a Change Scene behavior into the rule that detects the attribute numberCarrots equals 0. Change the setting of Change Scene to Go to scene: "New" as per Figure 5-29.

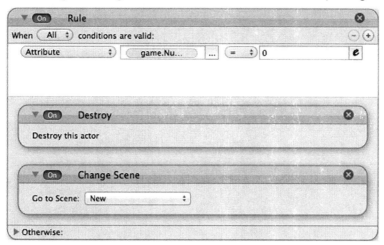

Figure 5-29. *Changing the scene*

Summary

You have created a classic shoot 'em up game! You can design your own shooting game with various levels, several enemy types, and big losses.

In this chapter, you have:

- Reinforced your basic project creation, actors, rules, and behavior design skills.

- Learned about parametric equations.

- Created visual effects of movement.

- Discovered the Interpolate behavior and implemented its application to manage the energy bar.

- Learned how to transition from one scene to another with the Change Scene behavior.

Part 2

Let's Spice Up the Salad with Advanced Functions and Effects in GameSalad

Learning Gravity, Basic Physics, and Camera Controls: An Angry Birds-like Game, Part I

Unless you spent the past two years on a deserted island, you must have heard about Angry Birds. Angry Birds is one of the biggest success stories among game developers. This small, simple, but very addictive game is a worldwide phenomenon. First released on iOS in 2009, Angry Birds has been downloaded more than 300 million times on multiple platforms and logs more than one million hours of game time each day.

In the next two chapters, I will cover the development of a similar game in GameSalad. Then it will be up to you to find the next Angry Birds success with a game you design with GameSalad.

If you are not familiar with the gameplay, you can download a free version of Angry Birds from the App Store. Alternatively, you can play in a Firefox web browser or on Facebook.

As mentioned, the gameplay is simple but yet efficient. Using a slingshot, you throw birds at pigs on the other side of the scene. The goal is to destroy all pigs.

As the purpose of the two coming chapters is to cover the fundamental mechanisms of the gameplay, I will not use any image element. I will stick to the basic shapes in GameSalad.

In this chapter, you will learn to:

- Build a complete slingshot system.

- Simulate an elastic slingshot element in GameSalad.

- Control the camera.

- Implement gravity for your game.

- Use advanced camera settings.

- Manage a defined number of attempts to destroy targets.

Building a Slingshot: Elastic and Pullback Force

Building the slingshot is one of the keys to your game. In doing so, you will learn some new functions like magnitude and vectorToAngle.

Anatomy of a Slingshot

A slingshot is a catapult that has a T-shape with two elastics attached to it. It is used to throw small projectiles by hand. Figure 6-1 shows a drawing of a slingshot.

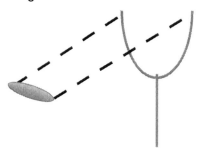

Figure 6-1. *Drawing of a slingshot*

You will position the slingshot on the ground. The projectile will have a limited area of movement. The more you pull back on the elastic, the farther you will send the projectile, as shown in Figure 6-2.

Figure 6-2. *Throwing a projectile with a slingshot*

You can't imagine how many metal cans I shot at when I was a kid. I lived in a pretty rural area and slingshot competitions were common among young boys. We weren't using birds as projectiles and we weren't shooting at animals…but we may have had a few fights. I also replaced quite a few glass windows in my neighborhood.

Enough memories! Let's play with a digital slingshot now. I will show you the basic components of the slingshot in GameSalad.

Creating the Project File

Create a new project in GameSalad and save the file as "CanonShowPartI.gameproj." You're calling it "CanonShow" because in the gaming area, all concepts used in this chapter are referred as Canon physics.

In the Project Info tab, use the information in Table 6-1.

Table 6-1. *Canon Show Part I Project Info*

Title	Canon Show Part I
Platform	iPhone Landscape
Resolution Independence	Unchecked
Description	A Angry Bird-like game created with GameSalad
Instructions	Use your finger to fire a slingshot
Tags	Gravity, Slingshot, Angry Birds

Building the Slingshot Frame

The slingshot frame will be built with three components: one foot and two arms. To make it simple, you will use only one simple white actor and change the shape and rotation of the instances of this actor. You will modify the instances directly on the scene.

Open the initial scene of your new project in the Scene Editor. Create a new actor in the Actor Editor and name it "Slingshot Component." The actor attributes should not be changed.

Drag the actor on the scene. Select the instance by clicking the actor on the scene. A frame with circles will appear inside the actor. Click the frame to change the shape of the actor. Alternatively, double-click the instance and change the size of the actor instance. Modify the shape to make a vertical rectangle (Width: 24 and Height: 100). Position the actor on the ground as per Figure 6-3.

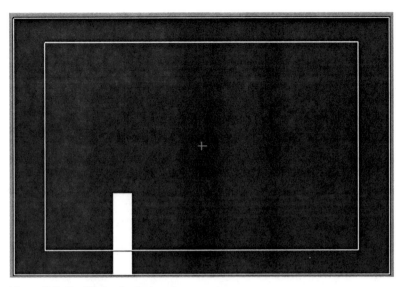

Figure 6-3. *Positioning the foot on the ground*

Drag another instance of the actor on the scene. Replicate the previous shape by holding the Option key and clicking and dragging the instance. Double-click the instance of the actor and change the Rotation attribute to 330. Position the instance at the top of the foot as per Figure 6-4.

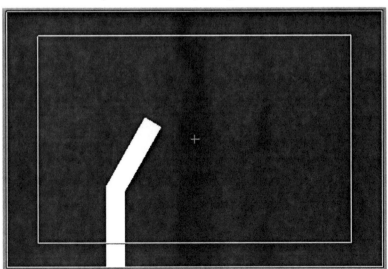

Figure 6-4. *Positioning the right frame of the slingshot*

Drag a third instance of the actor on the scene. Replicate the previous shape by holding the Option key and clicking and dragging the instance. Double-click the instance of the actor and change the Rotation attribute to 30. Position the instance at the top of the foot as per Figure 6-5.

Figure 6-5. *Positioning the left frame of the slingshot*

You have the base of the slingshot. You will now focus on building the pullback force.

Building the Pullback Force

The pullback force is proportional to the distance you move the block to throw back to the left side. You will move the block by pressing the touch; when you release the touch, it will throw the block to the right side of the scene. You will limit the area in which you can pullback the block, as shown in Figure 6-6.

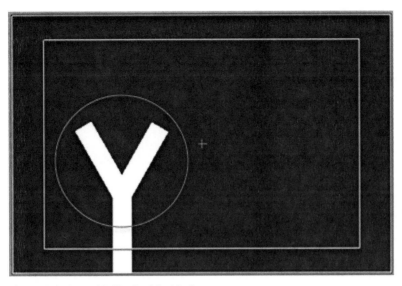

Figure 6-6. *Area of Pullback of the block*

A circle will define this area. The radius of the circle will be the maximum of the force of the pullback. You will use a game attribute to store this maximum value; name it "MaxPower."

Before building this pullback, let's look at two new functions of GameSalad: magnitude and vectorToAngle.

magnitude Function

magnitude is a function that calculates the distance between two actors, as shown in Figure 6-7. The syntax of the function is magnitude (Actor1X-Actor2X, Actor1Y-Actor2Y)

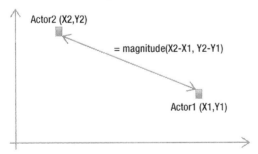

Figure 6-7. *Distance between two actors*

You will use magnitude to calculate the distance from the origin point of the block to the current position of the block while pulling back.

vectorToAngle Function

vectorToAngle is a function that calculates the angle to the horizontal and the line formed between two actors, as shown in Figure 6-8. The syntax of the function is:

vectorToAngle(Actor1X-Actor2X, Actor1Y-Actor2Y)

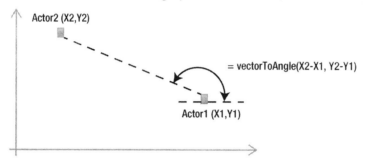

Figure 6-8. *vectorToAngle function*

Using magnitude and vectorToAngle with the Slingshot

Figure 6-9 shows how to use the magnitude and vectorToAngle functions with the slingshot.

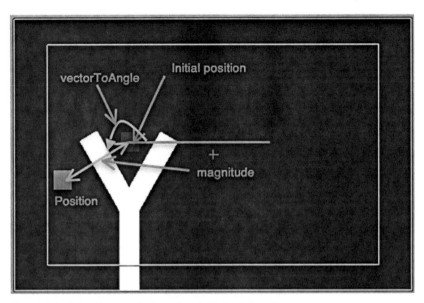

Figure 6-9. *Using the magnitude and vectorToAngle functions*

With your finger, you will touch the projectile and pull it back. When the touch is released, you will use a Change Velocity for the direction, which will depend on the vectorToAngle value, and the speed, which will depend on the magnitude.

Using the mouse position when the touch is pressed, you will constrain the position of the projectile. But you don't want the projectile to be outside of the circle shown back in Figure 6-6.

Creating the Projectile

In the Scene Editor, create a new actor and named it "Projectile." Change the attributes of the actors as per Table 6-2.

Table 6-2. *Projectile Actor Attributes*

Name	Projectile
Size\Width	25
Size\Height	25
Color\Red	1
Color\Green	0
Color\Blue	0

This small red actor will be thrown by the slingshot.

Storing the Initial Position

In order to store the initial position of the projectile, you will use two game attributes. The reason for using game attributes instead of actor attributes is because you will need to access this initial position from other actors (the subsequent projectiles).

Return to the Scene Editor and create two real game attributes named "InitialProjectileX" and "InitialProjectileY."

Use a Change Attribute behavior to store the initial position of the projectile in the two attributes you just created. Open the Projectile actor in the Actor Editor; drag and drop a Change Attribute behavior and change game.InitialProjectileX to Projectile.Position.X as shown in Figure 6-10.

Figure 6-10. *Change Attribute of InitialProjectX*

Drag and drop a second Change Attribute behavior (or duplicate the previous one) into the Projectile actor and change game.InitialProjectileY to Projectile.Position.Y.

Cosinus and Sinus

Next, create a rule to detect the touch on the projectile. You will use the mouse device position to constrain the position of the projectile. But you want to constrain this position within a circle. Use the Cosine and Sine functions, as shown in Figure 6-11.

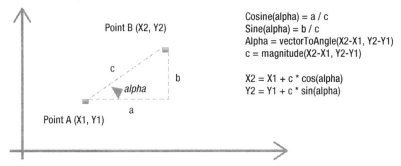

Figure 6-11. *Cosine and Sine*

Cosines and Sines are trigonometric functions, meaning they are functions of an angle, that link angles of a right triangle with the sides of this triangle. In a right triangle, the cosine of an angle (alpha) is defined by

Cosine(alpha) = (adjacent side of the angle alpha)/(opposite side to the right angle – hypotenuse)

The sine of an angle (alpha) is defined by

Sine(alpha) = (opposite side of the angle alpha)/(opposite side to the right angle – hypotenuse)

As you want to constrain the projectile within the circle that is defined by the attribute MaxPower, the value you use for c will be the minimum of MaxPower and the distance between A and B. This way the maximum value that c will be able to take is MaxPower.

Let's implement all this.

Moving the Projectile with a Touch

Open the Scene Editor and create an Integer game attribute named "MaxPower." Set a default value of 75.

Create a new rule named "Touch." The condition will be "Actor receives event""touch" is "pressed." This will detect that the actor is touched.

Drag and drop a Constrain Attribute into the rule and changeProjectile.Position.X to game.InitialProjectX + min(game.MaxPower, magnitude(game.Mouse.Position.X - game.InitialProjectX, game.Mouse.Position.Y – game.InitialProjectY) * cos(vectorToAngle(game.Mouse.Position.X - game.InitialProjectX, game.Mouse.Position.Y – game.InitialProjectY)).

Going back to Figure 6-11,

- X2 is Projectile.Position.X

- X1 is game.InitialProjectX

- c is min(game.MaxPower,magnitude(game.Mouse.Position.X - game.InitialProjectX, game.Mouse.Position.Y – game.InitialProjectY))

- alpha is vectorToAngle(game.Mouse.Position.X - game.InitialProjectX, game.Mouse.Position.Y – game.InitialProjectY)

Drag and drop a Constrain Attribute into the rule and change Projectile.Position.Y to game.InitialProjectY + min(game.MaxPower , magnitude(game.Mouse.Position.X - game.InitialProjectX, game.Mouse.Position.Y – game.InitialProjectY) * sin(vectorToAngle(game.Mouse.Position.X - game.InitialProjectX, game.Mouse.Position.Y – game.InitialProjectY)).

Going back to Figure 6-11,

- Y2 is Projectile.Position.Y

- Y1 is game.InitialProjectY

- c is min(game.MaxPower,magnitude(game.Mouse.Position.X - game.InitialProjectX, game.Mouse.Position.Y – game.InitialProjectY))

- alpha is vectorToAngle(game.Mouse.Position.X - game.InitialProjectX, game.Mouse.Position.Y – game.InitialProjectY

The rule is shown in Figure 6-12.

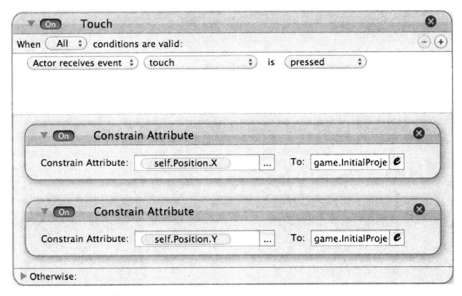

Figure 6-12. *Touch rule*

Return to the Scene Editor. Drag and drop the projectile on the scene and position it between the two arms of the slingshot.

Hit the Preview button and play around with the projectile.

Throwing the Projectile

The next step is to be able to throw the projectile when you remove your finger from the screen. The power will be defined based on the distance between the point of origin and the pullback, and the direction will be from vectorToAngle.

You will use the Change Velocity behavior to set the direction and the speed of the projectile once you release the touch.

Intuitively, you might think to use a new rule with the condition "Actor receives event" "touch" is "released." This approach is OK while you remain within the circle restriction, but if you go out of the circle and release the touch, it won't work. Instead, you will use a small trick with an attribute and the existing Touch rule. Create a Boolean actor attribute that is false by default. Then, once the Touch is pressed, change the attribute to True. In the Touch rule, add a sub-rule in the Otherwise section. The sub-rule condition is that the attribute is True. This will avoid the possibility of the projectile being thrown before Touch is pressed.

Open the Projectile actor in the Actor Editor. Create a Boolean actor attribute and name it "HasBeenTouched."

In the Touch rule, add a Change Attribute behavior above the Constrain Attribute behavior. Change HasBeenTouched to true, as shown in Figure 6-13.

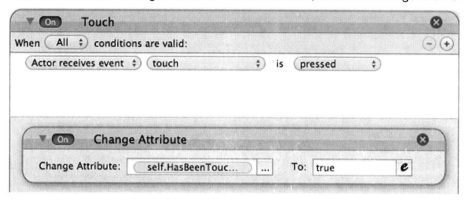

Figure 6-13. *Changing HasBeenTouched attribute*

Then add a Change Attribute behavior at the top of the Behaviors window so that the HasBeenTouched attribute is reset to false when you initiate the scene. Set Projectile.HasBeenTouched to false.

Then expand the Otherwise section of the rule and add a new rule in this section. Name this sub-rule "Throwing." The condition is "Attribute" "Projectile.HasBeenTouched" is "true." Then drag and drop a Change Velocity behavior into the Throwing rule. Change the settings of this behavior to

- Direction: 180 + vectorToAngle(Projectile.Position.X-gameInitialX, Projectile.Position.Y-gameInitialY)

- Relative to: scene

- Speed: 10*magnitude(Projectile.Position.X-gameInitialX, Projectile.Position.Y-gameInitialY)

The rule is shown in Figure 6-14.

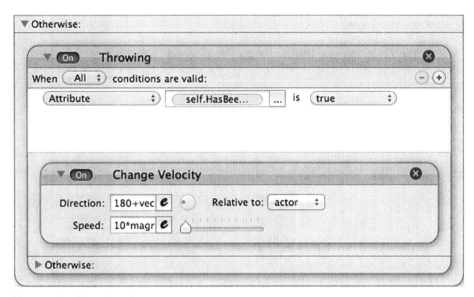

Figure 6-14. *Throwing rule*

The direction has been set to 180 + vectorToAngle() because vectorToAngle provides the direction from the origin point to the location of the pullback. You want to throw the projectile in the opposite direction, so this is why you use the "180 +".

For the speed, use a multiplicator to increase the effect. I've suggested 10 but you can play with different values.

Hit the Preview button to test your rule.

How to Simulate an Elastic in GameSalad

Simulating the elastic in GameSalad is based on modifying the size of the actor used as a graphical representation of the elastic.

You will have two instances of the same elastic actor on the scene. Each of them will connect to a different arm of the slingshot. The behaviors will be different for each instance; as such, you will edit the instances on the scene. Also, you will need to access some of the attributes of the scene instances.

Changing Instance Actor Name

To create the slingshot, you used a single actor called "Slingshot Component." In order to easily identify the instances, you will change the names of the instances in the scene.

Open the Scene Editor and double-click the foot of the slingshot. This will open the instance in the Actor Editor, as shown in Figure 6-15.

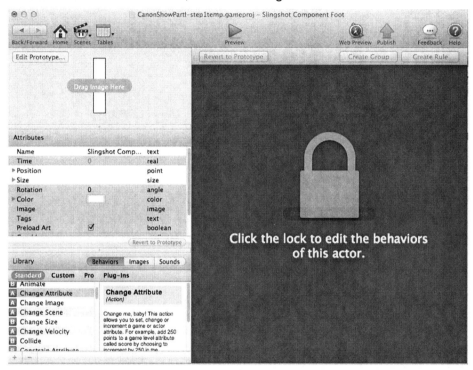

Figure 6-15. *Foot of the slingshot in the Actor Editor*

In the attributes of the instance, modify the name to "Slingshot Component Foot."

Repeat the same operation for the right arm of the slingshot and name it "Slingshot Component Right." Do it one more time for the left arm of the slingshot and name it "Slingshot Component Left."

You performed this renaming operation because you will need to access some of the attributes of these instances from the instance of elastic on the scene.

Getting the Real-Time Position of the Projectile

In order to correctly position the elastic, you will need to access the real-time position of the projectile. This is fairly easy to do so using game attributes and Constrain Attribute behaviors. But you only need this information when the project is grabbed. You don't want your elastic to follow the projectile once it is thrown. You will use the Touch rule of the projectile to constrain the position when the rule is verified; otherwise you will bring back the elastic to the original position.

Create two real game attributes named "ProjectileX" and "ProjectileY."

Open the Projectile actor in the Actor Editor. Drag and drop a Constrain Attribute into the Touch rule and changegame.ProjectileX to Projectile.Position.X. Drag and drop another Constrain Attribute behavior into the Touch rule and change game.ProjectileY to Projectile.Position.Y. These two behaviors are shown in Figure 6-16.

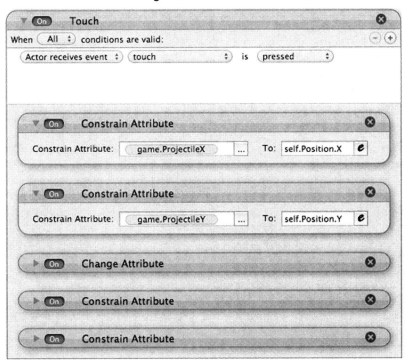

Figure 6-16. *Constraining the position of the projectile*

This will ensure that when the projectile is grabbed, the position of the bird is contained in the two game attributes ProjectileX and ProjectileY.

Next, when the bird is not grabbed (the Otherwise section of the Touch rule), change the value of the ProjectileX and ProjectileY attributes to the initial position of the projectile, which is contained in InitialProjectileX and InitialProjectileY.

Expand the Otherwise section of the Touch rule, and drag and drop a Change Attribute behavior in this section. Change game.ProjectileX to game.InitialProjectileX. Drag and drop another Change Attribute behavior and change game.ProjectileY to game.InitialProjectileY. These two additional behaviors are shown in Figure 6-17.

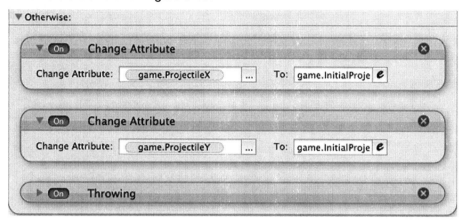

Figure 6-17. *Back to initial position*

Now you have attributes ProjectileX and ProjectileY set. Let's spend some time on the elastic.

Elastic Theory

The elastic will be a basic actor of a very small size (5x5) that will modify its shape (width), position, and rotation depending on the position of the projectile. Figure 6-18 illustrates how the elastic interacts with the projectile.

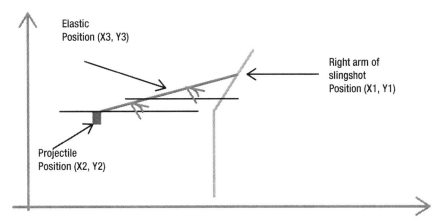

Figure 6-18. *Projectile, elastic, and slingshot arm*

For the elastic, you will constrain its width to the distance between the projectile and the right arm of the slingshot, giving the impression that the length is changing (elastically) when moving the projectile. The position X3 is made by adding half of the distance between X2 (the projectile) and X1 (the arm) to X2. It's the same for Y3, which is made by adding half of the distance between Y2 and Y1 to Y2.

To finalize the effect, you will constrain the rotation of the elastic to the same angle between the projectile and the arm of the slingshot. As you can see in Figure 6-18, these two angles are equal.

Let's do all the above.

Creating the Elastic Actor

In the Scene Editor, create a new actor named "Elastic." Change the attribute of this actor as per Table 6-3.

Table 6-3. *Elastic Actor Attribute*

Name	Elastic
Size\Width	5
Size\Height	5
Color\Red	0.5
Color\Green	0
Color\Blue	0.5

Drag the Elastic actor and drop it on the scene at about the center of the right arm. Repeat the same action, but drop the second instance in about the center of the left arm, as shown in Figure 6-19.

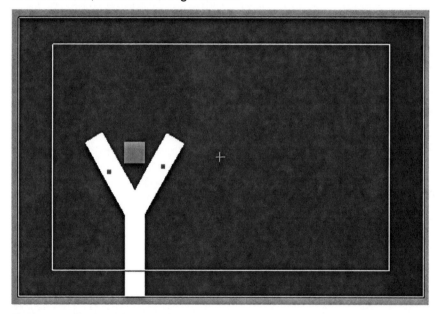

Figure 6-19. *Elastic positioned on the scene*

Let's now configure each of the instances.

Implementing the Right Elastic

Double-click the right elastic instance on the scene to open it in the Actor Editor. Rename the instance actor to "elastic right." Click the lock icon shown in Figure 6-20. This will unlock the instance behaviors.

Figure 6-20. *Unlock the instance of actor*

Drag and drop a Constrain Attribute behavior and change elastic right.Position.X to game.ProjectileX + (Current Scene.Layers.Background.Slingshot Component Right.Position.X – game.ProjectileX)/2.

Drag and drop a Constrain Attribute behavior and change elastic right.Position.Y to game.ProjectileY + (Current Scene.Layers.Background.Slingshot Component Right.Position.Y – game.ProjectileY)/2.

Drag and drop a Constrain Attribute behavior and change elastic right.Size.Width to magnitude(Current Scene.Layers.Background.Slingshot Component Right.Position.X – game.ProjectileX ,Current Scene.Layers.Background.Slingshot Component Right.Position.Y – game.ProjectileY).

Drag and drop a Constrain Attribute behavior and change elastic right.Rotation to vectorToAngle(game.ProjectileX - Current Scene.Layers.Background.Slingshot Component Right.Position.X ,game.ProjectileY - Current Scene.Layers.Background.Slingshot Component Right.Position.Y).

These behaviors are shown in Figure 6-21.

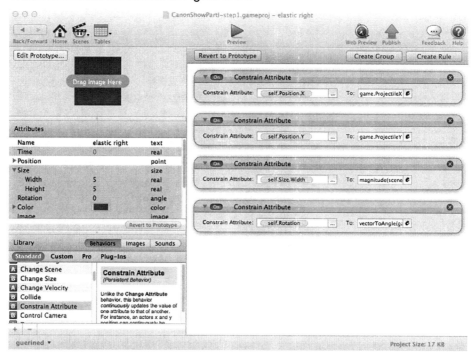

Figure 6-21. *Elastic Right behaviors*

Let's do the same for the left elastic.

Implementing the Left Elastic

Double-click the left elastic instance on the scene to open it in the Actor Editor. Rename the instance actor to "elastic left." Click the lock icon.

Drag and drop a Constrain Attribute behavior and change elastic left.Position.Xto game.ProjectileX + (Current Scene.Layers.Background.Slingshot Component Left.Position.X – game.ProjectileX)/2.

Drag and drop a Constrain Attribute behavior and change elastic left.Position.Y to game.ProjectileY + (Current Scene.Layers.Background.Slingshot Component Left.Position.Y – game.ProjectileY)/2.

Drag and drop a Constrain Attribute behavior and change elastic left.Size.Width to magnitude(Current Scene.Layers.Background.Slingshot Component Left.Position.X – game.ProjectileX ,Current Scene.Layers.Background.Slingshot Component Left.Position.Y – game.ProjectileY).

Drag and drop a Constrain Attribute behavior and change elastic left.Rotation to vectorToAngle(game.ProjectileX - Current Scene.Layers.Background.Slingshot Component Left.Position.X ,game.ProjectileY - Current Scene.Layers.Background.Slingshot Component Left.Position.Y).

These behaviors are shown in Figure 6-22.

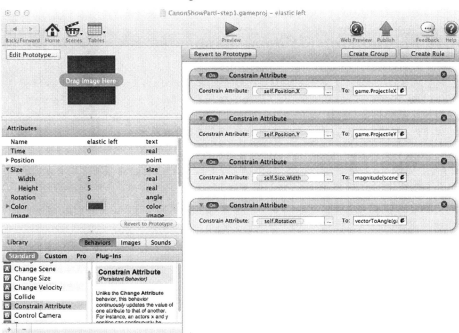

Figure 6-22. *Elastic Left behaviors*

Hit the Preview button to play with the projectile.

You can open the file CanonShowPartI-step1.gameproj located in the folder Chapter6_Files.

Controlling the Camera: Scrolling Across the Scene

Next, you will learn about the camera in GameSalad. The camera in GameSalad is not a way to control the iPhone camera (this is not possible yet with GameSalad, but it would be a very cool feature). The simplest way to understand the camera is to think that you are seeing the game through the camera. Then you can play with the scrolling features to enhance the player experience in your Canon Show!

The Screen vs. the Scene

In GameSalad, there is only one camera. The camera is the point of view, the way you see the game. The visible area of the game is on your screen and you will implement controls to play with the camera: to move it left, right, up, and down.

So far, you have made projects where the size of the scene was equal to the size of the screen. This is good when you are building a project where scrolling is not required. However, in this game you want to have a much bigger scene in which the visible part is equal to the size of the screen.

A key concept of the camera in GameSalad is that an actor is controlling the camera. You will use a behavior named Control Camera and affect it to an actor. Thus, when the actor moves, the camera follows.

The camera view is the screen, but there is another tool that accompanies the camera: the camera zone. This zone is the key to controlling the camera. As long as the actor moves within this zone, the camera will not move; as soon as the actor moves out of the zone, the camera will follow.

To access the camera zone, click the camera icon shown in Figure 6-23.

Figure 6-23. *The camera icon*

This activates the camera mode and shows the camera zone (seeFigure 6-24).

Figure 6-24. *The camera zone view*

The actor controlling the camera can move freely in the central black area before bumping into the camera zone and moving the camera along with the actor.

You can use the handles to reduce or increase this zone. You can also use the Scene-Camera-Tracking Area to edit the values with exact numbers.

But what is the point of being able to move the camera if your scene is the size of your screen? None! In order to use the camera, you need to have a much bigger scene.

Implementing the Scrolling

Let's implement the scrolling for the Canon Show. The first step is to make the size of the scene bigger.

In the Scene Editor, click the Scene tab to open the scene attributes, as shown in Figure 6-25.

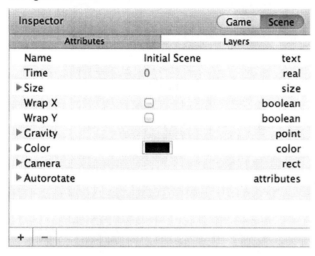

Figure 6-25. *Scene attributes*

Expand the size attributes and change the size of the scene to Width: 1920 and Height: 1280, as shown in Figure 6-26.

▼Size		size
Width	1920	real
Height	1280	real

Figure 6-26. *Scene size*

Let's add the camera control to the projectile now.

Open the Projectile actor in the Actor Editor. Drag and drop a Control Camera behavior into the Projectile actor, as shown in Figure 6-27.

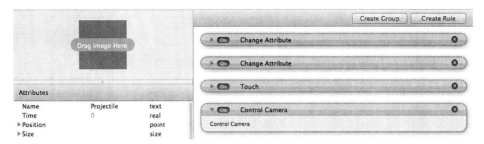

Figure 6-27. *Control the camera*

Hit the Preview button to play with the projectile.

You can open the file CanonShowPartI-step2.gameproj located in the folder Chapter6_Files.

Flying and Falling Down: Gravity Concepts

You now have a projectile that is thrown but it only goes up and very rapidly out of the scene. You need to implement a way to get down to earth so you can try to reach the targets you will later create. Also, when an object flies in the air, the air causes some friction that slows down the speed, so you need to define this.

Once Upon a Time, There Was an Apple

Gravity is a natural phenomenon by which physical bodies attract a force proportional to their mass. The concept of gravity is attributed to Sir Isaac Newton in the 17th century. It is denoted by g and is the acceleration that Earth imparts to objects on or near its surface. It's why you stick to the ground. As you can see in Figure 6-28, it is measured in meters per second per second of about 9.8m/s^2.

9.8 m/s^2

Figure 6-28. *Illustration of gravity*

> About Apple:
>
> The very first Apple logo was actually a representation of Sir Isaac Newton sitting under an apple tree with an apple falling on his head. It is said that the Apple name was an homage to Sir Newton.

Flying and Dragging

Personally I do not use the GameSalad gravity feature. It is located within the scene attributes. You can enter a real number on X and Y that will simulate a force in the X and Y direction.

As gravity is an acceleration, instead I prefer to use the Accelerate behavior. It gives more flexibility because you can trigger it through rules. Imagine having a space scene with several planets, each having their own gravity…

Implement the gravity and drag it into your project. Drag is used to simulate the friction of the air for an object. Drag is an attribute of an actor.

Open the Projectile actor in the Actor Editor. Expand the Otherwise section of the Touch rule. Then, drag and drop an Accelerate behavior into the Throwing rule. Change the settings to:

- Direction: 270
- Relative to: scene
- Acceleration: 200

This will simulate the gravity.

Then, drag and drop a Change Attribute behavior next to the Accelerate behavior. Change Projectile.Physics.Drag to 100. Figure 6-29 shows these two behaviors. This drag will simulate the air friction.

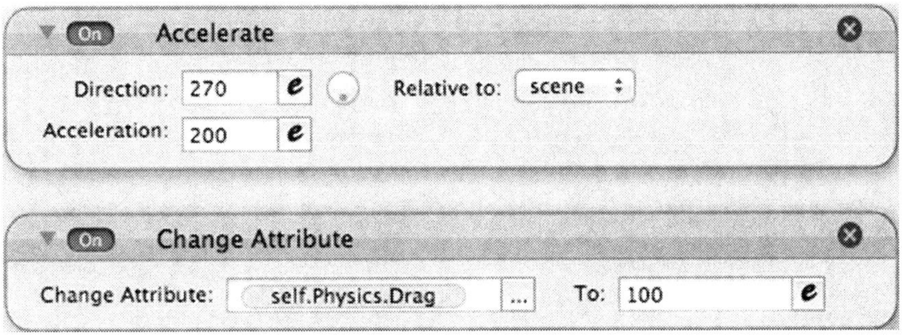

Figure 6-29. *Accelerate and drag*

The last step is to position a background to make it easier to visualize the movement of the projectile. Import the image Background.png and create a new actor named "Background." Drag the actor on the scene, right-click the actor to send it to the back, and then resize the background to cover the complete scene.

Hit the Preview button to play with the projectile.

You can open the file CanonShowPartI-step3.gameproj located in the folder Chapter6_Files.

More Camera Controls: Zooming In/Out While Flying

When you watch action movies, a common moviemaker trick to give more emphasis on a scene is to zoom in or zoom out. Wouldn't it be nice to be able to do the same in GameSalad while your projectile is flying? Imagine that you can zoom out at the beginning of the fly and then zoom it when you are close to the landing. It would certainly give a very nice visual effect.

Let's do it!

Zooming Out

There is one set of attributes I didn't mention yet for the camera: the camera size. As discussed, the display of the camera is the screen. So what happens is that you change the camera size. Obviously, your physical screen is not going to expand (Apple is magical, but not that magical). So what happens if you increase the size of the screen? You would have more to cover in the same display size. It will generate a visual effect as if the camera was going further (zooming out) to show more on the display. This is exactly the effect you want.

The camera attributes are scene attributes. If you want a behavior to modify them, you need to be able to access the scene attributes. What type of actors can access the scene attributes? The unlocked actor instance!

Open the Scene Editor. Double-click the instance of the Projectile actor on the scene. Unlock the instance by clicking the lock icon as per Figure 6-30.

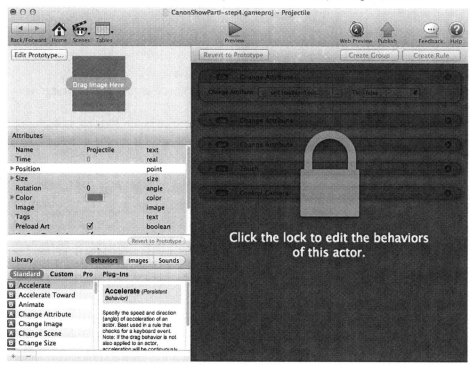

Figure 6-30. *Unlocking the Projectile instance*

Expand the Otherwise section of the Touchrule. Then expand the Throwing rule. Drag and drop an Interpolate behavior into the Throwing rule and, as shown in Figure 6-31, change the settings to:

- Interpolate Attribute: Current Scene.Camera.Size.Width

- To: 920

- Duration: 2

- Function: Linear

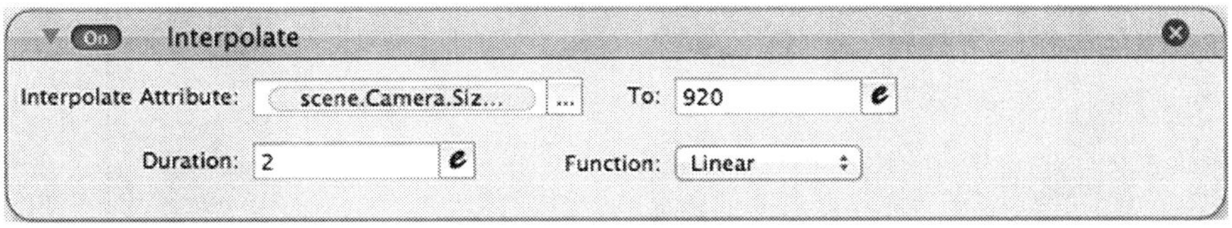

Figure 6-31. *Interpolate the width of the camera size*

You can play with the value of the width as well as the duration. I used 920 because I like the effect of doubling the value over 2 seconds. I recommend that you play around to find values you prefer.

Drag and drop an Interpolate behavior into the Throwing rule and change the settings to:

- Interpolate Attribute: Current Scene.Camera.Size.Height

- To: 640

- Duration: 2

- Function: Linear

Hit the Preview button to try this new effect.

Zooming In

Intuitively, you can say that if you reduce the camera size, you will create a zoom-in effect. And you are absolutely right!

In order to trigger the effect after the zoom out, add a timer of 2 seconds. In the next chapter, you will change the time to add a rule that will trigger the zoom-in when there is a contact with a target.

Drag and drop a Timer behavior into the Throwing rule of the Projectile actor instance and change the settings to "After" "2" seconds.

Duplicate these two Interpolate behaviors (drag+Option key) into the timer. Change the settings of the Interpolate behaviors you just duplicated to Width: 460 and Height: 320, as shown in Figure 6-32.

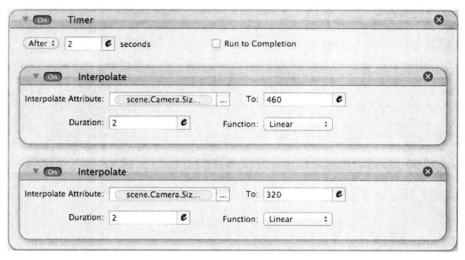

Figure 6-32. *Zoom-in effect*

You now have good zoom-out and zoom-in effects, but with a very small trick, you can make it even better.

Fine-Tuning

To fine-tune the effect, there is a small trick. Reducing the tracking area will produce a much better effect.

Open the Scene Editor and click the Scene tab to display the scene attributes. Expand the Camera attributes and then the Tracking Area attributes. Change the Width attribute to 200 and Height attribute to 150, as shown in Figure 6-33.

▼ Camera		rect
▶ Origin		point
▶ Size		size
▼ Tracking Area		size
Width	200	real
Height	150	real

Figure 6-33. *Reducing the tracking area*

Hit the Preview button to play with the projectile.

You can open the file CanonShowPartI-step4.gameproj located in the folder Chapter6_Files.

Projectile Management: Managing the Attempts

The final step for this chapter is to implement a maximum number of attempts per scene. You will have some projectiles on the bottom left part of the screen, and the number will decrease by one after throwing each projectile.

Adding Boundaries

Before going into projectile management, you need to define some walls around the playing area. As you may have noticed, when you throw projectiles, they fall and go under the scene, as there is no ground floor. You will create some walls around the scene. The projectile will collide with the walls.

Open the Scene Editor and create a new actor named "wall." Double-click the actor to open it in the Actor Editor. In the attributes of the actor, change the restitution to 0 and uncheck the movable box.

Go back to the Scene Editor. Drag and drop four instances of the Wall actor on the scene. Change the shape of each of them to position them on the four borders of the scene, as shown in Figure 6-34.

Figure 6-34. *Adding walls to the scene*

Next, double-click the Projectile actor instance on the scene. Remember that because you have edited this instance (unlock), it will not incorporate changes made on the prototype. Drag and drop a Collide behavior on the top of the behaviors and change the settings to Bounce when colliding with "actor of type" "Wall," as shown in Figure 6-35.

Figure 6-35. *Bouncing on the walls*

Hit Preview to test your work.

Creating Dummy Projectiles

The very cool trick to manage the various projectiles is that in reality you will only use one projectile. You will create dummy projectiles that will just disappear one by one after each attempt while the main projectile is brought back to the slingshot.

The dummy projectiles will have the same appearance as the projectile. But they will just contain one rule and one Change Attribute behavior in this rule.

Create a game attribute to define the number of attempts left to complete the scene. I set this number of attempts to 4 (you can choose any other number that suits you), so you will need three dummy projectiles. As you have one on the slingshot, it will initially display four projectiles on the scene. After each attempt, you will decrement by one the game attribute. The rule in the dummy projectile will check the game attribute compared to a position number. If the game attribute is lower, you will make invisible (color alpha to 0) the dummy projectile. And the magic is done!

In the Scene Editor, create a new game attribute of type integer, name it "Attemptleft," and set its default value to 4, as shown in Figure 6-36.

Attemptleft	4	integer

Figure 6-36. *Game Attribute attemptleft*

Next, create a new actor and rename it "dummy projectile" and change the following attributes in the Actor Editor:

- Size/Width: 25
- Size/Height: 25
- Color/Red: 1
- Color/Green: 0
- Color/Blue: 0

Next, create a new rule with the condition "Attribute""game.Attemptleft" "<""4." Drag and drop a Change Attribute and change dummy projectile.Color.Alpha to 0, as shown in Figure 6-37.

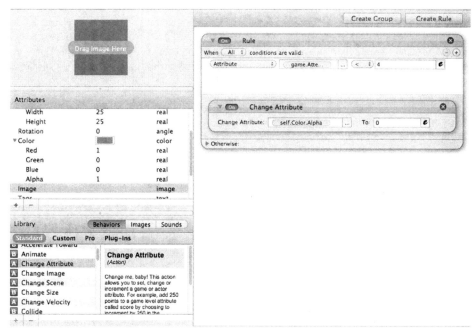

Figure 6-37. *Dummy projectile*

Drag and drop three instances of the dummy projectile actors and position them on the bottom left of the scene, as shown in Figure 6-38.

Figure 6-38. *Positioning the dummy projectiles*

Starting from the left side, open the first instance of the dummy projectile and unlock it. Change the condition of the rule to "Attribute""game.Attemptleft""<""2," as shown in Figure 6-39.

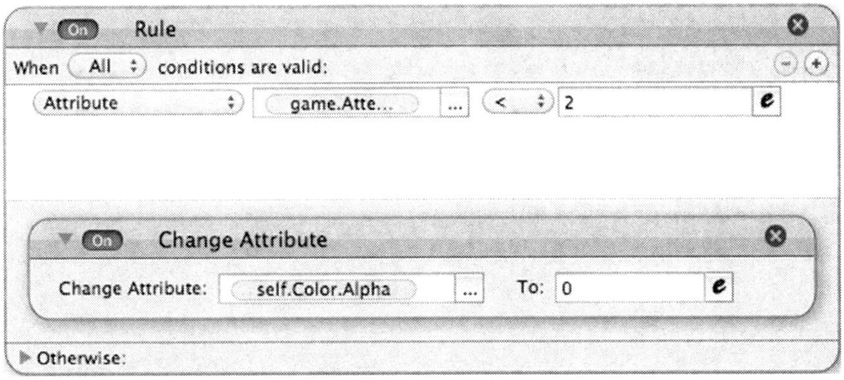

Figure 6-39. *Modifying dummy projectile one*

Starting from the left side, open the second instance of the dummy projectile and unlock it. Change the condition of the rule to "Attribute""game.Attemptleft""<""3," as shown in Figure 6-40.

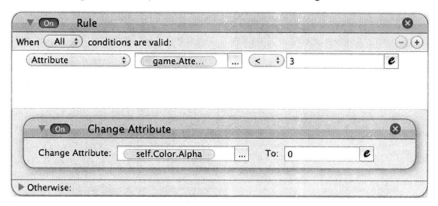

Figure 6-40. *Modifying dummy projectile two*

Modifying the Projectile Instance

The next part of the work is to modify the projectile instance. You will need to implement a detection when the projectile stops moving, which will trigger the projectile to return to its original position. You will also reset the key attributes, decrement the number of attempts, and implement a game reset when the four attempts have been done. You will also use a Boolean attribute to set a state when you change the projectile. This Boolean will be used as a condition in a rule to trigger some resets.

Detecting when the Projectile Stops Moving

In the Scene Editor, create a new Boolean game attribute named "Change Projectile." To detect when the projectile stops moving, you will use the linear velocity motion attributes.

Open the Projectile actor instance by double-clicking the actor on the scene. Create a new rule into the Throwing rule and name it "Change projectile." Add the following conditions into the rule with the criteria "All:"

- "Attribute""Projectile.Motion.Linear Velocity.X""=""0"
- "Attribute""Projectile.Motion.Linear Velocity.Y""=""0"

Then, drag and drop a Change Attribute behavior into the rule and change Projectile.Color.Alpha to 0. Next, drag and drop a Change Attribute behavior into the same rule and change game.Change Projectile to true. Last, drag and drop a last Change Attribute behavior into the rule and change game.Attemptleft to game.Attemptleft -1. The rule is shown in Figure 6-41.

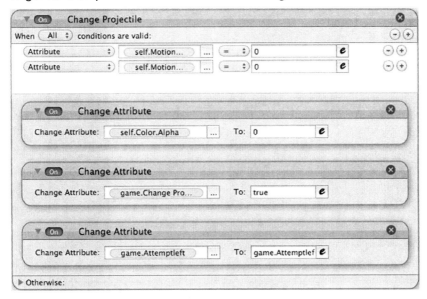

Figure 6-41. *Change Projectile rule*

Moving Back to the Original Position

You will move the projectile back to its original position via a rule when the attribute Change Projectile is true. Use the Interpolate behavior to move it back to its original position, which is stored in the attributes InitialProjectileX and InitialProjectileY.

Create a new rule in the Projectile actor instance and name it "Back to Position." The condition of the rule is "Attribute""game.Change Projectile""is""true." Drag and drop an Interpolate behavior into the rule and change the settings to:

- Interpolate Attribute: Projectile.Position.X
- To: game.InitialProjectileX
- Duration: 1
- Function: Linear

Repeat the same operation with the following settings:

- Interpolate Attribute: Projectile.Position.Y

- To: game.InitialProjectileY

- Duration: 1

- Function: Linear

The Back to Position rule is shown in Figure 6-42.

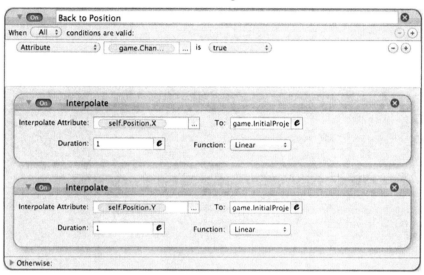

Figure 6-42. *Back to Position rule*

Resetting Key Attributes

Next, you need to reset the HasBeenTouched attribute, make projectile visible, and change the status of Change Projectile to false.

Drag and drop a Change Attribute behavior into the Back to Position rule and change Projectile.HasBeenTouched to false.

Drag and drop a new rule into the Back to Position rule, name it "attribute reset," and add the following conditions to "All:"

- "Attribute" "Projectile.Position.X"
  "="""game.InitialProjectileX"

- "Attribute" "Projectile.Position.Y" "="
  "game.InitialProjectileY"

This will detect that the projectile is back to its original position.

Drag and drop a Change Attribute behavior into the Attributes reset rule and change projectile.Color.Alpha to 1. Drag and drop a second Change Attribute and change game.Change Projectile to false. The Attributes reset rule is shown in Figure 6-43.

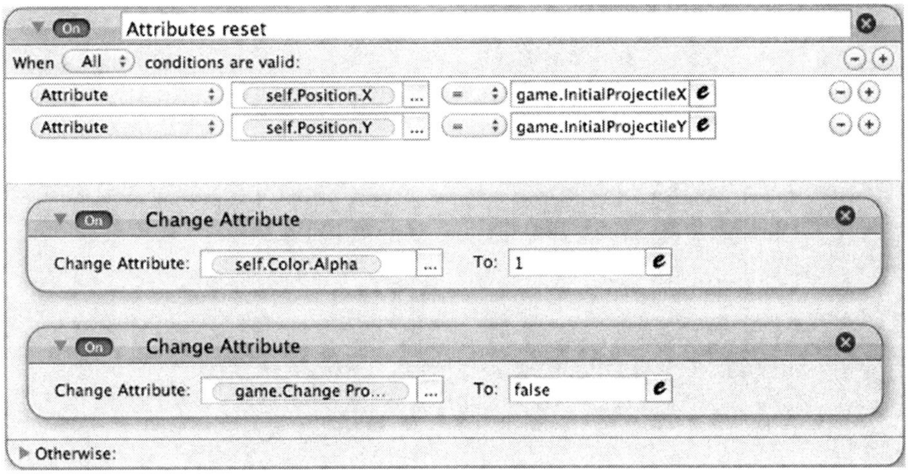

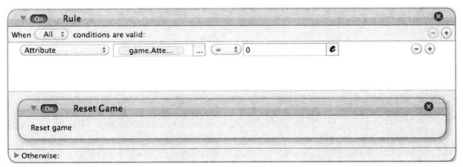

Figure 6-43. *Attributes reset rule*

Resetting the Game After Four Attempts

This last step is very easy. Just create a new rule in the Projectile actor instance and name it "Reset the Game." The condition of the rule is "Attribute" "game.Attemptleft" "=" "0." Then drag and drop a Reset Game behavior into the rule. The Reset the Game rule is shown in Figure 6-44.

Figure 6-44. *Reset the Game rule*

Hit the Preview button to play with the projectile.

You can open the file CanonShowPartI-step5.gameproj located in the folder Chapter6_Files.

Summary

Ready to throw any objects at targets? With your brand new slingshot you will be in a position to improve your targeting skills.

In this chapter, you have learned how to:

- Build a slingshot system.
- Simulate an elastic element.
- Control the camera.
- Implement gravity.
- Use advanced camera settings.
- Manage a limited number of attempts.

Creating a Game Menu and a Particles Effect: An Angry Birds-like Game, Part II

In the previous chapter you learned how to build the basics for an Angry Birds-like game. But you still have a lot to learn. You need a target to aim at and blocks to protect the target. It's also an opportunity to introduce tables, which perform some very advance optimization. Last but not least, you will build a very cool menu system.

In this chapter, you will:

- Build the target and blocks.
- Use the Particles effect feature.
- Learn about GameSalad tables.
- Optimize your game with tables.
- Create a cool menu system.

Aiming at a Target: Destroying Blocks

What would a canon game be without target and blocks to protect the target? In this section, you will increase the game experience by creating three categories of blocks to be destroyed and you'll create the required interactions to play the game.

Creating the Blocks: Hard, Soft, and the Target

You will create three types of blocks: hard, soft, and the target blocks. The target is the aim. A single hit by the projectile and the level is completed. The soft block will simulate easy-to-destroy blocks; a double hit will be required to destroy these blocks. Last, hard blocks will simulate a rock-solid block; a triple hit will be required to destroy these blocks.

Target

Open the scene in the Scene Editor and create a new actor. Name the actor "Target." Change the attributes as per Table 7-1.

Table 7-1. *Target Actor Attributes*

Name	Target
Size\Width	50
Size\Height	50
Color\Red	0.8
Color\Green	0.2
Color\Blue	1
Physics\Restitution	0

Soft Block

Create a new actor and name it "Soft Block." Change the attributes as per Table 7-2.

Table 7-2. *Soft Block Actor Attributes*

Name	Soft Block
Size\Width	100
Size\Height	100
Color\Red	0.15
Color\Green	0.95
Color\Blue	1
Physics\Restitution	0

Hard Block

Create a new actor and name it "Hard Block." Change the attributes as per Table 7-3.

Table 7-3. *Hard Block Actor Attributes*

Name	Hard Block
Size\Width	100
Size\Height	100
Color\Red	0.55
Color\Green	0.22
Color\Blue	0.09
Physics\Restitution	0

Make Them Collide

You will use a tag to make it easier to define the collideable objects.

Click the Home button and then click the Actors tab. Create a new tag for all collideable objects. Click the + sign on the tag pane and rename the new tag "Collidable." Then drag and drop the following actors into the Collidable tag:

- Projectile
- Target
- Soft Block
- Hard Block
- Wall

The result is shown in Figure 7-1.

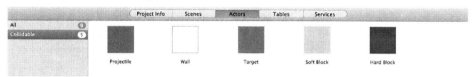

Figure 7-1. *The Collidable-tagged actors*

Open the Target actor in the Actor Editor. Drag and drop a Collide behavior and change the settings to Bounce when colliding with "actor with tag" "Collidable," as shown in Figure 7-2.

Figure 7-2. *Collide behavior*

Repeat the same for actors Soft Block and Hard Block.

Ground Them on Earth: Gravity

As you are implementing gravity through acceleration, you will need to define an Acceleration behavior.

Open the Target actor in the Actor Editor. Drag and drop an Acceleration behavior and change the settings to:

- Direction: 270
- Relative to: scene
- Acceleration: 200

Refer to Figure 7-3. "Relative to" applies to the direction. If you select scene, it will be compare to the referential of the scene. A direction of 90 relative to the scene will go up. If you select actor, it will be relative to the actor. So if you select 90 and your actor's rotation equals 90, the effect will be to go to the left in the scene (90 + 90).

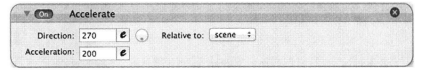

Figure 7-3. *Gravity for the target*

Repeat the same for actors Soft Block and Hard Block.

Let the Actors Enter the Scene

Drag and drop into the scene one instance of Target, one instance of Soft Block, and two instances of Hard Block. Position and reshape the actors to approximately match Figure 7-4. Try to position them on the right side of the scene.

Figure 7-4. *Positioning the target on the scene*

Hit the Preview button to play with the projectile.

You can open the file CanonShowPartII-step1.gameproj located in the folder Chapter7_Files.

At this stage, you still have more work to do in order to make it a little bit more playable. Next, you will focus on making sure that some of the blocks are destroyed after a certain amount of hits.

With a Touch of Style: The Particle Effect

The particle effect is a great feature of GameSalad. Basically, it will spawn multiple elements (particles) in a specified amount of time at a defined rate. It can be used in many different ways. It can deliver multiple results depending on the settings: dust, thrust, explosion. This section explains each of the setting parameters of the particle effect, and then you will implement it for the destruction of the target.

The Parameters of the Particle Effect

The particle effect is a behavior named Particles. It can be found in the standard behavior library and needs to be dragged and dropped into an actor. Although the effect is great, one downside is that you are not spawning actors. This means that particles don't have the same properties. For example, they can't collide or have behaviors.

The Particles behavior is composed of six tabs of parameters:

- Spawn Rate: Defines the number of particles, their life duration, and the spawn speed.

- Velocity/Position: Defines the speed of the particles and where they should be spawned.

- Size: Defines the size of the particles.

- Color: Allow some color effects on the particle.

- Rotation: Options to add some settings for the rotation of the particles.

- Image: Instead of a basic shape, this section lets you to choose an image from your library for the particle.

Spawn Rate

Figure 7-5 shows the Spawn Rate tab of the Particles behavior.

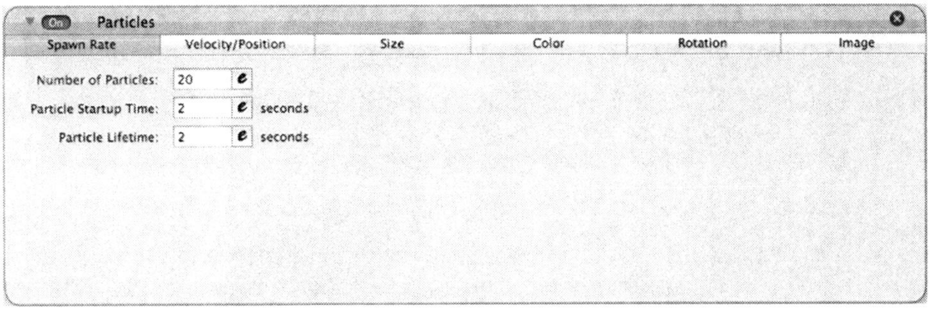

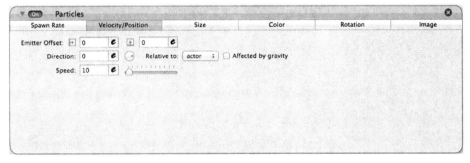

Figure 7-5. *Spawn Rate tab of the Particles behavior*

In this tab, you have three setting parameters:

- Number of Particles: Here you enter the number of particles to be spawned during the occurrence of the behavior. Be careful; setting a high number of particles here may slow down your game.

- Particle Startup Time: Enter the time required to spawn the complete number of particles that you just defined above. The unit is second.

- Particle Lifetime: Here you define the life duration of a particle before it is destroyed. The unit is second.

Velocity/Position

The Velocity/Position tab is shown in Figure 7-6.

Figure 7-6. *The Velocity/Position tab of the Particles behavior*

Here you can define the speed and direction of the particles that you spawn as well as their origins. This tab contains six setting parameters:

- Emitter Offset x: This parameter offsets the position on the x-axis for the origin of the particles compared to the center of the actor that has the particles behavior.

- Emitter Offset y: This parameter offsets the position on the y-axis for the origin of the particles compared to the center of the actor that has the particles behavior.

- Direction: Defines the direction of the spawned particles.

- Relative to: You can choose if you want the direction to be relative to the actor or to the scene. For example, if you select 270 degrees for the direction relative to the scene, it will always go down, whatever the position of the actor. If you select 270 degrees for the direction relative to the actor, if will go to the bottom of the actor, which will depend on the rotation of the actor.

- Affected by gravity: If you have defined the scene gravity, check this box if you want your particles to be affected by the gravity.

- Speed: Enter a value to define the speed of the particles.

Size

The Size tab of the Particles behavior is shown in Figure 7-7.

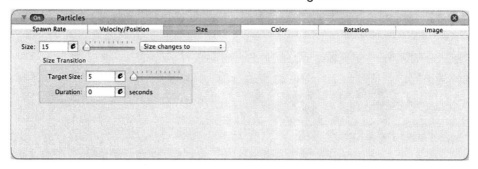

Figure 7-7. *Size tab of the Particles behavior*

The Size tab defines the size of the particles, a start size, and a target size to be reached within a specified time. The parameters are:

- Size: Enter a value here. The unit is pixel.

- Size does not change: Select if you want to have a constant size over the life of the particle or if you want the size to change.

If you have selected "Size changes to," the Size Transition settings will appear on the screen. The setting parameters are:

- Target Size: Enter the size to reach in a specified amount of time set in the below parameter.

- Duration: Enter the time to change the size. Unit is second.

Color

Figure 7-8 shows the Color tab of the Particles behavior.

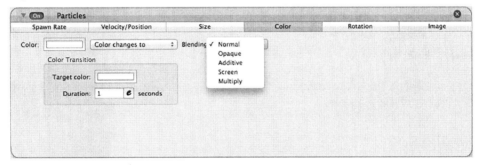

Figure 7-8. *The Color tab of the Particles behavior*

The Color tab not only defines the color of the particles but it also enables you to have a start color and a target color to be reached within a specified time.

The parameters are:

- Color: Pick a color here.

- Color does not change: Select if you want to have a constant color over the life of the particle or if you want the color to change.

If you have selected "Color changes to", the Color Transition settings will appear on the screen. The setting parameters are:

- Blending mode: You can choose between various blending modes. Experiment to find the setting that best suits you.

      ◾ Target color: Pick the color to set in a specified amount of time (set in the below parameter).

      ◾ Duration: Enter the time to change the color. Unit is second.

Rotation

The Rotation tab is shown on Figure 7-9.

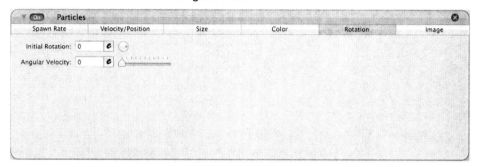

Figure 7-9. *The Rotation tab*

You can define the initial rotation angle as well as the angular velocity (the speed of rotation of the particles).

Image

Figure 7-10 shows the Image tab.

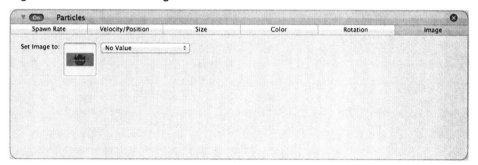

Figure 7-10. *The Image tab of the Particles behavior*

Instead of having a basic square, you can use an image from the image library by selecting the image from the drop button. The previous settings continue to apply.

An Explosion of Colors

Before playing a little bit with the Particles behavior, you need to follow a few additional steps in your gameplay.

Open Soft Block in the Actor Editor and create a new integer actor attribute named "NbHit" with a default value of 0. This attribute will increment itself by one for each collision with the projectile.

Create a new rule named "Collision Increment." The condition of the rule is "Actor receives event" "overlaps or collides" with "actors of type" "Projectile." Then drag and drop a Change Attribute behavior into the rule and change Soft Block.NbHit to Soft Block.NbHit+1.

Next, create a second rule named "Block Destruction." This rule will destroy the actor after two hits from the projectile. The condition of the rule is "Attribute""Soft Block.NbHit""≥""2." Then drag and drop a Destroy behavior into the rule.

The Actor Editor view of Soft Block is shown in Figure 7-11.

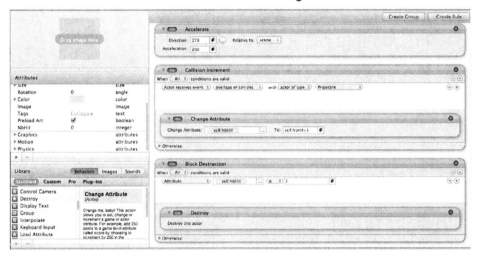

Figure 7-11. *Actor Editor view of Soft Block*

Repeat the same for the Hard Block actor, but instead of two hits required to destroy the actor, set it for destruction after three hits. The actor is shown in Figure 7-12.

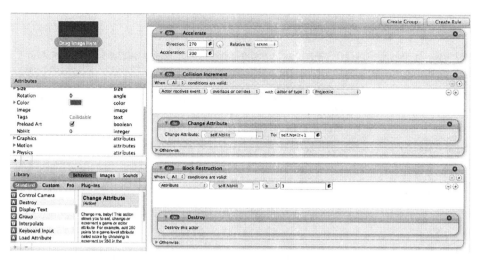

Figure 7-12. *Actor Editor view of Hard Block*

Now, let's play a little with the Particles behavior.

Import the image located in the Chapter7_Files folder named `star.png` into the Image library of your project.

Open the Target actor in the Actor Editor. Create a new rule and name it "Target Destruction." The condition of the rule is "Actor receives event" "overlaps or collides" with "actor of type" "projectile." Drag and drop a Particles behavior and change the settings to:

- Number of Particles: 200
- Particle Startup Time: 1
- Particle Lifetime: 1
- Emitter Offset: 0 & 0
- Direction: random(0,359)
- Relative to: actor
- Speed: 100
- Size: 20
- Size changes to:
    - Target Size: 0
- Duration: 1

- Color: pick a blue and set opacity to 50%
- Color changes to:
    - Blending: Normal
- Target color: pick a yellow green and set opacity to 50%
- Duration: 1
- Initial Rotation: random(0,359)
- Angular Velocity: 50
- Image: star

Drag and drop another Particles behavior and change the settings to (or duplicate the previous behavior by dragging it while pressing the Option key)

- Number of Particles: 200
- Particle Startup Time: 1
- Particle Lifetime: 1
- Emitter Offset: 0 & 0
- Direction: random(0,359)
- Relative to: actor
- Speed: 100
- Size: 20
- Size changes to:
    - Target Size: 0
- Duration: 1
- Color: pick a green and set opacity to 50%
- Color changes to:
    - Blending: Normal
- Target color: pick a yellow green and set opacity to 50%
- Duration: 1
- Initial Rotation: random(0,359)
- Angular Velocity: 50
- Image: star

Drag and drop another Particles behavior and change the settings to:

- Number of Particles: 200
- Particle Startup Time: 1
- Particle Lifetime: 1
- Emitter Offset: 0 & 0
- Direction: random(0,359)
- Relative to: actor
- Speed: 100
- Size: 20
- Size changes to:
    - Target Size: 0
- Duration: 1
- Color: pick a red and set opacity to 50%
- Color changes to:
    - Blending: Normal
- Target color: pick a yellow green and set opacity to 50%
- Duration: 1
- Initial Rotation: random(0,359)
- Angular Velocity: 50
- Image: star

Drag and drop another Particles behavior and change the settings to:

- Number of Particles: 200
- Particle Startup Time: 1
- Particle Lifetime: 1
- Emitter Offset: 0 & 0
- Direction: random(0,359)
- Relative to: actor
- Speed: 100

- Size: 20
- Size changes to:
  - Target Size: 0
- Duration: 1
- Color: pick a green and set opacity to 50%
- Color changes to:
  - Blending: Normal
- Target color: pick a grey and set opacity to 50%
- Duration: 1
- Initial Rotation: random(0,359)
- Angular Velocity: 50
- Image: star

Hit the Preview button to play with the projectile.

You can open the file CanonShowPartII-step2.gameproj located in the folder Chapter7_Files.

Performance Optimization with Tables

Version 0.9.90 of GameSalad introduced the tables. Tables are two-dimension arrays that allow you to store data of different types. At the time of writing this book, tables are only in a read-only mode, but it is in the GameSalad roadmap to make them writable from the game logic.

Introduction to Tables in GameSalad

The tables can be seen on the Tables tab next to Actors tab, as show in Figure 7-13.

Figure 7-13. *The Tables tab view*

To create a new table, you simply need to click the + sign on the bottom left of the screen. You can rename the table name by clicking on its name. Tables will appear as game attributes and you will use specific functions to access the content of the tables. Tables can also be imported from Excel or any other software that exports CSV format.

You can open a table in the Table Editor by double-clicking the table. The Table Editor is shown in Figure 7-14.

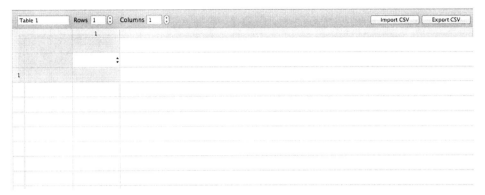

Figure 7-14. *Table Editor*

You can modify the name of the table in the Table Editor also. You will be able to add rows and columns by modifying those parameters next to the table name.

You will select the type of data that will be contained in the table by column. This means that each column will be a specific type of data. As usual, you can select Text, Integer, Boolean, Real, and Angle. You can also name your columns and lines as shown in Figure 7-15.

City Position	Rows 3	Columns 3		
		1	2	3
		Longitude	Latitude	City Name
		Real	Real	Text
1	Row 1	0	0	
2	Row 2	0	0	
3	Row 3	0	0	

Figure 7-15. *A simple table*

Another very useful feature of the Table Editor is the ability to import and export CSV files. If you have big files of data, you can immediately import them from a CSV file.

Last but not least, let's quickly review the functions to use with tables. Figure 7-16 shows the three functions to access table information.

tableCellValue
tableColCount
tableRowCount

Figure 7-16. *Table function*

Let's examine the syntax and the outcome of each function.

tableCellValue() returns the value of a specified cell in a specified table. The syntax is:

tableCellValue(table,row,col)

- Table: The name of the table. You need to use the attribute browser to select the table.

- Row: The row number

- Col: The column number

tableColCount() returns the number of columns in a specified table. The syntax is:

tableColCount(table)

- Table: The name of the table. You need to use the attribute browser to select the table.

tableRowCount()returns the number of rows in a specified table. The syntax is:

tableRowCount(table)

- Table: The name of the table. You need to use the attribute browser to select the table.

Let's put in practice the usage of tables.

Managing Several Scenes in One Scene

Let's go through a very advanced utilization of the tables. You will do some recycling of the actors and use tables to store the different levels of a game.

Creating Tables

You will create a table for each actor you will recycle. Basically, you will have tables for Hard Block1, Hard Block2, Soft Block, and Target. The tables will contain the positions of the blocks for each level. You will have two columns (X and Y) and three rows (three levels). If you were to create more levels, you would create more rows.

Go to the Tables tab and create a new table. Rename this table "Hard Block1." Open this table in the Table Editor by double-clicking it. Type the values inside this table as per Figure 7-17.

Hard Block1	Rows 3	Columns 2
	1	2
	X	Y
	Real	Real
1	1,630	88
2	1,609	113
3	1,326	165

Figure 7-17. *Hard Block1 table*

Repeat the operation by creating another table named "Hard Block2" and add the values shown in Figure 7-18.

Hard Block2	Rows 3	Columns 2
	1	2
	X	Y
	Real	Real
1	1,763	88
2	1,646	113
3	1,400	164

Figure 7-18. *Hard Block2 table*

Repeat the operation by creating another table named "Soft Block" and insert the values shown in Figure 7-19.

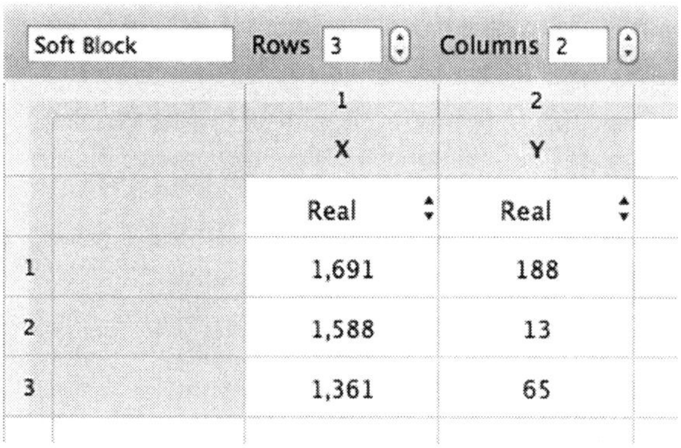

Soft Block		Rows 3 ⬍	Columns 2 ⬍
		1	2
		X	Y
		Real ⬍	Real ⬍
1		1,691	188
2		1,588	13
3		1,361	65

Figure 7-19. *Soft Block table*

Repeat the operation again to add another table named "Target" and add the values shown in Figure 7-20.

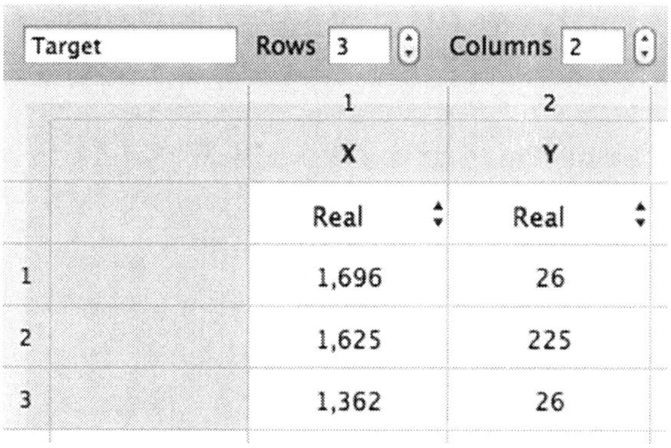

Target		Rows 3 ⬍	Columns 2 ⬍
		1	2
		X	Y
		Real ⬍	Real ⬍
1		1,696	26
2		1,625	225
3		1,362	26

Figure 7-20. *Target table*

You now have your tables all set. You will modify your actors accordingly.

Implementing the Recycling

The purpose of recycling is very simple. You position a block and when it is time to destroy the block, instead of using the Destroy behavior, you will move the actor out of the visible scene. When you go to the next level, you will again change the position of the block back to where it should be for the next level. This way you can have hundreds of levels with just one scene, which is very efficient on memory.

You will use a game attribute to store the current level. Open the scene in the Scene Editor and create a new integer game attribute named "WhatLevel." The default value is 1.

Open the instance of the Hard Block actor located in the far right of the scene in the Actor Editor, as shown in Figure 7-21.

Figure 7-21. *The far right Hard Block selected*

Unlock the instance of the actor. Rename the instance "Hard Block1."

Drag and drop a Change Attribute behavior into the instance and change Hard Block1.Position.X to tableCellValue(game.Hard Block1, game.WhatLevel,1). Drag and drop another Change Attribute behavior into the instance and change

Hard Block1.Position.Y to tableCellValue(game.Hard Block1, game.WhatLevel,2). These two behaviors are shown in Figure 7-22.

Figure 7-22. *Initial positioning of Hard Block1*

Open the second instance of the Hard Block actor and rename it "Hard Block2."

Drag and drop a Change Attribute behavior into the instance and change Hard Block2.Position.X to tableCellValue(game.Hard Block2, game.WhatLevel,1). Drag and drop another Change Attribute behavior into the instance and change Hard Block2.Position.Y to tableCellValue(game.Hard Block2, game.WhatLevel,2). These two behaviors are shown in Figure 7-23.

Figure 7-23. *Initial positioning of Hard Block2*

Open the instance of the Soft Block actor.

Drag and drop a Change Attribute behavior into the instance and change Soft Block.Position.X to tableCellValue(game.Soft Block, game.WhatLevel,1). Drag and drop another Change Attribute behavior into the instance and change Soft Block.Position.Y to tableCellValue(game.Soft Block, game.WhatLevel,2). These two behaviors are shown in Figure 7-24.

Figure 7-24. *Initial positioning of Soft Block*

Open the instance of the Target actor.

Drag and drop a Change Attribute behavior into the instance and change Target.Position.X to tableCellValue(game.Target, game.WhatLevel,1). Drag and drop another Change Attribute behavior into the instance and change Target.Position.Y to tableCellValue(game.Target, game.WhatLevel,2). These two behaviors are shown in Figure 7-25.

Figure 7-25. *Initial positioning of Target*

Re-open the Hard Block1 instance. In the Block Destruction rule, remove the Destroy behavior by clicking the circled cross on the right side of behavior.

Drag and drop a Change Attribute behavior into the rule and change Hard Block1.Position.X to 640. Drag and drop a Change Attribute behavior into the rule and change Hard Block1.Position.Y to 1500. The updated Block Destruction rule is shown in Figure 7-26.

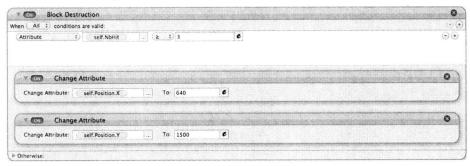

Figure 7-26. *Updated Block Destruction rule*

Make similar changes for Hard Block2 (shown in Figure 7-27) and for Soft Block (shown in Figure 7-28).

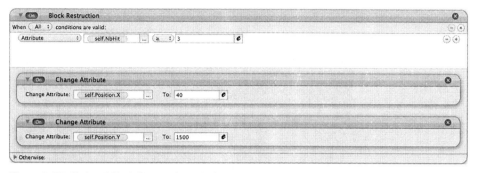

Figure 7-27. *Updated Block Destruction rule for Hard Block2*

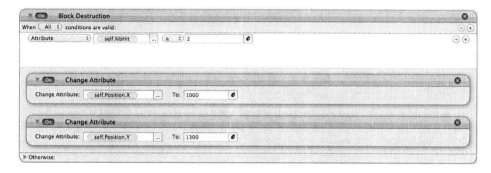

Figure 7-28. *Updated Block Destruction rule for Soft Block*

Next, open the instance of the Target actor. Drag and drop a Timer behavior into the Target Destruction rule below the last Particles behavior. Change the settings of the Timer behavior to "After" "0.5" seconds with "Run to completion" checked.

Drag and drop a Change Attribute behavior into the Timer and change Target.Position.X to 1400. Drag and drop a Change Attribute behavior into the Timer and change Target.Position.Y to 1300. The updated Target Destruction rule is shown in Figure 7-29.

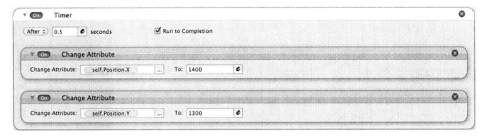

Figure 7-29. *Updated Target Destruction rule*

You use a Timer here because you want to see the particles effects.

Knowing When the Target Has Been Destroyed

You will need another game attribute in order to know when the target has been destroyed. Create a new Boolean game attribute named "TargetDestroyed."

Add a new Change Attribute behavior into the Timer you just created and change game.TargetDestroyed to true, as shown in Figure 7-30.

Figure 7-30. *TargetDestroyed is set to true*

You will now know when the target has been destroyed; this indicates that it's time to move to the next level and reposition the actors on the scene per their next level coordinates. Let's do that.

Still in the instance of the Target actor, create a new rule named "Level Up" that will meet the following two conditions:

- "All"
- "Attribute" "game.TargetDestroyed" is "true"
- "Attribute" "game.Change Projectile" is "true"

Add the condition for the Change Projectile to be true in order to reset the scene when the projectile goes back to the slingshot.

Drag and drop a Change Attribute behavior and change game.WhatLevel to game.WhatLevel+1. This moves the level up.

Next, you will reposition the target. But before doing that, you need to ensure that the target has no momentum movement. This would be a movement from the previous scene. As you will re-use this for other blocks, I will show you how to create a custom behavior.

Creating a Custom Behavior

Basically, to ensure that the target is not moving, you will reset to 0 all velocity (linear and angular) as well as the rotation angle.

In the Level up rule, create a new group named "No Movement." Use Change Attribute behaviors to set the following (shown in Figure 7-31):

- Self.Motion.Linear Velocity.X to 0
- Self.Motion.Linear Velocity.Y to 0
- Self.Motion.Angular Velocity to 0
- Self.Rotation to 0

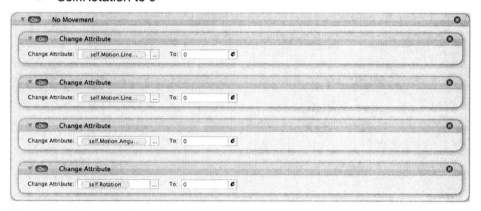

Figure 7-31. *No movement*

Now, click the Custom tab in the Behaviors library. Drag the No Movement group over to the Behavior library, as shown in Figure 7-32.

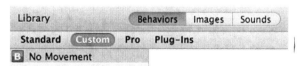

Figure 7-32. *No Movement custom behavior*

That's it! You have created your first custom behavior. You will use this behavior later.

Positioning the Target on the New Level

In the Level up rule, drag and drop a Change Attribute behavior and change Target.Position.X to tableCellValue(game.Target, game.WhatLevel, 1).

Drag and drop another Change Attribute behavior and change Target.Position.Y to tableCellValue(game.Target, game.WhatLevel, 2).

The updated Level up rule is shown in Figure 7-33.

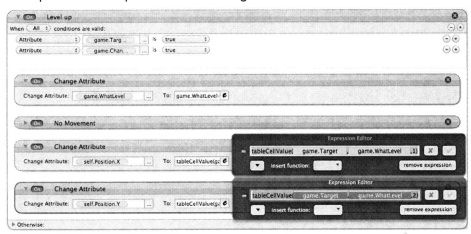

Figure 7-33. *Updated Level up rule*

One last modification on the Target instance: you need to reset the TargetDestroyed attribute at the start of each game.

Drag and drop a Change Attribute behavior into the Target instance and change game.TargetDestroyed to false, as shown in Figure 7-34.

Figure 7-34. *Resetting the Target Destroyed attribute*

Replacing the Blocks

Let's modify the hard and soft blocks so they reposition themselves after the target is destroyed.

Open the instance Hard Block1 in the Actor Editor. Create a new rule and rename it "Level Up." The triggers for this rule are the two attributes TargetDestroyed and Change Projectile set to true. So modify the conditions to:

- "All"
- "Attribute" "game.TargetDestroyed" is "true"
- "Attribute" "game.Change Projectile" is "true"

Then, drag and drop a Timer and change the settings to "After" "1" seconds with "Run to Completion" checked. You use a Timer before re-positioning the blocks to ensure that the projectile has enough time to fly out of the scene. If you don't wait, a collision may occur that could mess your gameplay.

Now drag and drop the No Movement custom behavior into the Timer.

Drag and drop two Change Attributes into the Timer and change:

- Hard Block1.Position.X to tableCellValue(game.Hard Block1, game.WhatLevel, 1)
- Hard Block1.Position.Y to tableCellValue(game.Hard Block1, game.WhatLevel, 2)

You will also need to reset the number of hits for the block. Drag and drop a Change Attribute behavior and change Hard Block1.NbHit to 0.

The Level Up rule for Hard Block1 is shown in Figure 7-35.

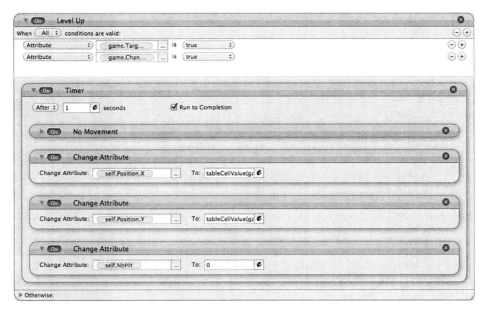

Figure 7-35. *Level Up rule for Hard Block1*

Open Hard Block2 in the Actor Editor. Create a new rule named "Level Up." Modify the conditions area to:

- "All"

- "Attribute" "game.TargetDestroyed" is "True"

- "Attribute" "game.Change Projectile" is "True"

Then, drag and drop a Timer and change the settings to "After" "1" seconds with "Run to Completion" checked. Now drag and drop the No Movement custom behavior into the timer. Drag and drop two Change Attributes into the timer and change:

- Hard Block2.Position.X to tableCellValue(game.Hard Block2, game.WhatLevel, 1)

- Hard Block2.Position.Y to tableCellValue(game.Hard Block2, game.WhatLevel, 2)

Drag and drop a Change Attribute behavior and change Hard Block2.NbHit to 0.

Repeat the same steps for the Soft block instance. Create a new rule named "Level Up." Modify the conditions area to:

- "All"

- "Attribute" "game.TargetDestroyed" is "true"
- "Attribute" "game.Change Projectile" is "true"

Then, drag and drop a Timer and change the settings to "After" "1" seconds with "Run to Completion" checked. Now drag and drop the No Movement custom behavior in the timer. Drag and drop two Change Attributes into the timer and change

- Soft Block.Position.X to tableCellValue(game.Soft Block, game.WhatLevel, 1)
- Soft Block.Position.Y to tableCellValue(game.Soft Block, game.WhatLevel, 2)

Drag and drop a Change Attribute behavior and change Hard Block2.NbHit to 0.

The last steps are to take care of the projectiles.

Modifying the Projectiles to Start a New Level

You will use the end of the re-positioning of the projectile to finish resetting your parameters.

Open the instance of Projectile in the Actor Editor. Expand the Attributes reset rule located in the Back to Position rule.

Drag and drop a Change Attribute behavior into the Attributes reset rule and change game.TargetDestroyed to false.

Within the Back to Position rule, create a new rule that you will position on top position. The condition is "Attribute" "TargetDestroyed" is "true." Then drag and drop a "Change Attribute" behavior in this rule and change game.Attemptleft to 4. This will reset the number of attempts back to 4 when you change levels.

The last modification you need make is to delay the repositioning because putting the projectile back to its original position will reset the attributes. You need to have the necessary time to reposition all the blocks.

Drag and drop a Timer behavior into the Back to Position rule and change the settings to "After" "0.2" seconds with "Run to Completion" checked. Next, drag and drop the rule and two behaviors into the Timer, as shown in Figure 7-36.

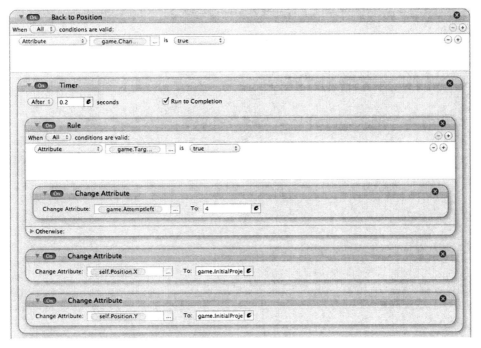

Figure 7-36. *Reset the number of attempts left after a level up*

Also, you need to replace the interpolate behaviors in the Back to position rule because they could trigger an unwanted collision with blocks when going back to slingshot position. You will use Change Attribute behaviors instead.

Remove the two Interpolate behaviors from the Back to Position rule. Drag and drop two Change Attribute behaviors and change the settings to the following (shown in Figure 7-37):

- Projectile.Position.X to game.InitialProjectileX
- Projectile.Position.Y to game.InitialProjectileY

Last, you need to modify the dummy projectile. It will re-appear when the number of attempts is reset.

Open each of the dummy projectile instances and expand the Otherwise section of the existing rule. Drag and drop a Change Attribute behavior in the Otherwise section and change Dummy Projectile.Color.Alpha to 1. This will make the trick work.

Hit the Preview button to play with the projectile.

You can open the file CanonShowPartII-step3.gameproj located in the folder Chapter7_Files.

Adding a Cool Menu

In the last section of this chapter, you will create a very cool sliding menu. You will limit it to three levels, with each level displayed on one page. But you can have many more levels on a page and as many pages as you want. In addition, only the first level will be unlocked and you will need to win the level to unlock the following levels.

Creating the Menu Scene

Create a new scene named "Menu" and position it before the Initial Scene, as shown in Figure 7-37.

Figure 7-37. *Menu scene*

Double-click the Menu scene to open the Scene Editor.

As you are working on an iPhone Landscape project, the size of the screen is 480 x 320. As you want to have three pages of menu, you will need to change the width to 1440.

Display the scene attribute and change Width to 1440, as shown in Figure 7-38.

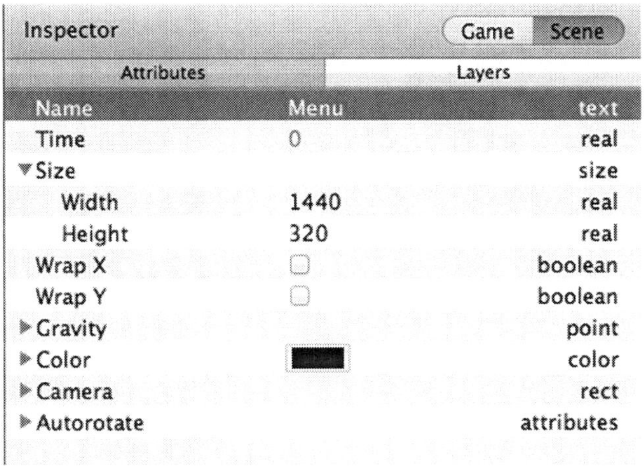

Figure 7-38. *Menu scene attributes*

Managing Unlocked Levels

In order to manage levels, you will use an integer game attribute that will contain the maximum level unlocked. By default, it will start at one. Then during the game, every time you do a level up, you will check that the new WhatLevel attribute is higher than MaxLevel. If this is the case, you will replace the value of MaxLevel with the value of WhatLevel.

On the Menu Scene, you will use an actor to display either the level number of the box or a red cross if the level has not been unlocked yet. The level number of the box will be an actor attribute with a different value per instance on the scene.

Let's do all this!

Create a new integer game attribute named "MaxLevel." The default value is 1. Open Initial Scene in the Scene Editor. Open the target instance and locate the increment of WhatLevel in the Level Up rule. Just below this increment, create a new rule with the condition "Attribute" "game.WhatLevel" ">" "game.LevelMax." Then drag and drop a Change Attribute behavior to the rule and change game.MaxLevel to game.WhatLevel, as shown in Figure 7-39.

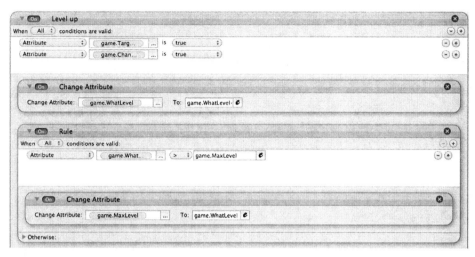

Figure 7-39. *MaxLevel update*

Next, create a new actor named "BoxLevel." Double-click this actor to open it in the Actor Editor. Create an actor attribute of type integer named "Level."

Create a new rule with the condition "Attribute" "BoxLevel.Level" "≤" "game.MaxLevel." Drag and drop a Display Text behavior and select BoxLevel.Level as an attribute to display. Change the size to 60.

Expand the Otherwise section of the rule and drag and drop a Display Text behavior. Type a capital X letter to display. Change the size to 60 and the color to red.

The rule is shown in Figure 7-40.

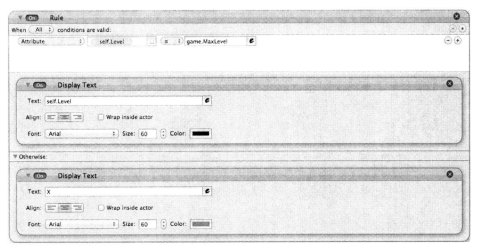

Figure 7-40. *What content to display for Level box*

Position three instances of the BoxLevel actor on the Menu scene, as per Figure 7-41.

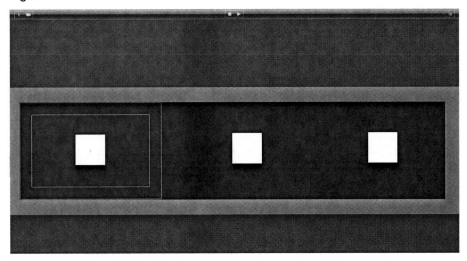

Figure 7-41. *Positioning the boxes*

Open each instance of the actor on the scene and change the level attribute from one to three, starting from left to right.

Next, you will implement the sliding effect.

Implementing the Sliding Effect

To implement the sliding effect, you will need two actors. Basically, the first one will register the finger movement and the second one will control the camera based on the data collected from the first actor.

Touch Actor

The Touch actor will be used to register the finger movements. It will be made invisible on the scene.

Create an actor named "Touch." Drag and drop an instance of the Touch actor on the scene and double-click the instance to open it in the Actor Editor. Click the lock icon to unlock the instance.

Create a new rule with the condition "Actor receives event" "mouse button" is "down." This will detect that the finger has been positioned on the screen. Contrary to the previous chapter, you don't use Touch to detect the finger touch. You do use the mouse button detection because this gives you the possibility to detect the touch anywhere on the screen, not related to position of the actor.

Then drag and drop a Change Attribute behavior into the rule and change Touch.Position.X to Device.Mouse.Position.X. Then drag and drop a Constrain Attribute behavior into the rule and change Touch.Motion.Linear Velocity.X to 10*(game.Mouse.Position.X – Touch.Position.X). Those two behaviors will ensure that as long as the finger is on the screen there is no inertia. It moves with the finger.

Last, drag and drop a Constrain Attribute behavior into the rule and change Touch.Motion.Linear Velocity.X to Touch.Motion.Linear Velocity.X*0.95. This last behavior will make an inertia that will slow down by itself with the 95% reduction (*0.95).

The rule is shown in Figure 7-42.

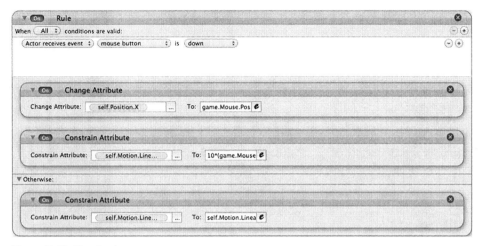

Figure 7-42. *Touch rule*

One last modification, which is critical, is that this actor should be positioned on a non-scrollable layer. In the Scene Editor, click the Scene tab to display the scene attributes inspector. Click the Layers tab, as shown in Figure 7-43.

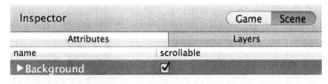

Figure 7-43. *Layers inspector*

Create a new layer by clicking the + sign in the layer inspector. By default, it will create a new layer named "Layer 1." Uncheck the box below "scrollable."

Expand the background layer, move down to the Touch actor in the layer inspector to Layer 1, as shown in Figure 7-44.

Inspector		Game	Scene
Attributes		Layers	
name	scrollable		
▼ Background	☑		
BoxLevel	☐		
BoxLevel	☐		
BoxLevel	☐		
▼ Layer 1	☐		
Touch	☐		

Figure 7-44. *Touch in Layer 1*

Lastly, open the Touch actor instance in the Actor Editor and uncheck the Visible box.

CameraControl Actor

Let's work on the CameraControl actor.

Create a new actor named "CameraControl." Change its color to a vivid green. This actor will be invisible but it will be helpful when positioning the actor.

Drag and drop an instance of CameraControl on the scene. Try to position the actor at the center of the scene and reshape the actor to be as small as possible, as shown in Figure 7-45.

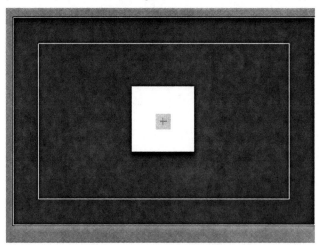

Figure 7-45. *Positioning the CameraControl on the scene*

Click the Camera icon to set up the camera zone. Reduce the camera zone to a very small zone on the CameraControl actor, as shown in Figure 7-46.

Figure 7-46. *Modified camera zone*

Go back to the Scene Editor. Double-click the instance of CameraControl actor. Click the lock icon to unlock the instance.

Drag and drop a Control Camera behavior into the actor.

Next, drag and drop a Constrain Attribute behavior and change CameraControl.Motion.Linear Velocity.X to - Current Scene. Layers.Layer 1.Touch.Motion.Linear Velocity.X, as shown in Figure 7-47.

Figure 7-47. *Moving the camera*

You put a minus sign in front of the velocity value from Touch because you want the camera to move in the opposite direction of the finger. If you move your finger from right to left, you want to see what is on the right of the screen (opposite direction).

Now you will add boundaries to the left and right sides. It will be a minimum of 240 and a maximum of (1440-240) for the x-axis value. Drag and drop two Constrain Attribute behaviors and change:

- CameraControl.Position.X to max(240,CameralControl.Position.X)

- CameraControl.Position.X to min(1200,CameralControl.Position.X)

This is shown in Figure 7-48.

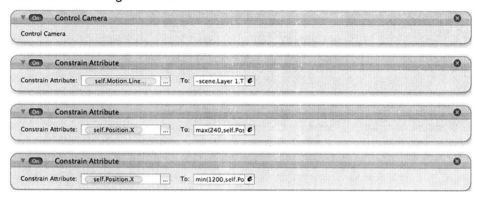

Figure 7-48. *CameraControl behaviors*

Last but not least, uncheck the visible attribute, which is located in the actor attribute for this actor.

Enabling Level Selection

You now need a way to be able to click on a box to play an unlocked level. You will use a very simple trick. When you touch to slide, the Touched and Released position will not be the same. But if you intend to click a box, the Touch and Release position will be the same.

Create two game attributes of type real named "TouchedX" and "ReleasedX." You will use those attributes to store the value of the Touch and the Release.

Next, open the BoxLevel actor prototype in the Actor Editor.

Create a new rule with the condition "Actor receives event" "touch" is "pressed." Then drag and drop a Change Attribute behavior in the rule and change game.TouchX to devices.Mouse.Position.X, as shown in Figure 7-49.

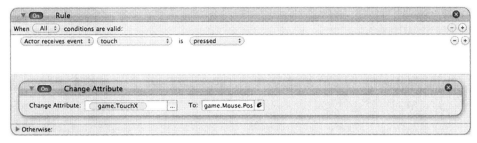

Figure 7-49. *Registering the Touch X value*

Create a new rule with the condition "Actor receives event" "touch" is "released." Then drag and drop a Change Attribute behavior in the rule and change game.ReleaseX to devices.Mouse.Position.X, as shown in Figure 7-50.

Figure 7-50. *Registering the Release X value*

Next, create a rule that will check when Touch is release if the x positions are the same and if the level is unlocked.

Create a new rule with the conditions of:

- "All"
- "Actor receives event" "touch" is "released"
- "Attribute" "game.ReleaseX" "=" "game.TouchX"
- "Attribute" "BoxLevel.Level" "≤" "game.MaxLevel"

Then drag and drop a Change Attribute behavior into the rule and change game.WhatLevel to BoxLevel.Level. Last, drag and drop a Change Scene behavior and change the settings to "Go to Scene:" "Initial Scene," as per Figure 7-51.

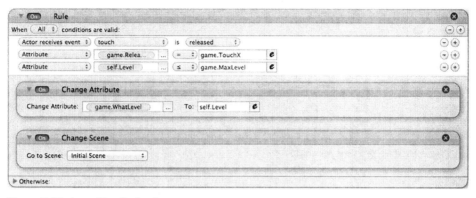

Figure 7-51. *Launching the level*

Let's finish up this project by adding a Menu button on the initial scene.

Adding a Menu Button on the Initial Scene

Open the Initial Scene in the Scene Editor.

Create a new actor named "Menu." Change the Color\Alpha to 0.

In the Actor Editor, add a Display Text behavior into the Menu actor and type "Menu" as text to display.

Next, create a new rule with the condition "Actor receives event" "touch" is "pressed." Last, drag and drop a Change Scene behavior into the rule and select the Menu scenes.

The actor behaviors are shown in Figure 7-52.

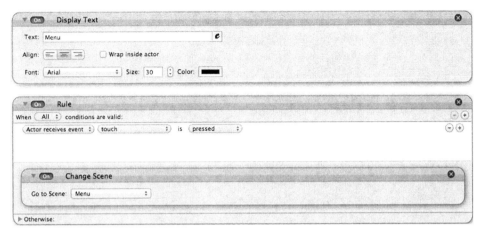

Figure 7-52. *Menu actor behaviors*

Last but not least, drag and drop the actor on the Initial Scene at the top right of the scene.

Hit the Preview button to play with your menu.

You can open the file CanonShowPartII-step4.gameproj located in the folder Chapter7_Files.

Summary

Whoa! What a long road you just travelled! You build the entire game mechanics of a game such as Angry Birds. In this chapter, you have:

- Created the blocks and target.
- Discovered the Particles behavior.
- Used tables in GameSalad.
- Implemented recycling of actors.
- Optimized your performance with tables.
- Created a very powerful and advanced menu.

Graphics and Sound Effects: Labyrinth

When I was a kid, video games were not commonly found in households. At that time, we had other games. Yes, we had non-video games. Ball-in-a-maze puzzles were very popular; they were available in every drugstore in different sizes, shapes, and colors (Figure 8-1).

Figure 8-1. *Ball-in-a-maze picture from Wikipedia*

These games date back to the 19th century. Why am I talking about non-video games in a book about video games? Well, because in this chapter you will transform a retro game into a retro video game. You will implement a Labyrinth game with GameSalad.

Implementing a Labyrinth game in GameSalad is fairly easy and gives you unlimited number of games to design. In the previous chapters, you learned some serious game logic, and you will use this knowledge to lay down the basics of the Labyrinth game. You will be implementing accelerometer movements again as well as the Timer behavior.

Then I will show you how to implement some cool lighting special effects using a few tricks in GameSalad. Lastly, I will cover Sound Import and how to use sound behaviors to create spatial sound effects.

Creating the Labyrinth Game Project

Start by opening the GameSalad creator. Under New Project, select My Great Project template and click Edit in GameSalad Creator.

Configure the project info as per Table 8-1.

Table 8-1. *Labyrinth Project Info*

Title	Labyrinth
Platform	iPhone Landscape
Description	Put the ball in the hole
Instruction	Move the phone
Tags	

Click File ➤ Save As to save your project. Name it Labyrinth.gameproj.

Creating Actors for the Labyrinth Game

In this game you will use the following actors:

- Ball
- Background
- Wall

- Door

- Open Door

- Victory Hole

- Losing Hole

Ball

The Ball is the main actor of the game in the sense that it is the actor controlled by the player. Because it's a ball, you will change the collision shape to circle, which will provide a more realistic collision effect.

Create a new actor and double-click it to open the Actor Editor. Edit the actor attributes with the parameters in Table 8-2.

Table 8-2. *Ball Actor Attributes*

Name	Ball
Size/Width	20
Size/Height	20
Physics/Density	3
Physics/Restitution	0
Physics/Fixed Rotation	Checked
Physics/Collision Shape	Circle

Import the image named ball.png located in the chapter_08 folder. Drag and drop ball.png into the actor.

Background

The Background actor is just used to display a background image in your game.

Create a new actor and double-click it to open the Actor Editor. Edit the actor attributes with the parameters in Table 8-3.

Table 8-3. *Background Actor Attributes*

Name	Background
Size/Width	480
Size/Height	320

Import the wood background.png image located in the chapter_08 folder. Drag and drop it into the actor.

Wall

The Wall actor is used to define the collidable boundaries for your ball. It is important to change the restitution to 0 to avoid bounciness. In addition, the walls are fixed position, so you will uncheck the Moveable attribute.

Create a new actor and double-click it to open the Actor Editor. Edit the actor attributes with the parameters in Table 8-4.

Table 8-4. *Wall Actor Attributes*

Name	Wall
Color/Red	0.6
Color/Green	0.4
Color/Blue	0.2
Physics/Restitution	0
Physics/Moveable	Unchecked

Door

The Door actor is used to add a little bit more complexity to the game. It prevents access to the winning area. The player will have to perform some steps to open the door and get access to the winning area.

Create a new actor and double-click it to open the Actor Editor. Edit the actor attributes with the parameters in Table 8-5.

Table 8-5. *Door Actor Attributes*

Name	Door
Size/Width	5
Size/Height	100
Color/Red	0
Color/Green	0
Color/Blue	0
Physics/Restitution	0
Physics/Fixed Rotation	Checked
Physics/Moveable	Unchecked

Open Door

The Open Door actor is used as a switch button to open the access to the victory hole.

Create a new actor and double-click it to open the Actor Editor. Edit the actor attributes with the parameters in Table 8-6.

Table 8-6. *Open Door Actor Attributes*

Name	Open Door
Size/Width	20

Name	Open Door
Size/Height	20
Physics/Moveable	Unchecked

Victory Hole

The Victory Hole actor acts as the aim for the ball. Your target as a player is to put the ball in the hole. The actor should be slightly bigger than the ball for good visual effects.

Create a new actor and double-click it to open the Actor Editor. Edit the actor attributes with the parameters in Table 8-7.

Table 8-7. *Victory Hole Actor Attributes*

Name	Victory Hole
Size/Width	25
Size/Height	25
Physics/Moveable	Unchecked

Losing Hole

To make the game a little bit harder, you will use some traps: holes that make you lose. These are losing holes.

Create a new actor and double-click it to open the Actor Editor. Edit the actor attributes with the parameters in Table 8-8.

Table 8-8. *Losing Hole Actor Attributes*

Name	Losing Hole
Size/Width	25
Size/Height	25
Physics/Moveable	Unchecked

Defining the Game Logic with Rules and Behaviors

Now it's time to define the game logic. You will re-use rules and behaviors that have been covered in the previous chapters. This is an excellent opportunity to review the Timer behavior and the accelerometer usage.

Ball Rules and Behaviors

In order to move the ball, you will use the accelerometer as you did in Chapter 4. You will implement the four directions. Remember that if you were to publish this game, you would need to implement the auto-rotate in order to keep valid movements.

Open the Ball actor in the Actor Editor. Create a new group and name it "accelerometer."

Create a new rule and name it "up." The condition of the rule is "attribute""device.Accelerometer.X""<""-0.1." Then drag and drop an Accelerate behavior and change the settings to:

- Direction: 270
- Relative to: actor
- Acceleration: max(100, min(1400, abs(device.Accelerometer.X * 1000)

The rule is shown in Figure 8-2.

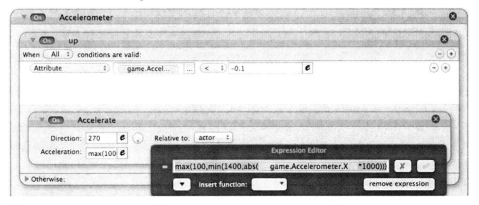

Figure 8-2. *Up Accelerometer rule*

The formula will ensure that you will have analog acceleration. It's linked to the value of the accelerometer axis, so the stronger you move, the faster it will go.

Repeat the previous steps three more times.

Duplicate the rule you just created by holding the option key while dragging down the existing rule. Name it "right." The condition of the rule is "attribute""device.Accelerometer.Y"">""0.1." Then drag and drop an Accelerate behavior and change the settings to:

- Direction: 180

- Relative to: actor

- Acceleration: max(100, min(1400, abs(device.Accelerometer.Y * 1000)

The rule is shown in Figure 8-3.

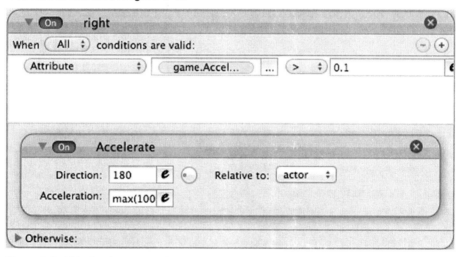

Figure 8-3. *Right Accelerometer rule*

Create a new rule and name it "down." The condition of the rule is "attribute""device.Accelerometer.X"">""0.1". Then drag and drop an Accelerate behavior and change the settings to:

- Direction: 90

- Relative to: actor

- Acceleration: max(100, min(1400, abs(device.Accelerometer.X*1000)

The rule is shown in Figure 8-4.

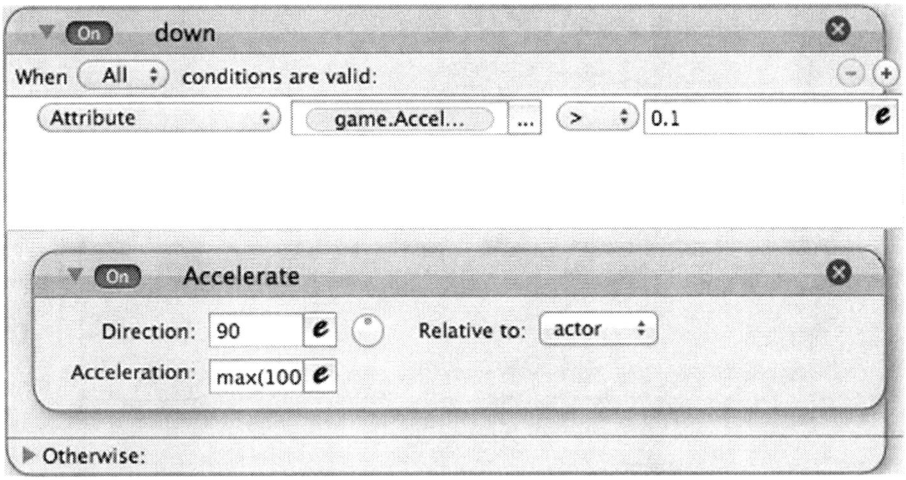

Figure 8-4. *Down Accelerometer rule*

Create a new rule and name it "left." The condition of the rule is "attribute""device.Accelerometer.Y""<""-0.1". Then drag and drop an Accelerate behavior and change the settings to:

- Direction: 0

- Relative to: actor

- Acceleration: max(100, min(1400, abs(device.Accelerometer.Y*1000)

The rule is shown in Figure 8-5.

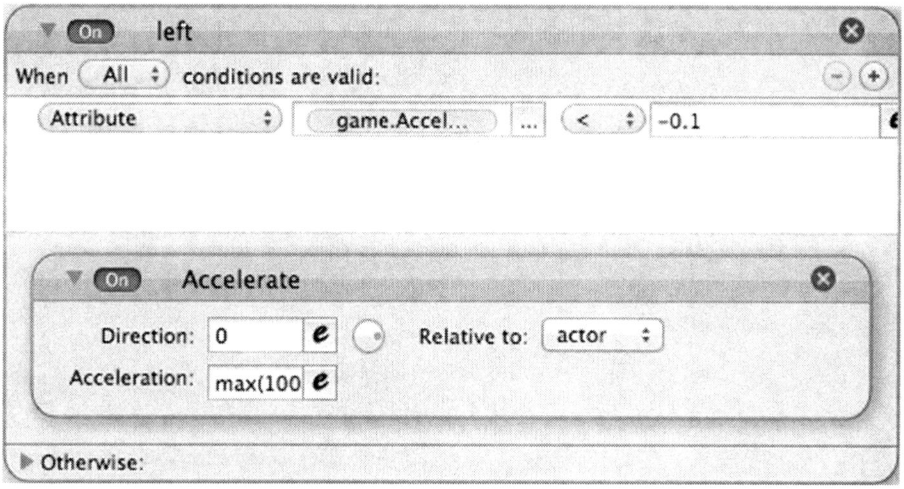

Figure 8-5. *Left Accelerometer rule*

> **TIP:** Should you want to design a game that will be published, do not
> forget to handle screen rotation as explained in Chapter 4.

Next, you need to ensure that the ball is bouncing off the Wall and Door actors.
Drag and drop a Collide behavior and change the settings to Bounce when
colliding with "actor of type" "Wall." Repeat the operation by dragging and
dropping a second Collide behavior, but change the settings to make it collide
with "actor of type" "Door" as per Figure 8-6.

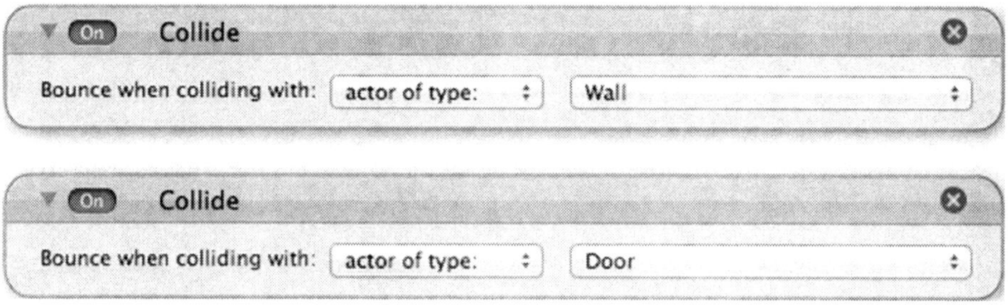

Figure 8-6. *Collision rules for Ball*

Background Rules and Behaviors

The background contains a couple of Change Attribute behaviors that will be used to perfectly position the actor at the center of the screen.

Open the Background actor in the Actor Editor. Create a new group and name it "Position the background." Drag and drop a Change Attribute behavior in the group and change Background.Position.X to 240. Repeat the operation with an additional Change Attribute behavior and change Background.Position.Y to 160. The group is shown in Figure 8-7.

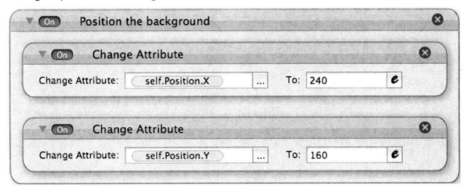

Figure 8-7. *Position the background*

Open Door Rules and Behaviors

You need to open the door that blocks the access to the winning hole. The player has to move the ball over a button that will trigger the opening of the door. The button works as an on/off button. This means that if the ball touches the button, it will open the door. If the ball touches the button again, it will close the door, and this cycle will continue.

In the Open Door actor, you will detect the collision with the Ball actor. This will trigger a change in a Boolean game attribute. Depending on the value of the previous attribute, the door will move from one position to the other. But, in order to have time to move the ball off the button before it hits the button again, you need to add a timer of 2 seconds. If you don't use this timer and let the ball keep moving over the button, it will keep changing state from true to false so quickly you won't even notice it by eye.

Create a new game attribute of type Boolean and name it "Open Door." Open the Open Door actor in the Actor Editor. Create a new actor attribute of type Boolean and name it "Timer."

Create a new rule and name it "Change to False." Apply "All" to the following conditions:

- "Attribute" "game.OpenDoor" is "true"
- "Actor receives event" "overlaps or collides" with "actor of type" "ball"
- "Attribute" "Open Door.Timer" "=" "0"

Then drag and drop a Change Attribute behavior and change game.OpenDoor to 0.

Drag and drop a second Change Attribute behavior and change Open Door.Timer to 1.

Next, drag and drop a Timer behavior and change the settings to "After" "2" seconds with "Run to completion" checked.

Lastly, drag and drop a Change Attribute behavior into the Timer and change Open Door.Timer to 0.

The complete rule is shown in Figure 8-8.

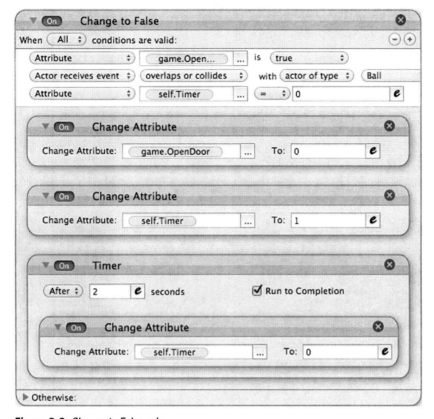

Figure 8-8. *Change to False rule*

Duplicate the rule by dragging it down while pressing the Option key. Name it "Change to True." You will basically reverse the results. Apply "All" to the following conditions:

- "Attribute" "game.OpenDoor" is "false"

- "Actor receives event" "overlaps or collides" with "actor of type" "ball"

- "Attribute" "Open Door.Timer" "=" "0"

Then drag and drop a Change Attribute behavior and change game.OpenDoor to 1.

Drag and drop a second Change Attribute behavior and change Open Door.Timer to 1.

Next, drag and drop a Timer behavior and change the settings to "After" "2" seconds with "Run to completion" checked.

Lastly, drag and drop a Change Attribute behavior into the timer and change Open Door.Timer to 0.

The complete rule is shown in Figure 8-9.

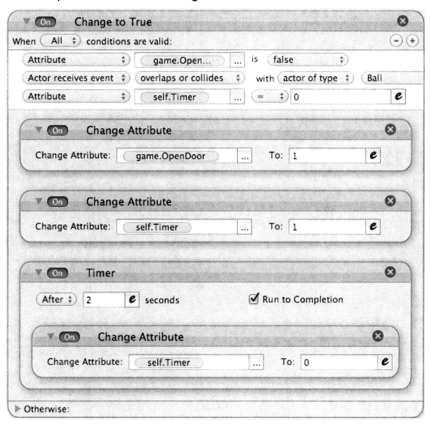

Figure 8-9. *Change to True rule*

Door Rules and Behavior

Assume that the door is located in a top position on the screen and will open by going down (you could easily adapt the settings if you want it to go up or left or right). Store the initial value of the Y position in an actor attribute and interpolate back and forth the Y position value minus the height of the actor.

First, create a new actor attribute of type real and name it "InitialY."

Next, drag and drop a Change Attribute behavior and change Door.InitialY to Door.Position.Y as per Figure 8-10.

Figure 8-10. *Storing the initial Y position value*

Then, create a new rule and name it "OpenDoor is True." This rule will be used to open the door. Apply "All" to the following conditions:

- "Attribute" "game.OpenDoor" is "True"
- "Attribute" "Door.Position.Y" "=" "Door.InitialY"

The second condition will check that the door is closed.

Drag and drop an Interpolate behavior and change the settings to "Door.Position.Y" "Door.InitialY – Door.Size.Height" "0.5" "Linear."

The complete rule is shown in Figure 8-11.

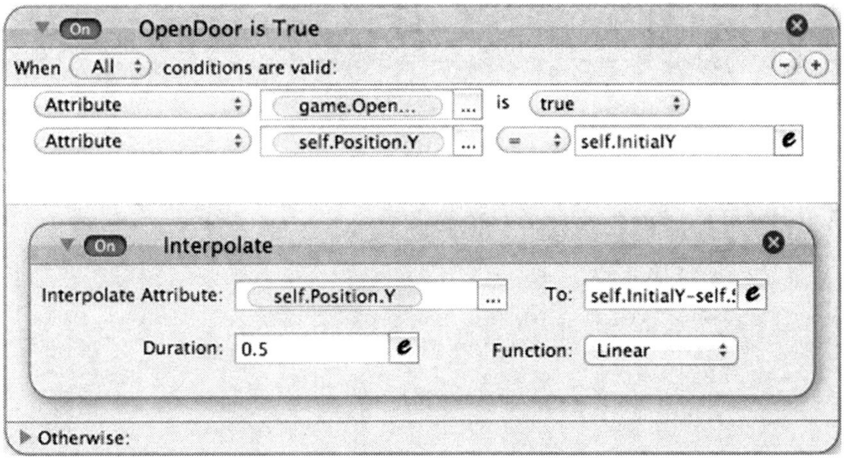

Figure 8-11. *OpenDoor is True rule*

Last, create a new rule and name it "OpenDoor is False." This rule will be used to close the door. Apply "All" to the following conditions:

- "Attribute" "game.OpenDoor" is "False"

> "Attribute" "Door.Position.Y" "≠" "Door.InitialY"

The second condition will check that the door is closed.

Drag and drop an Interpolate behavior and change the settings to "Door.Position.Y" "Door.InitialY" "0.5" "Linear."

The complete rule is shown in Figure 8-12.

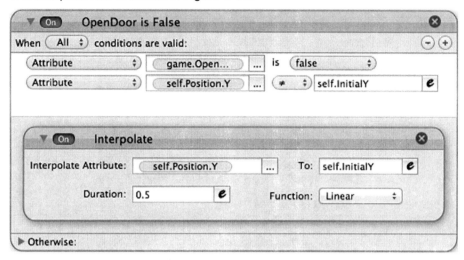

Figure 8-12. *OpenDoor is False rule*

Victory Hole Rules and Behaviors

The final step in this part is to reset the game when the ball touches the Victory Hole actor. For a real game, you would change scene to the next level.

Create a new rule with the condition "Actor receives event" "overlaps or collides" with "actor of type" "ball." Then drag and drop a Reset Game behavior into the rule as per Figure 8-13.

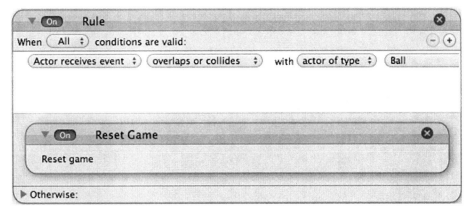

Figure 8-13. *Victory Hole rule*

Designing the Game Area by Laying Out the Scene

It's time to lay out the scene. First, drag and drop the Background actor and try to position it approximately in the center of the scene.

Then you will use multiple instances of the Wall actor in different sizes. GameSalad allows you to have multiple instances of an actor with different sizes but still sticking to the prototype for the rules and behaviors.

Drag and drop the Wall actor on the scene. With the mouse pointer positioned on the side of the actor (on the white circle) as per Figure 8-14, press click and maintain the click to resize the actor.

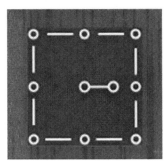

Figure 8-14. *Resizing an actor*

Change the size to the minimum width and match the height to the height of the scene. Then move the wall to the left side of the scene as per Figure 8-15.

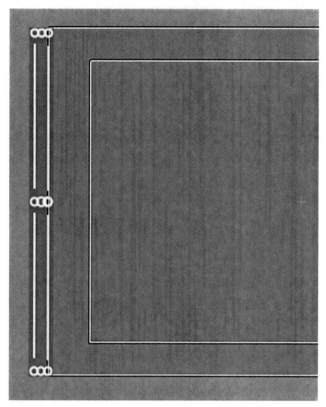

Figure 8-15. *Positioning the first wall*

Now repeat the operation in order to have a labyrinth similar to Figure 8-16.

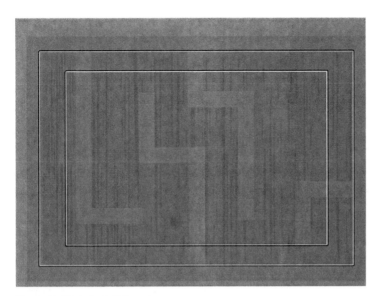

Figure 8-16. *Labyrinth layout*

Lastly, drag and drop the Ball, Victory Hole, Open Door, and Door actors on the scene as per Figure 8-17.

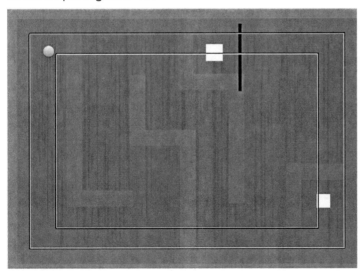

Figure 8-17. *Finished layout*

Try the game on your device.

Implementing Lighting Special Effects

LightFX are known as special effects with lighting. They are commonly used in video games to add more interactivity or enhance the player experience.

You can start directly at this stage by opening the file Labyrinth-step1.gameproj.

I will show you a very cool trick now. This is what I call "The light is off." Imagine the labyrinth game with only a small amount of light around the ball; the scene is completely dark. Of course the light will have to follow the ball and you will discover the area via the ball. If you already have a labyrinth game for iOS, you know that this is a common feature.

The trick is very simple. You will use a black image with a transparent disk at its center. The size of the disk depends on how difficult you want to make the game. Also, the size of the image should be twice the size of the scene. The center of the disk will be constrained to the position of the ball. With this size, the entire scene will be covered wherever the ball is going.

You will use some game attribute in order to store the position of the ball. Create two game attributes named "BallX" and "BallY."

Open the Ball actor in the Actor Editor. Drag and drop a Constrain Attribute behavior and change game.BallX to Ball.Position.X. Repeat the same operation with BallY and Position.Y as per Figure 8-18.

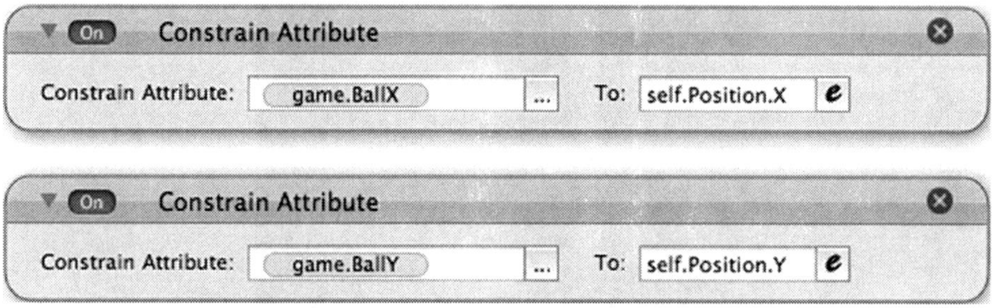

Figure 8-18. *Constraining the ball*

Import the image named Light Off.png located in the Chapter_8 folder. Create a new actor and drag and drop the image on the new actor. Rename the actor "Light_Off."

Open the actor in the Actor Editor and drag and drop a Constrain Attribute behavior with the settings "Light_Off.position.X" "game.BallX." Repeat the operation with Light_Off.position.Y and game.BallY.

Position the Light_Off actor on the scene.

Try the game on your device.

Implementing Sound Special Effects

SoundFX are known as special effects with sounds. You will use sounds to make your game more interactive and more lively. It will also provides an additional level of information to the player.

You can start directly at this stage by opening the file Labyrinth-step2.gameproj.

In order to make the game more realistic, you will use a small sound special effect—nothing fancy, just a small sound when the ball hits a wall. This will illustrate how to use the Play Sound behavior.

I will focus on the Play Sound behavior here, but Play Music works in much the same way. There are additional behaviors called Pause Music and Resume Music that I will talk about a little bit later.

> **NOTE:** Play Sound vs. Play Music
>
> When the sound is less than 30 seconds, you can use Play Sound. When the sound is longer than 30 seconds, you should use Play Music. Keep in mind that GameSalad will play only one music clip at a time but can play multiple sounds simultaneously.

Similar to images, you need to import sounds into your library in order to be able to use them.

Click the Sounds tab in either the Actor Editor or Scene Editor as per Figure 8-19.

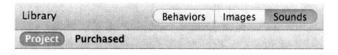

Figure 8-19. *Sounds tab*

Click on the + sign to import a new audio file. Select the file named brick.mp3 to import it. Then you need to select if you want to import the file as music or sound as per Figure 8-20.

Figure 8-20. *Music or Sound import*

Select "Import as Sound."

Next, create a rule within the Ball actor to play the sound every time there is a collision with a wall. Open the Ball actor in the Actor Editor. Create a new rule and the condition will be "Actor receives event" "overlaps or collides" with "actor of type" "Wall." As per Figure 8-21, drag and drop a Play Sound behavior into the rule and change the settings to Sound: "brick" and Volume: "0.50" with "Run to completion" checked.

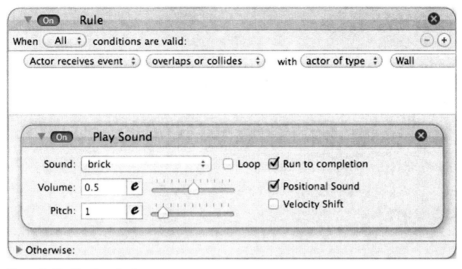

Figure 8-21. *Play Sound rule*

I recommend using Positional Sound as often as you can. The Positional Sound feature adds a great deal of interactivity. If the actor playing the sound is on the left side of the screen, it will give the impression that the sound is coming from the left, which is very nice effect. In addition, if the actor moves while playing the sound, the sound will "move" with the actor.

You can try the game on your device.

> MP3 or other formats
>
> GameSalad supports multiple sound formats such as Caf, ogg, mp3, and m4a.

> About Pause Music and Resume Music:
>
> If you implement a Pause function in your game and have background music, you may want to pause the music and resume it after the player unpauses the game. In order to do so, you will need to use the Pause Music and Resume Music behaviors.

Summary

In this chapter, you reviewed the basics of creating a new project and defining the gameplay. You also learned some very powerful and simple special effects that definitely spice up the game and the player experience.

You have:

- Reviewed GameSalad new project creation.
- Reinforced the use of rules and behaviors to define the gameplay.
- Learned how to implement lighting special effects.
- Learned how to use sounds behavior to implement sound special effects.

Part 3

Prepping for the App Store: Polishing, Publishing, and Promoting Your Game

Bonuses, Game Center, and iAd: Break a Wall

In this chapter, you will finalize the game you started in Chapter 4. I have prepared a file named BreakaWallPartII.gameproj that includes background images and actor images. These improvements won't be covered in this chapter. Refer to previous chapters for a refresher on how to implement graphics and sounds.

In this chapter, I want to focus on the finalization of a few elements before you submit your game to the App Store. You will learn how to:

- Create a Start Screen.
- Implement a scoring system.
- Add game interactivity with in-game bonuses.
- Post scores on Game Centerleaderboard.
- Monetize your game with iAd.

You can download my version of Break A Wall, used in this chapter and Chapter 4 to illustrate game-building concepts, for free at

http://itunes.apple.com/us/app/break-a-wall/id496154190?ls=1&mt=8

Have fun and try to rank first on the leaderboard!

Designing the Start Screen

Every game starts with a Start Screen, also called the menu page. I am not talking about the Splash Screen that may or not appear as the first screen when you launch the game. A Splash Screen will not offer interactivity with the player; it's just a way to promote your brand.

The Start Screen is a very important step in the player experience as it will guide him/her through different choices. The most obvious choice will be to play the game, of course, but you may provide some instructions, too.

Note about instruction:

Apple loves apps that are intuitive. Nevertheless, some games require a level of instruction to play the game or to understand the rules.

The following are the guidelines that I systematically apply to my games:

1) If your game is very simple and very intuitive to use, don't add instructions. Keep it straightforward.

2) If your game is simple and intuitive but you would like to give non-intuitive additional instructions, create a scene to contain the instructions and make it accessible from the menu.

3) If your game requires some learning, use the first levels or create an interactive scene for the player to learn the game. You may also add instructionsinto the game when a new situation arises.

To design a Start Screen in GameSalad, you will create a specific scene. This scene will be the first one in the order (from left to right).

Open the file BreakaWall-partII-step1.gameproj in GameSalad.

Create a new scene and name it "Home." Drag and drop the scene in the first position (the very left side) as shown in Figure 9-1.

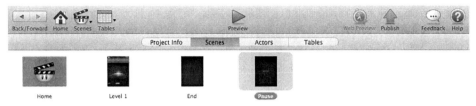

Figure 9-1. *Home scene*

Placing the Homescene in this location will ensure that it will be the first scene when you start the game.

> Note about Splash Screens:
>
> As you will see in Chapter 11, you can create a customized splash screen during the publishing process, but this is limited to a static image. By default, it will be a GameSalad Splash Screen. A trick is to replace the Splash Screen with a black image and have an animation in the first scene that acts as an animated Splash Screen.

Creating the Actors

In this section, you will create a few additional actors for use on your Home screen. A Background actor will be used to contain the background image. You will also create a couple of buttons to add controls for the player.

Home

Create a new actor and double-click it to open the Actor Editor. Edit the actor attributes with the parameters in Table 9-1.

Table 9-1. *Home Attributes*

Name	Home
Size/Width	768
Size/Height	1024

Click the Images tab to display the images resources and drag and drop
Home.png into the actor.

Start Game

Create a new actor and double-click it to open the Actor Editor. Edit the actor
attributes with the parameters in Table 9-2.

Table 9-2. *Start Game Attributes*

Name	Start Game
Size/Width	294
Size/Height	57

Click the Images tab to display the images resources and drag and drop
play1.png into the actor.

Speaker

Create a new actor and double-click it to open the Actor Editor. Edit the actor
attributes with the parameters in Table 9-3.

Table 9-3. *Speaker Attributes*

Name	Speaker
Size/Width	90
Size/Height	90

Click the Images tab to display the images resources and drag and drop
Speaker.png to the actor.

Implementing Rules and Behaviors

It's now time to define the logic behind your actors. The most important logic
will reside in the control actors you just created. The Start Game actor will let
you start playing and the Speaker actor will control the volume (on or off).

Home

In order to perfectly position the background object, you will use the trick of changing the position attributes.

Open the Home actor in the Actor Editor. Drag and drop a Change Attribute behavior and change Home.Position.X to 384.

Drag and drop a Change Attribute behavior and change Home.Position.Y to 512.

The two behaviors are shown in Figure 9-2.

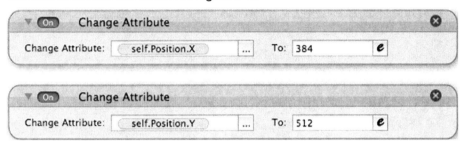

Figure 9-2. *Positioning the background with Change Attributes*

Now drag and drop the actor on the scene and position it approximately in the center.

Start Game

The Start Game actor will be used as a button. You will implement a rollover effect so that the color of the font changes when the button is pressed. But, because it is an image, you will use the Change Image behavior and use a different image to replace the active one.

You will proceed in two steps. First, you will change the image to an image with a different font color when the actor is pressed. Then you will change the image back to the original when the actor touch is released. This is only one of the many ways to createa button-pressing effect. Another approach could be to change either alpha to 0.5 or RGB colors to 0.5.

Open the Start Game actor in the Actor Editor. Create a new rule and name it "Touch is Pressed." The condition is "Actor receives event" "touch" is "pressed."

Then drag and drop a Change Image behavior into the rule and select "play2" from the drop-down next to "Set Image to."

Let's proceed to the second phase of the rollover.

Create a new rule and name it "Touch is Released." The condition is "Actor receives event" "touch" is "released." This could also be done in the "otherwise" section of the "Touch is pressed" rule.

Then drag and drop a Change Image behavior into the rule and select "play1" from the drop-down next to "Set Image to."

The two new rules are shown in Figure 9-3.

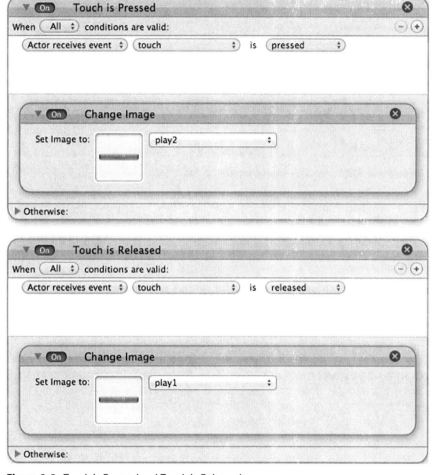

Figure 9-3. *Touch is Pressed and Touch is Released*

You've got the visual effect in place, but the purpose of the Start Game actor is to allow you to start the game.

In order to reach this goal, you will add some behaviors in the rule "Touch is Released." In order to have a smooth transition, I often use a short timer before implementing the change scene. This will improve the user experience by giving the player the time to see the change of states of the button.

Drag and drop a Timer behavior below the Change Image behavior in the "Touch is Released" rule. Set the timer to "After""0.5"seconds. Then drag and drop a Change Scene behavior in the timer and set it to Level 1 as per Figure 9-4.

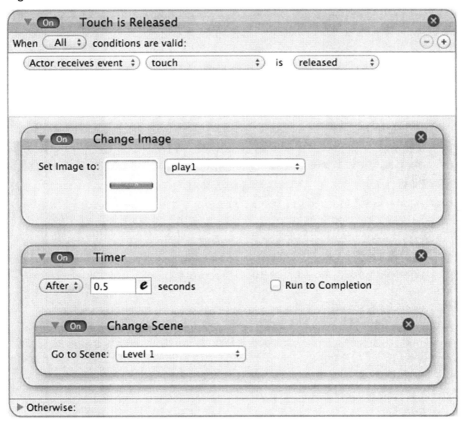

Figure 9-4. *Updated Touch is Released rule*

Position the Start Gameactor in the scene.

Speaker

You will use the speaker actor to control the sounds and music. In this example, you will only focus on sound but you could use the same approach with music.

A touch on the speaker will change the state of a game attribute to either 0 or 1. You could use rules and Boolean, but instead I will show you a cool trick with the modulo operator.

Wikipedia defines modulo operation as a function that returns "the remainder of division of one number by another."

In other words, if you divide 9 by 4, you get 9 = 2 x 4 + 1. The remainder of 9 divided by 4 is 1. Let's take another example. If you divide 50 by 14, you get 50 = 3 x 14 + 8. The remainder of 50 divided by 14 is 8.

With modulo notation (%), you have 9 mod 4 = 1 or 9%4=1.

Now, if you take any number (integer) and you do modulo 2 this number, you only have two possible results: 0 and 1. If the number is even, the remainder of this number divided by two is null (0). If the number is odd, the remainder of this number divided by two is 1.

So with a simple equation of a unitary increment and modulo two, you have a result that goes from zero to one and from one to zero. The equation is soundOn = (soundOn+1)%2.

By default, you want to have the sound on. So the initial value is soundOn=1. When you press the Speaker actor, you get SoundOn = (1+1)%2 = (2)%2 = 0. The next time you press the Speaker actor, you get SoundOn = (0+1)%2 = (1)%2 = 1. And so on…

When you want to have sound, SoundOn is equal to 1 and when you don't want to have sound, SoundOn is equal to 0. All the rules on sound are based on the state of the SoundOn attribute.

To make it simple to manage, instead of creating a rule for every PlaySound behavior, you will control the volume instead. When SoundOn is equal to 1, volume is equal to 1. Respectively, when SoundOn is equal to 0, volume is equal to 0.

You will also implement a rollover with a crossed speaker icon when the sound is turned off.

Let's do all this now!

Create a new game attribute of type Integer and name it "SoundOn." Give this attribute the default value of 1 as per Figure 9-5.

Inspector		Game	Scene
Actors	Attributes		Devices
Name	default name		text
Time	0		real
▶ Display Size			size
Actor Tags	Collidable		text
ActiveBall	☐		boolean
BrickCount	24		integer
TextToDisplay			text
lives	3		integer
SoundOn	1		integer

Figure 9-5. *SoundOn attribute*

Open the Speaker actor in the Actor Editor. Create a new rule and name it
"Touch is pressed." The condition is "Action receives event" "touch" is
"pressed." Next, drag and drop a Change Attribute behavior and change
game.SoundOn to (game.SoundOn+1)%2 as per Figure 9-6.

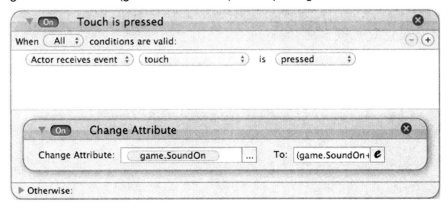

Figure 9-6. *Touch is pressed rule*

Now, create a new rule and name it "SoundOn is equal to 1." The condition will
be "Attribute""game.SoundOn""=""1". Next, drag and drop a Change Image
behavior and set the image to speaker. Lastly, drag and drop a Change Attribute
behavior and change Device.Audio.Sound Volume to 1 as per Figure 9-7.

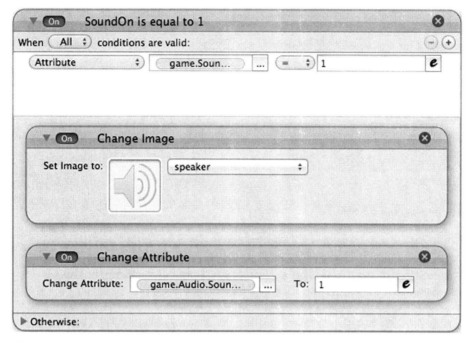

Figure 9-7. *SoundOn is equal to 1 rule.*

Last but not least, create a new rule and name it "SoundOn is equal to 0." The condition is "Attribute""game.SoundOn""=""0". Next, drag and drop a Change Image behavior and set the image to speaker off." Lastly, drag and drop a Change Attribute behavior and change Device.Audio.Sound Volume to 0 as per Figure 9-8.

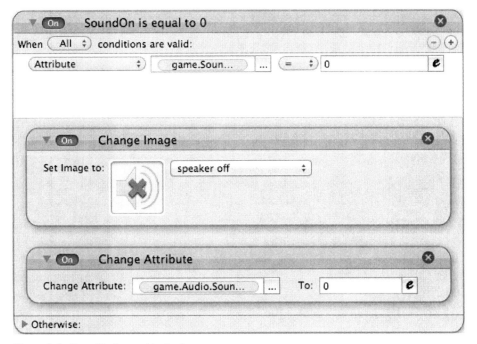

Figure 9-8. *SoundOn is equal to 0 rule*

Position the Speaker actor on the scene at the bottom left corner.

You can now test your work in the Preview window of GameSalad.

Adding Score Keeping

Later in the chapter I will cover Game Center. But first you need to have a scoring system. You will make it very simple. Every time a blue brick is destroyed, one point will be added to the score. And every time a red brick is destroyed, you will add two points to the score. To follow the project from this point, open the file named BreakaWall-partII-step2.gameproj.

A game attribute of type Integer will be used to keep up with the score. You will ensure a manual reset every time you start the game. And you will increment the score every time a brick is hit. Last but not least, you will display the score on the top right zone of the screen, so the player can keep up with his/her progress.

First, let's create the score attribute. Create a new game attribute of type Integer and name it "Score." Keep the default value to zero.

Open the Start Game actor into the Actor Editor. Drag and drop a Change Attribute behavior into the rule "Touch is Released" and change game.Score to 0, as per Figure 9-9.

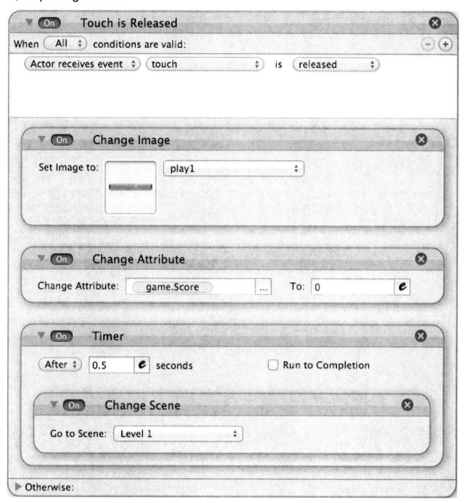

Figure 9-9. *Updated Touch is Released rule*

Open the Brick1 actor in the Actor Editor. Drag and drop a Change Attribute into the existing rule and change game.Score to game.Score+1, as per Figure 9-10.

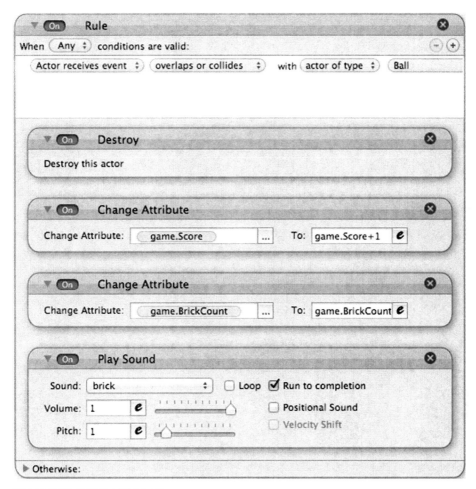

Figure 9-10. *Updated Brick1 rule*

Repeat the same operation with Brick2 but add two points for each Brick2. Open the Brick2 actor in the Actor Editor. Drag and drop a Change Attribute into the existing rule and change game.Score to game.Score+2, as per Figure 9-11.

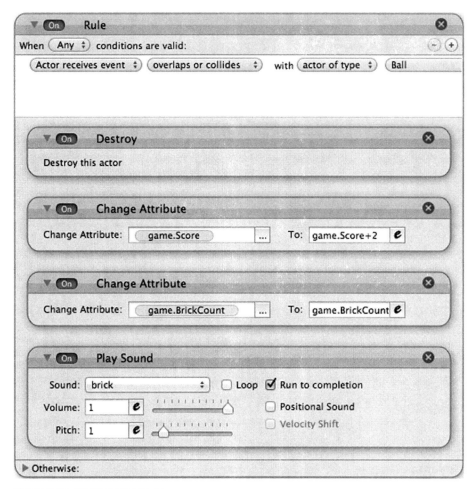

Figure 9-11. *Updated Brick2 rule*

You are keeping up with the score but wouldn't it be nice to display it to the player?!

ScoreDisplay Actor

Create a new actor and double-click it to open the Actor Editor. Edit the actor attributes with the parameters in Table 9-4.

Table 9-4. *ScoreDisplay Attributes*

Name	ScoreDisplay
Size/Width	260
Size/Height	100
Color/Alpha	0

ScoreDisplay Rules and Behaviors

Drag and drop a Display Text behavior into the ScoreDisplay actor. Change the settings as follows (and shown in Figure 9-12):

- Text: "Score:"..game.Score
- Font: Cochin
- Color: purple

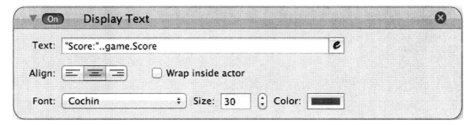

Figure 9-12. *Display Text for ScoreDisplay actor*

Open the Level 1 scene in the Scene Editor and position the ScoreDisplay actor in the scene at the top in the middle as per Figure 9-13.

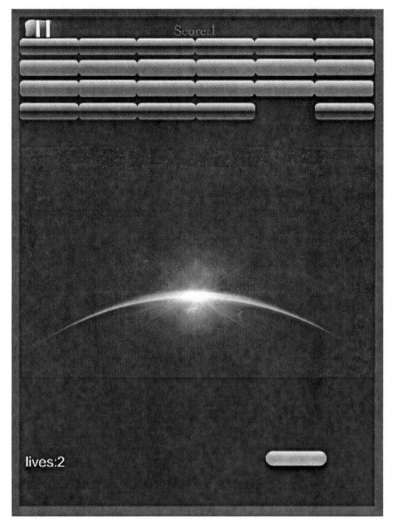

Figure 9-13. *Level 1 Scene*

Creating the Extra-Bonus Actors

In order to make it more fun, you will add the following bonuses into some of the bricks:

- A 50-point bonus
- A 100-point bonus
- A auto-bullet bonus

The point bonuses will be spawned by the bricks that hide them and will be added to the score if the racket collides with them. The same principle will apply to the auto-bullet, but instead of adding points, it will have the racket trigger bullets automatically. These bullets will destroy the bricks. The bullets will be automatically fired as long as a Boolean game attribute AutoBullet is set to true. By default, it is set to false. Catching the capsule will set it to true. Losing the ball will set it back to false.

To follow the project from this point, open the file named `BreakaWall-partII-step3.gameproj`.

50 pt cap Actor

Create a new actor and double-click it to open the Actor Editor. Edit the actor attributes with the parameters in Table 9-5.

Table 9-5. *50 Pt Cap Actor Attributes*

Name	50 pt cap
Size/Width	81
Size/Height	54

Click the Images tab to display the images resources and drag and drop `50 pt.png` into the actor.

100 pt cap Actor

Create a new actor and double-click it to open the Actor Editor. Edit the actor attributes with the parameters in Table 9-6.

Table 9-6. *100 pt cap Actor Attributes*

Name	100 pt cap
Size/Width	81
Size/Height	54

Click the Images tab to display the images resources and drag and drop 100 pt.png into the actor.

Auto Bullet Actor

Create a new actor and double-click it to open the Actor Editor. Edit the actor attributes with the parameters in Table 9-7.

Table 9-7. *Auto Bullet Actor Attributes*

Name	Auto bullet
Size/Width	81
Size/Height	54

Click the Images tab to display the images resources and drag and drop Bullet.png to the actor.

Bullet Actor

Create a new actor and double-click it to open the Actor Editor. Edit the actor attributes with the parameters in Table 9-8.

Table 9-8. *Bullet Actor Attributes*

Name	Bullet
Size/Width	30
Size/Height	60

Click the Images tab to display the images resources and drag and drop `Bullet-img.png`into the actor.

Your newly created actors should be similar to Figure 9-14.

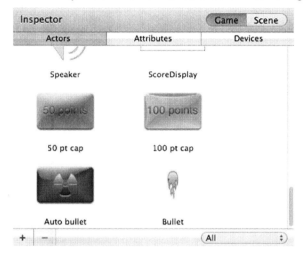

Figure 9-14. *Actor Inspector*

Implementing the Extra-Bonus Rules and Behaviors

Basically, you want the bricks containing the extra bonuses to spawn an extra-bonus actor. The extra-bonus actor will move down and when it overlaps with the racket, it will enable the bonus.

50 pt cap

Open the 50 pt cap actor in the Actor Editor. Drag and drop a Change Velocity behavior into the actor and change the settings to:

- Direction: 270
- Relative to: scene
- Speed: 150

Create a new rule and set the condition to "Actor receives event""overlaps or collides" with "actor of type""racket." Drag and drop a Change Attribute behavior and change game.Score to game.Score+50. Drag and drop a Destroy behavior. Depending on the number of actions to be executed, you may have an issue if you place the Destroy behavior before them. As a rule of the thumb, I recommend that you place the Destroy behavior last. The actor action pane should be as per Figure 9-15.

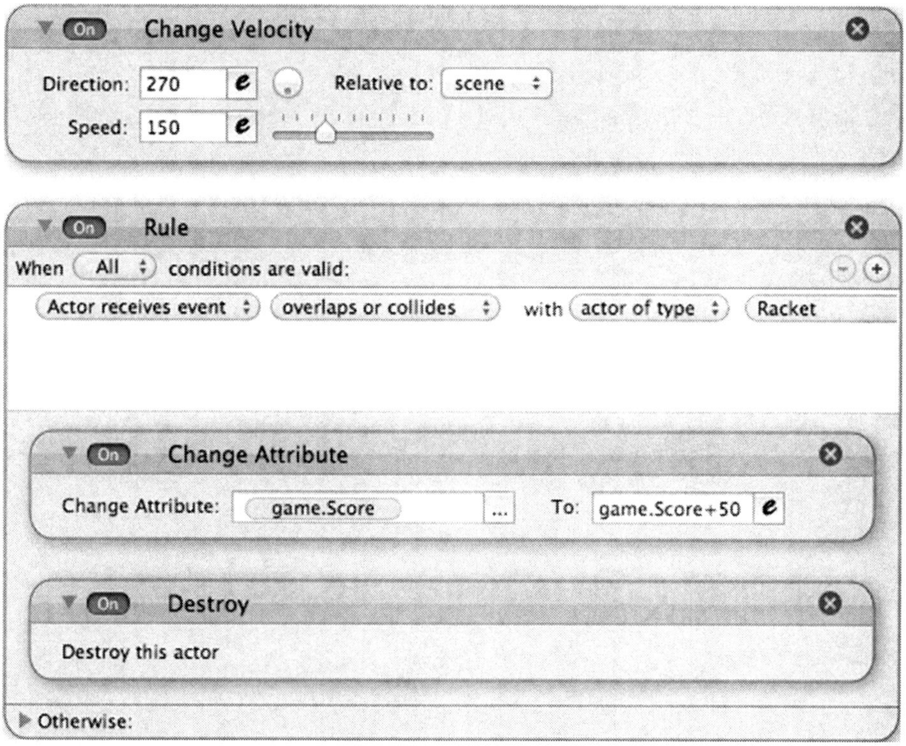

Figure 9-15. *50 pt cap action pane*

100 pt cap

Open the 100 pt cap actor in the Actor Editor. Drag and drop a Change Velocity behavior into the actor and change the settings to:

- Direction: 270
- Relative to: scene
- Speed: 150

Create a new rule and set the condition to "Actor receives event""overlaps or collides" with "actor of type""racket." Drag and drop a Change Attribute behavior and change game.Score togame.Score+100. Drag and drop a Destroy behavior. The actor action pane should be as per Figure 9-16.

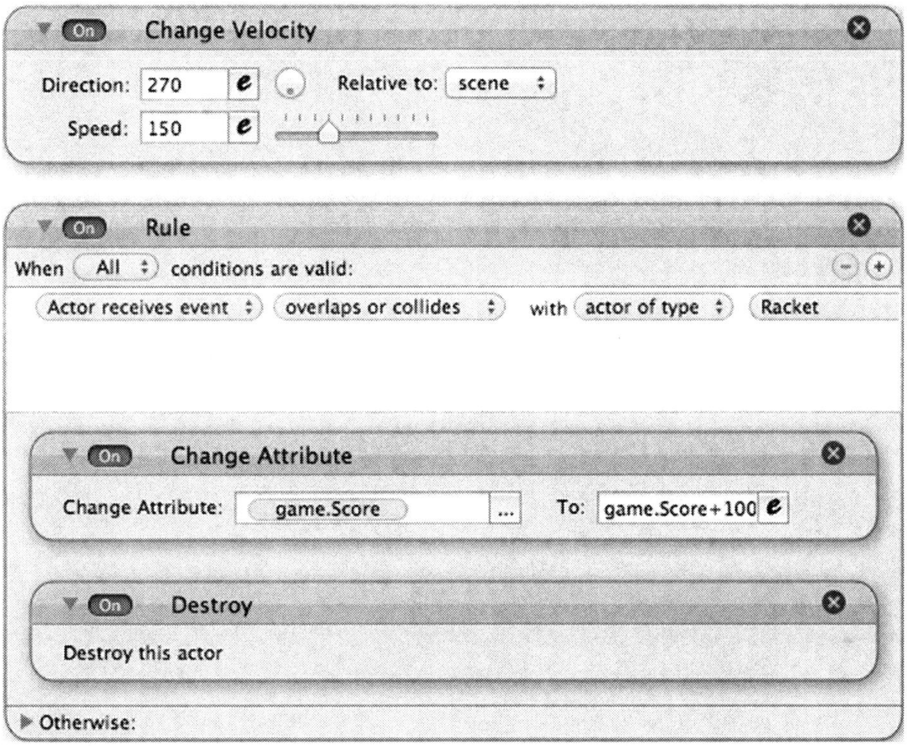

Figure 9-16. *100 pt cap action pane*

Auto bullet

Create a game attribute of type Boolean, name it "AutoBullet," and set the default value to false.

Open the Auto bullet actor in the Actor Editor.

Drag and drop a Change Velocity behavior into the actor and change the settings to:

- Direction: 270
- Relative to: scene
- Speed: 150

Create a new rule and set the condition to "Actor receives event" "overlaps or collides" with "actor of type" "racket." Drag and drop a Change Attribute behavior and change game.AutoBullet to 1. Drag and drop a Destroy behavior. The actor action pane should match Figure 9-17.

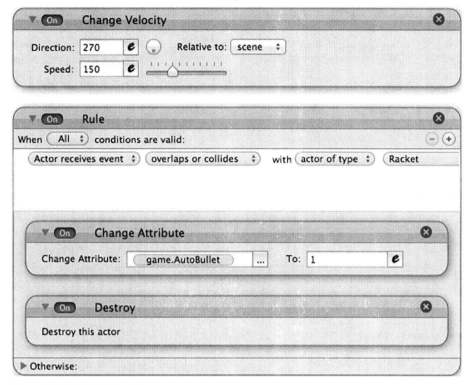

Figure 9-17. *AutoBullet action pane*

Bullet

Open the Bullet actor in the Actor Editor. Drag and drop a Change Velocity behavior into the actor and change the settings to:

- Direction: 90
- Relative to: scene
- Speed: 300

Create a new rule and set the condition of "Any" for "Actor receives event" "overlaps or collides" with "actor of type" "Brick1" and "Actor receives event" "overlaps or collides" with "actor of type" "Brick2." Drag and drop a Destroy behavior. The actor action pane should match Figure 9-18.

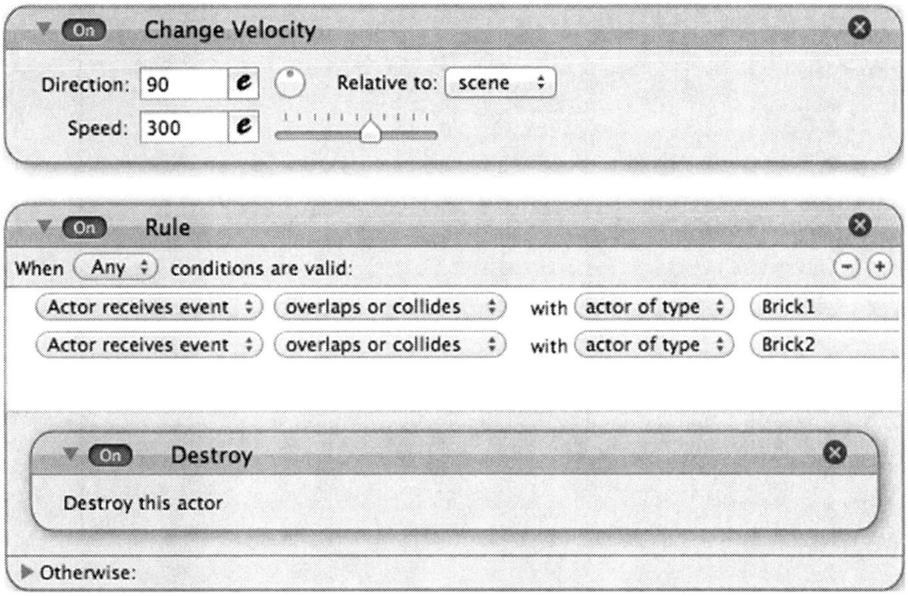

Figure 9-18. *Bullet action pane*

You now need to edit the following actors:

- Brick1
- Brick2
- Racket

Brick1

Open the Brick1 actor in the Actor Editor and add a condition set to "Any." The new rule is "Actor receives event" "overlaps or collides" with "actor of type" "Bullet" as per Figure 9-19.

Figure 9-19. *Modified Brick1 rule*

Brick2

Repeat the modification. Open the Brick2 actor in the Actor Editor and add a condition set to "Any." The new rule is "Actor receives event" "overlaps or collides" with "actor of type" "Bullet" as per Figure 9-20.

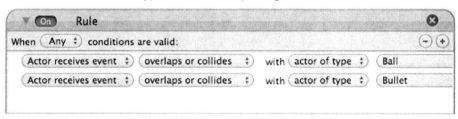

Figure 9-20. *Modified Brick2 rule*

Racket

Open the Racket actor in the Actor Editor and create a new rule. The condition is "Attribute" "game.AutoBullet" is "true." Drag and drop a Timer behavior set to "Every" "1" second. Then, drag and drop a Spawn Actor behavior and modify the settings to:

- Actor: Bullet
- Layer Order: in back of actor
- Direction: 0
- Position: 0&0
- Relative to: actor

Drag and drop a Play Sound behavior and change the settings to:

- Sound: bullet fire
- Run to completion: checked

- Volume: 1

- Pitch: 1

The new rule is shown in Figure 9-21.

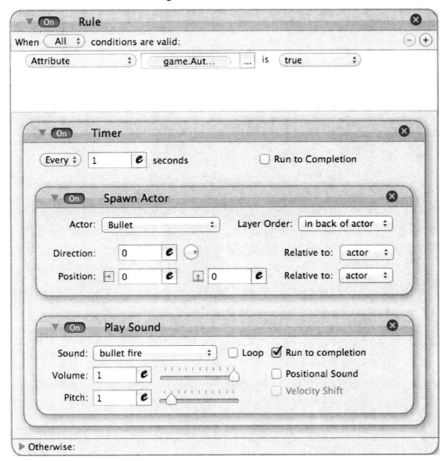

Figure 9-21. *New rule for Racket*

You will now position the bonuses randomly on the scene. Open the Level 1 scene in the Scene Editor. Double-click any of the bricks in the scene. This will open the instance of the actor prototype. Click the lock to edit the instance of the actor. Modifying the instance will only modify this instance in the scene and not all the actors. Add a Spawn Actor behavior into the rule of the instance and change the settings to:

- Actor: 50 pt cap
- Layer Order: in back of actor
- Direction: 0
- Position: 0&0
- Relative to: actor

The updated rule is shown inFigure 9-22.

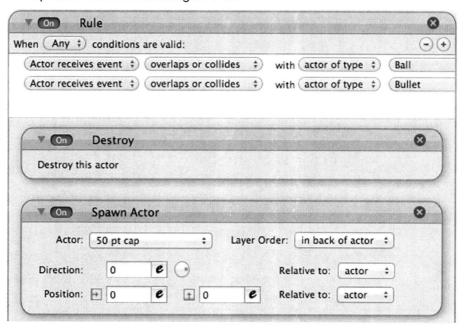

Figure 9-22. *Updated Brick rule*

Repeat this several times with various bricks with the following actors:

- 50 pt cap
- 100 pt cap
- Auto Bullet

100 pt cap and Auto Bullet implementations on random bricks are shown in Figures 9-23 and Figure 9-24.

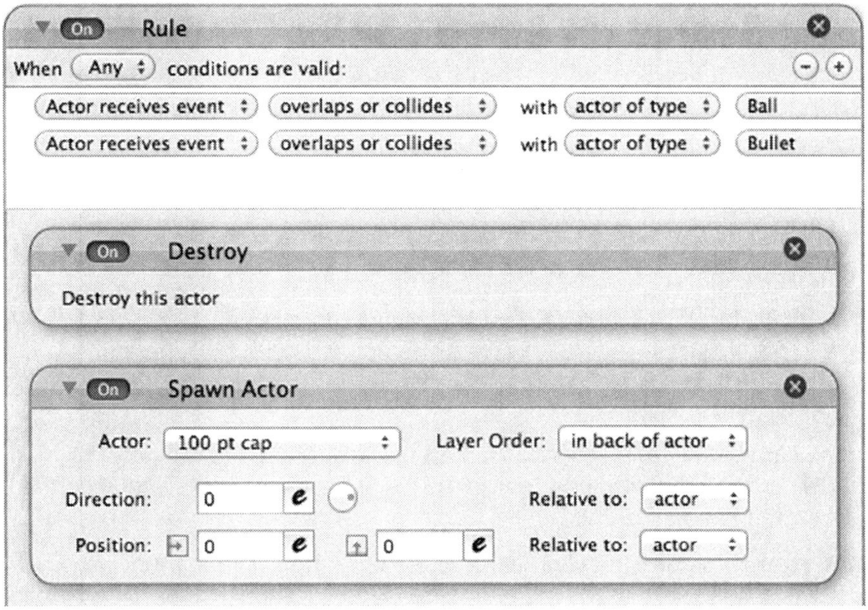

Figure 9-23. *100 pt cap implementation*

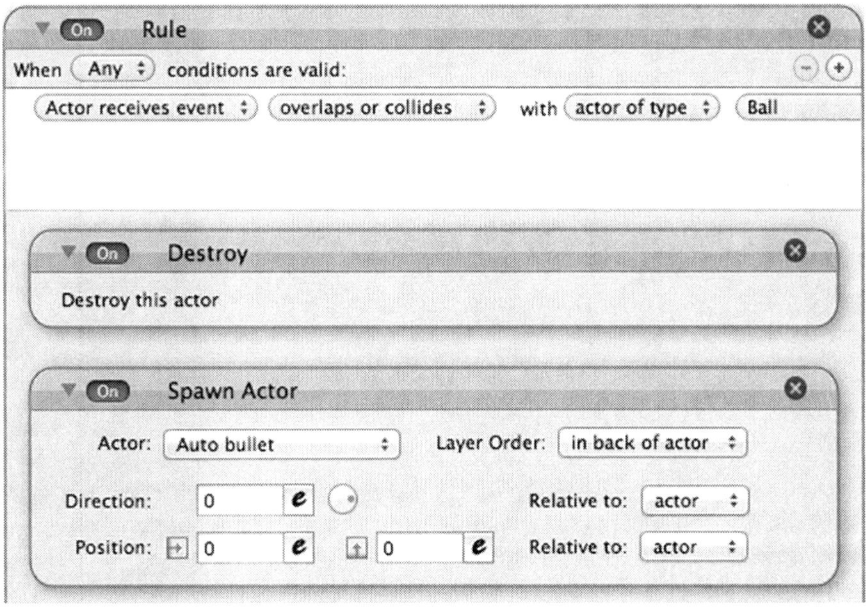

Figure 9-24. *Auto Bullet implementation*

Posting Scores on Game Center Leaderboard

To follow from this point, open the file named BreakaWall-partII-step4.gameproj.

Game Center is the social gaming platform of Apple. It lets players to share their gaming experiences by showing best results, achievements, and game recommendations. The Game Center features are only accessible to Pro members. Apple provides more information at www.apple.com/game-center/.

Basically, once you have authenticated yourself, you can post your scores in the area called Leaderboards and track specific game achievements in the area called Achievements. There are more features to Game Center but these two are the most important.

At the time I am writing this chapter, GameSalad has implemented only the Authentication and Leaderboards features. The Achievements section is on the roadmap for the first half of 2012.

Let's go deeper into authentication and the leaderboards. The authentication feature will enable your user to log into Game Center with their alias. The player uses their alias to validate their identity, manage lists of friends, and post status messages. After a player authenticates, he can post scores to Game Center. The scores posted on the leaderboards will rank all the players, the purpose of which is to develop a sense of competition.

Before setting up your GameSalad project, you will need to create a leaderboard in the Apple provisioning portal. You will decide the unit of achievement: time, money, or points. You can have several leaderboards per game. You could have leaderboards per type of gameplay (time when playing against the watch, points when playing arcade mode, etc.).

Let's implement the Game Center features in Break a Wall.

GameSalad offers three behaviors related to Game Center:

- Login
- Post a Score
- Show the Leaderboard

In order to properly configure the Game Center behaviors, you will need to have a Leaderboard ID. This will be necessary to post and show the scores. The creation of a Leaderboard ID is covered in Chapter 11. You will obtain a unique alphanumeric ID that you will use in the followings steps.

Login to Game Center

Open BreakaWall-partII-step4.gameproj. Open the Home scene. Select the Home actor in the Actor Editor.

Drag and drop a "Game Center – Login" behavior from the Pro tab as per Figure 9-25.

Figure 9-25. *Game Center behaviors*

The Home actor is shown inFigure 9-26.

Figure 9-26. *Home actor action pane*

Posting a Score

During a game, there will be two key moments to post your score:

- When you loose
- When you win

Posting the Score After You Lose

Open the Ball actor in the Actor Editor. Go to the rule with the condition "Attribute game.lives = 0". Drag and drop a "Game Center – Post Score" behavior into the rule. The attribute to post is "game.Score." Enter your Leaderboard ID. Your screen should look similar to Figure 9-27 (with a different Leaderboard ID, of course).

Figure 9-27. *Posting score when game is lost*

Posting the Score When You Win

The best moment to post the score is when the game has been won. The End actor tells you exactly when this happens. This actor is the control that resets the game. You need to post the score just before resetting the game.

Open the End actor in the Actor Editor. Drag and drop a "Game Center – Post Score" behavior into the rule. The attribute to post is "game.Score." Enter the Leaderboard ID. The screen should look similar to Figure 9-28.

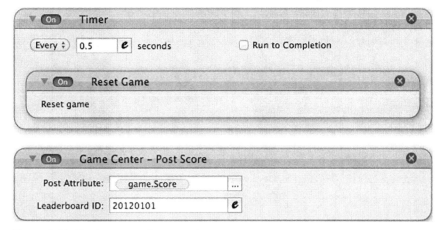

Figure 9-28. *Posting score when game is won*

Showing the Scores

On the Home scene, add a button to show the Leaderboard with the highest scores from all players across the world.

Create a new actor and double-click it to open the Actor Editor. Edit the actor attributes with the parameters in Table 9-9.

Table 9-9. *Leaderboards Actor Attributes*

Name	Leaderboards
Size/Width	294
Size/Height	57

Click the Images tab to display the images resources and drag and drop Leaderboard.png to the actor.

Open the actor in the Actor Editor. Create a new rule with the condition "Actor receives event""touch" is "pressed." Then drag and drop a "Game Center – Show Leaderboard" behavior and key-in the Leaderboard ID and the period for the score (today, this week, or all time). The screen should look similar to Figure 9-29.

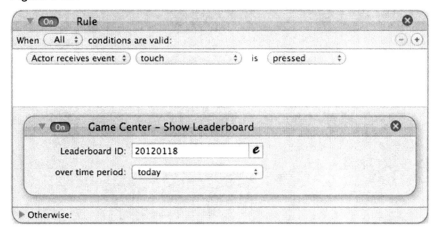

Figure 9-29. *Show Leaderboard*

Position the Leaderboards actor on the Home scene just below the Play actor.

iAd

iAd is the Apple advertising platform. It comes with the intent of developing the freemium model. What is the freemium model? Basically it's one in which you can develop an application/game that is free to users but that displays ads within the game spaceto generate revenue from advertising or iAP (in-app purchase).

iAd provides you with a complete framework to display either banner or full-screen ads in your application; these come directly from Apple. Thus you don't need to bother about selling the ad space. You just need to design the area for the ad space and then the iAd framework will manage it from there.

To use iAd in your GameSalad project, you must join the iAd network. In iTunesConnect, the first step is to setup your contract with Apple.

iAd was introduced with iOS 4. This means that all pre-iOS 4 will not be compatible with iAd. The iAd feature is only accessible to Pro members.

To follow from this point, open the file named `BreakaWall-partII-step5.gameproj`.

Configuring iAd is extremely easy. You need to activate iAd for your application as described in Chapter 11. Once iAd is activated, you need to implement the iAd behavior.

You need to take into consideration the area of display of the Ad so it does not interfere with your game user interface. On an iPhone, a portrait advertisement is 320 x 50 pixels and a landscape advertisement is 480 x 32 pixels. On an iPad, a portrait advertisement is 768 x 66 pixels and a landscape advertisement is 1024 x 66 pixels.

Open the Home actor in the Actor Editor. Drag and drop a Show iAd behavior into the actor. Select "Bottom" as the banner position as per Figure 9-30.

Figure 9-30. *Show iAd behavior*

That's it! You're all set for iAd. Real ads will only display once the application is published.

You can check the project by opening the file named BreakaWall-partII-step6.gameproj.

> Note about iAd:
>
> iAd is not a cash cow. The level of revenue is very low. Break a Wall has been downloaded about 1,400 times at the time of writing. So far, the iAd revenue is below US$2 (see Figure 9-31).

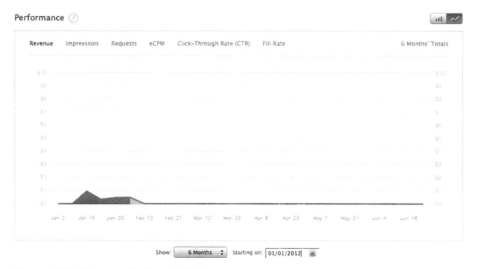

Figure 9-31. *iAd revenue for Break a Wall*

Summary

You have learned many new elements in this chapter. Your game has now a Start Screen and can post scores to Game Center. In addition, you have started to monetize your game with iAd. This will greatly increase the game experience and enable you to generate revenue from your games.

In this chapter, you learned how to:

- Design a Start Screen.
- Add game depth with extra bonuses.
- Implement score posting on Game Center.
- Enable iAd for your game.

Chapter 10

Device Internal Clock and Cyclic Movement: Non-Game Apps

Although the primary purpose of GameSalad is to create games, you can use it to create other applications, as long as your applications only require the framework available in GameSalad.

To illustrate this point, you will work on two projects. First, you will create an analog clock that will display the iOS device time and then you will create a metronome, as per Figure 10-1.

By using all your GameSalad knowledge you can create some very interesting apps. You will mostly use behaviors and concepts that you have seen previously, but I will introduce new concepts that could also be used in games.

Figure 10-1. *The analog clock and the metronome*

The purpose of this chapter is to illustrate that by thinking out of the box, you can extend the possibilities of GameSalad.

In this chapter, you will learn how to:

- Use standard GameSalad features to make an app, which is not a game.
- Access and use the device internal clock.
- Create cyclic movement using basic math.

Creating an Analog Clock with the Device Clock and Rotation

In this project you will build an analog clock that will display the time in hours, minutes, and seconds. This will be a relatively short and easy project. It should not take you more than 30 minutes to implement.

You will learn to implement behaviors based on the device internal clock. You will also learn how to modelize the movements of the clock hands through rotation and angle calculation.

Accessing the Device Clock

In order to display the current time, you will be using the clock from the device attributes, which is a great set of attributes. The clock gives you access to the device time from the year and up to the milliseconds as per Figure 10-2.

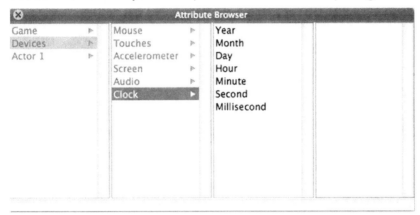

Figure 10-2. *The Clock set of attributes*

Although this example will only create a clock, you will cover some manipulation of the clock attributes which you can use to extend your ideas out of the box and integrate those attributes in new features of your games. For example, you could create a special icon on the Menu page that will only display on the 4th of July to celebrate Independence Day.

Creating the Clock Project

Open the GameSalad Creator and create a new project. Configure the project info as per Table 10-1.

Table 10-1. *Project Info for Yet Another Clock*

Title	Yet Another Clock
Platform	iPhone Portrait
Resolution Independence	Unchecked
Description	This project is to demonstrate that you can build non-game apps
Instruction	None
Tags	time, clock, analog

Name and save your file as YAC.gameproj.

Creating the Background and the Clock Hands

To design your clock, you need to create the following actors:

- Clock: This is the frame for the clock.
- Hours: This is the hour arrow.
- Minutes: This is the minute arrow.
- Seconds: This is the second arrow.
- Button: This is a graphic trick to hide the origin of the arrows.

Before creating the actors, import the images that you will be using for those actors.Open the Scene Editor and select the Images tab. Click the + sign and import the following files: chap10-button.png, chap10-clock.png, chap10-hours.png, chap10-minutes.png, and chap10-seconds.png. These pictures files are located in the chapter 10 file folder. Your Image tab should match Figure 10-3.

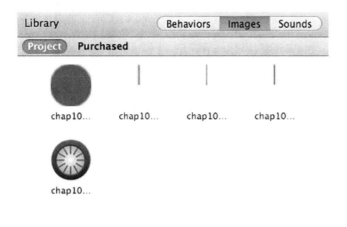

Figure 10-3. *Images*

As a bonus, I also provide the Illustrator file for each of the images if you want to customize your clock.

Take a close look on the arrows. Did you notice something strange? The image size is twice the double of the visible arrow. This is not a mistake. This is a trick! I will explain it later.

Clock

Create a new actor and double-click it to open the Actor Editor. Edit the actor attributes with the parameters in Table 10-2.

Table 10-2. *Clock Actor Attributes*

Name	Clock
Size/Width	320
Size/Height	320

Click the Images tab to display the images that you just imported and drag and drop Chap10-clock.png into the actor.

Seconds

Create a new actor and double-click it to open the Actor Editor. Edit the actor attributes with the parameters in Table 10-3.

Table 10-3. *Seconds Actor Attributes*

Name	Seconds
Size/Width	5
Size/Height	200

Click the Images tab to display the images that you just imported and drag and drop Chap10-seconds.png into the actor.

Minutes

Create a new actor and double-click it to open the Actor Editor. Edit the actor attributes with the parameters in Table 10-4.

Table 10-4. *Minutes Actor Attributes*

Name	Minutes
Size/Width	5
Size/Height	226

Click the Images tab to display the images that you just imported and drag and drop Chap10-minutes.png into the actor.

Hours

Create a new actor and double-click it to open the Actor Editor. Edit the actor attributes with the parameters in Table 10-5.

Table 10-5. *Hours Actor Attributes*

Name	Hours
Size/Width	9
Size/Height	194

Click the Images tab to display the images that you just imported and drag and drop the Chap10-hours.png into the actor.

Button

Create a new actor and double-click it to open the Actor Editor. Edit the actor attributes with the parameters in Table 10-6.

Table 10-6. *Button Actor Attributes*

Name	Button
Size/Width	27
Size/Height	27

Click the Images tab to display the images that you just imported and drag and drop Chap10-button.png to the actor.

Creating the Clock Mechanisms: Rules and Behaviors

Creating a real world mechanical clock could be a work of art. It is so small and the movements need to be perfect, so it can take several months. Fortunately for us, a virtual analog clock is much less complicated. The time information isdirectly accessed from the device internal clock. The behaviors of your actors will mostly ensure that the hands move correctly.

Clock

In order to perfectly position the clock on the screen, you will position it via change attribute behavior.

Open the Clock actor in the Actor Editor. Drag and drop a Change Attribute behavior into the actor and change clock.position.X to 160. Drag and drop a second Change Attribute behavior into the actor and change Clock.position.Y to 240. The Clock action view should match Figure 10-4.

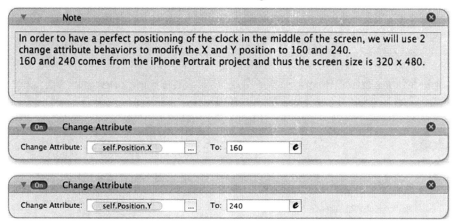

Figure 10-4. *Clock action view*

In order to be efficient and save some precious time, you will create a custom behavior that will position the actors in the center of the screen.

Create a new group and name it "Positioning in the center." Move the two Change Attributes you just created into the new group.

In the Behaviors inventory pane, select Custom, located next to Standard, by clicking it. Drag and drop your group into the pane as per Figure 10-5. That's it! You have just created your first custom behaviors. You will use these behaviors on every actor in this project to position them perfectly in the center of the screen.

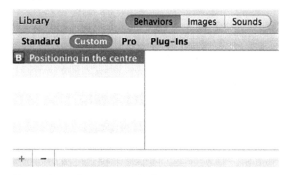

Figure 10-5. *Custom behavior inventory*

Button

Double-click the Button actor to open it in the Actor Editor. Drag and drop the "Positioning in the center" behavior from the custom behavior inventory.

Seconds

Double-click the Seconds actor to open it in the Actor Editor. Drag and drop the "Positioning in the center" behavior from the custom behavior inventory.

Coming back to the strange size of the image compare to the visible arrow, the trick is to implement a rotation of the actor per second. But the rotation attribute rotates the actor from its center. So having an actor double the size of the arrow provides the illusion that only the arrow is moving while in fact this is the complete actor.

Drag and drop a Constrain Attribute behavior and change Seconds.rotation to Devices.Clock.Seconds*6.

Why is there a minus sign? Chapter 2 discussed the way GameSalad measures the angle: counter-clockwise. So in order to have a clockwise movement, you need to make the seconds negative.

Also, the second arrows will cover the complete rotation in 60 seconds. A complete rotation is 360 degrees. So the arrow should cover 6 degrees per second (360/6).

The Seconds action view should match Figure 10-6.

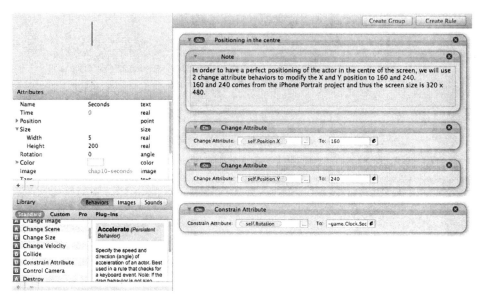

Figure 10-6. *Seconds action view*

MInutes

Double-click the Minutes actor to open it in the Actor Editor. Drag and drop the "Positioning in the center" behavior from the custom behavior inventory. Drag and drop a Constrain Attribute behavior and change Minutes.rotation to Devices.Clock.Minutes*6.

Hours

Double-click the Hours actor to open it in the Actor Editor. Drag and drop the "Positioning in the center" behavior from the custom behavior inventory.

Drag and drop a Constrain Attribute behavior and change Hours.rotation to Devices.Clock.Hours*6 – 30*Devices.Clock.Minutes/60.

You've added a few extra degrees in the case of the hour in order to show the movement between 2 hours. If the arrow were to move 30 degrees at once, the visual effect would not be nice. You know that the Hours arrow will do 30 degrees in 60 minutes. As such, it will be doing 0.5 degrees per minute.

The action view for the Hours actor should match Figure 10-7.

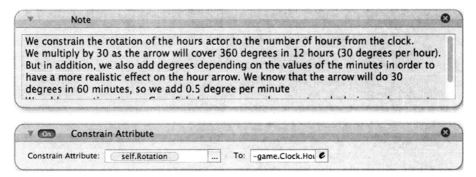

Figure 10-7. Hours constrain attribute

Assembling the Clock: Laying out the Scene

The layout of the scene is quite easy as you have positioned your actors using behaviors. But the order in which you position the actors is important for the visual aspect.

Position the actors about in the center of the scene in the following order as per Figure 10-8:

- Clock
- Hours
- Minutes
- Seconds
- Button

Figure 10-8. *The Clock scene*

Preview the project on your iPhone or in the Preview window.

Cyclic Movement: The Metronome

A metronome is a device that makes a regular beat (Figure 10-9). You can set the number of beats by seconds. It is used to help musicians follow a consistent tempo.

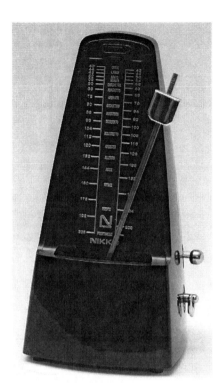

Figure 10-9. *A mechanical metronome*

In this section, you will learn how to implement a cyclic movement. This concept could easily be re-used in game projects.

To give you a better idea of the results, open the file `metronome_final.gameproj` and click Preview.

Creating the Metronome Project

Open the GameSalad Creator and create a new project. Configure the project info as per Table 10-7.

Table 10-7. *Project Info for the Metronome*

Title	The Metronome
Platform	iPhone Portrait
Resolution Independence	Unchecked
Description	This project is to demonstrate that you can build non-game apps
Instruction	Move the weight up and down and click on/off to start the metronome.
Tags	Metronome

Name and save your file as `Metronome.gameproj`.

Metronome Mechanical Components: Creating the Actors

To design your metronome, youneed to create the following actors:

- Metronome
- Weight
- Pendulum
- On
- Off

Before creating the actors, import the images for these actors. Open the Scene Editor and select the Images tab. Click the + sign and import the following files: `chap10-metronome.png`, `chap10-pendulum.png`, and `chap10-weight.png`. These pictures files are located in the chapter 10 file folder. Your Image tab should match Figure 10-10.

Figure 10-10. *Images*

As a bonus, I also provide the Illustrator file for each of the images if you want to customize your metronome.

Metronome

Create a new actor and double-click it to open the Actor Editor. Edit the actor attributes with the parameters in Table 10-8.

Table 10-8. *Metronome Actor Attributes*

Name	Metronome
Size/Width	301
Size/Height	478

As you may have noticed the actor size is odd. This is definitely not optimized for memory; if you are looking for performance, you should always optimize the actor size to a multiple of four.

Click the Images tab to display the images that you just imported and drag and drop Chap10-metronome.png into the actor.

Weight

Create a new actor and double-click it to open the Actor Editor. Edit the actor attributes with the parameters in Table 10-9.

Table 10-9. *Weight ActorAttributes*

Name	Weight
Size/Width	34
Size/Height	48

Click the Images tab to display the images that you just imported and drag and drop Chap10-weight.png into the actor.

Create two actors attributes for Weight as per Table 10-10.

Table 10-10. *Weight Actor Custom Attributes*

Name	Type	Default Value
InitX	Real	0
InitY	Real	0

Pendulum

Create a new actor and double-click it to open the Actor Editor. Edit the actor attributes with the parameters in Table 10-11.

Table 10-11. *Pendulum Actor Attributes*

Name	Pendulum
Size/Width	600
Size/Height	18
Rotation	90

Click the Images tab to display the images that you just imported and drag and drop Chap10-pendulum.png to the actor.

On

Create a new actor and double-click it to open the Actor Editor. Edit the actor attributes with the parameters in Table 10-12.

Table 10-12. *On Actor Attributes*

Name	On
Size/Width	100
Size/Height	100
Color/Alpha	0

Off

Create a new actor and double-click it to open the Actor Editor. Edit the actor attributes with the parameters in Table 10-13.

Table 10-13. *Off Actor Attributes*

Name	Off
Size/Width	100
Size/Height	100
Color/Alpha	0

Storing Information: Defining the Attributes

Create the game attributes as per Table 10-14.

Table 10-14. *Game Attributes*

Name	Type	Default Value
inMovement	Boolean	0
Speed	Real	1
Rotation	Real	0

Creating Mechanical Movements: Rules and Behaviors

The basic movement of a metronome is to go back and forth, thus having a cyclic movement. The speed of the cycle depends on the position of the weight. You will implement this logic using rules and behaviors.

Metronome Rules and Behaviors

Create a Group and name it "Position the metronome." Drag and drop a Change Attribute behavior and change metronome.Position.X to 160. Drag and drop a second Change Attribute behavior and change metronome.Position.Y to 240.

On Rules and Behaviors

Create a group and name it "Position the On button." Drag and drop a Change Attribute behavior and change on.Position.X to 60. Drag and drop a second Change Attribute behavior and change on.Position.Y to 30.

Drag and drop a Display Text behavior and type the text "On" inside. You can leave all other settings as the defaults. The action view should match Figure 10-11.

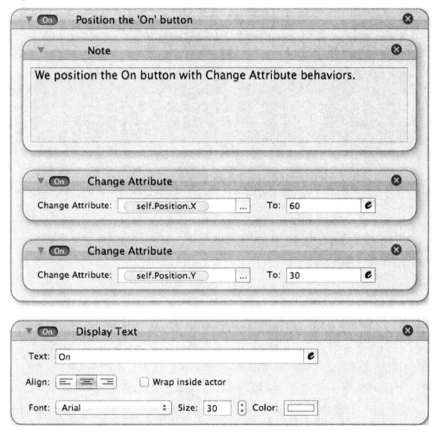

Figure 10-11. *On action view*

Lastly, create a new rule and name it "On is pressed." The condition is "Actor receives event" "touch" is "pressed." Then drag and drop a Change Attribute behavior and change game.InMovement to 1 as per Figure 10-12.

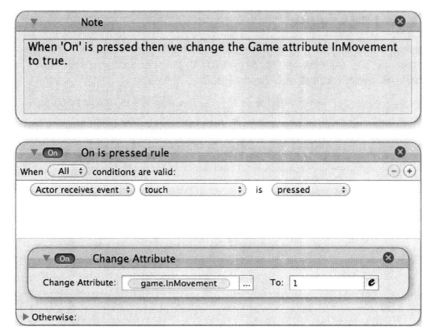

Figure 10-12. *On is pressed rule*

This rule is used to detect a touch in the On area and then it changes the InMovement attribute to true. You will use this attribute to authorize the movement of the pendulum.

Off Rules and Behaviors

Create a group and name it "Position the Off button." Drag and drop a Change Attribute behavior and change on.Position.X to 260. Drag and drop a second Change Attribute behavior and changeon.Position.Y to 30.

Drag and drop a Display Text behavior and type the text "Off" inside. You can leave all other settings as the defaults. The action view should match Figure 10-13.

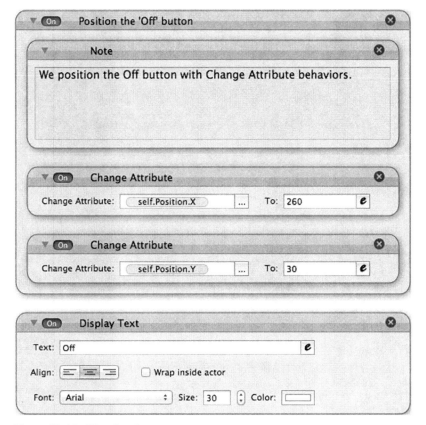

Figure 10-13. *Off action view*

Lastly, duplicate the On rule by dragging the rule down while pressing the Option key. Name it "Off is pressed." The condition is "Actor receives event" "touch" is "pressed." Then drag and drop a Change Attribute behavior and change game.InMovement to 0 as per Figure 10-14.

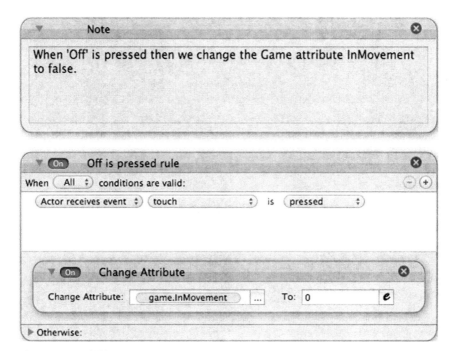

Figure 10-14. *Off is pressed rule*

This rule is used to detect a touch in the Off area and then it changes the InMovement attribute to false. You will use this attribute to stop the movement of the pendulum.

Pendulum Rules and Behaviors

Create a group and name it "Position the pendulum." Drag and drop a Change Attribute behavior and change on.Position.X to 160. Drag and drop a second Change Attribute behavior and change on.Position.Y to 100 as per Figure 10-15.

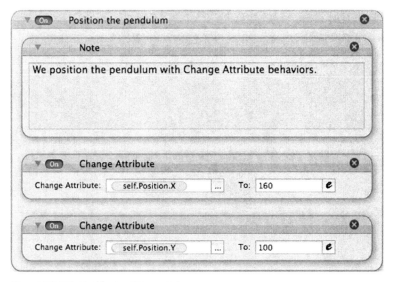

Figure 10-15. *Positioning the pendulum*

Open the Sound inventory view (click the Sounds tab next to Images tab). Click the + sign to import a new sound. Select the file named sound4.mp3 from the Chap4_files folder. Import the file as Sound.

You will now create the movement. To do so, you need to know the maximum rotation of the pendulum in both directions. Set a rotation angle of a total of 20 degrees: -10 to +10. But the originating angle is 90 degrees, so the pendulum will rotate from angle 80 to 100, back and forth. You will use the Interpolate behavior to make the movement adependent of a Speed attribute.

Create a new rule with the following conditions:

- "Attribute""Pendulum.Rotation""="80"
- "Attribute""game.InMovement" is "true"

Then drag and drop an Interpolate behavior and change the settings.

- Interpolate Attribute: Pendulum.Rotation
- To: 100
- Duration: game.speed
- Function: Linear

Next, drag and drop a Play Sound behavior and select sound4 as the sound to play. Leave all the other setting as the defaults.

The rule is shown in Figure 10-16.

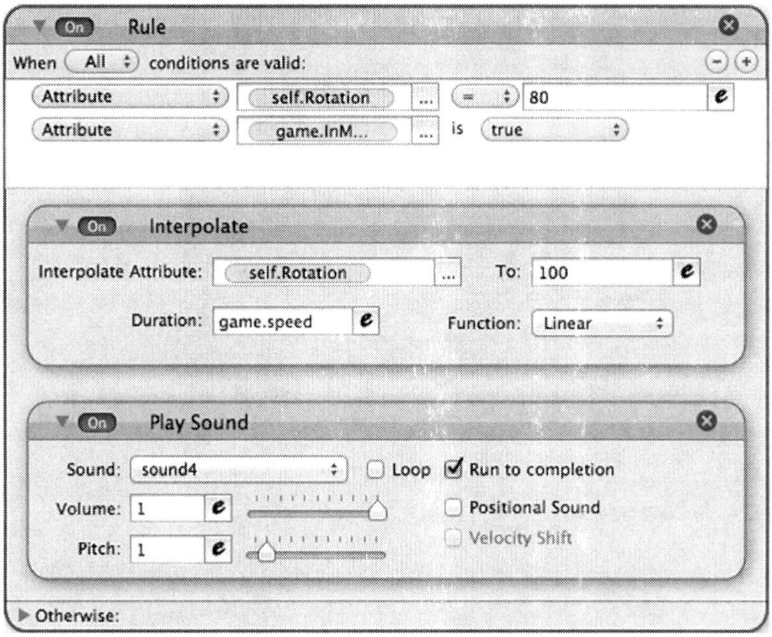

Figure 10-16. *Interpolate to 100 rule*

Create a new rule with the following conditions:

- "Attribute""Pendulum.Rotation""=""100"
- "Attribute""game.InMovement" is "true"

Then drag and drop an Interpolate behavior and change the settings.

- Interpolate Attribute: Pendulum.Rotation
- To: 80
- Duration: game.speed
- Function: Linear

Next, drag and drop a Play Sound behavior and select sound4 as the sound to play. Leave all the other setting as the defaults.

The rule is shown in Figure 10-17.

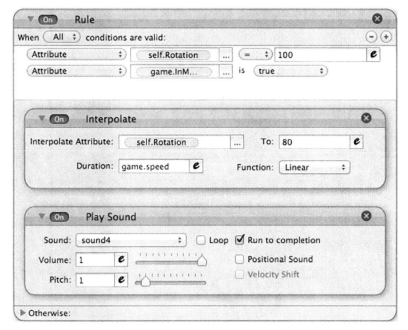

Figure 10-17. *Interpolate to 80 rule*

Create a new group named "Pendulum Movement" and place the two rules that you just created into this group.

Create a new rule with the condition "Attribute" "game.InMovement" is "false." Drag and drop a Constrain Attribute behavior into the rule and change pendulum.Rotation to 90. This rule will detect that the Off button has been pressed and set the pendulum into the initial position.

Create a new rule with the condition "Attribute" "game.InMovement" is "true." Drag and drop a Change Attribute behavior into the rule and change pendulum.Rotation to 100. This rule will position the pendulum to rotation at 100. Then the interpolate rules kicks off.

Create a new group and name it "On/Off rules." Drag and drop the two rules that you just created into this group as per Figure 10-18.

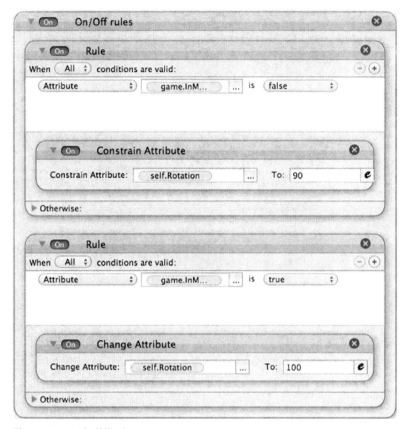

Figure 10-18. *On/Off rules*

Last but not least, drag and drop a Constrain Attribute behavior in the actor action view and change game.Rotation to pendulum.Rotation as per Figure 10-19.

Figure 10-19. *Constrain the Rotation attribute*

This last behavior aims at stocking at any time the Rotation value of the pendulum into the game attribute named Rotation. You will use this value later to synchronize the movement of the weight.

Weight Rules and Behaviors

Create a new group and name it "Position the Weight." Drag and drop two Change Attribute behaviors into the group and change:

- Weight.Position.X to 160
- Weight.Position.Y to 240

Create a second group and name it "Init." Drag and drop two Change Attribute behaviors into the group and change:

- Weight.InitX to Weight.Position.X
- Weight.InitY to Weight.Position.Y

At this stage, your action view should match Figure 10-20.

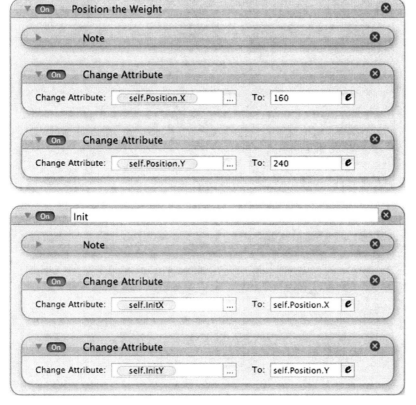

Figure 10-20. *Position and Init Groups*

Create a new rule and name it "Setting the Weight." The conditions for this rule are:

- "Attribute" "gameInMovement" is "false"
- "Actor receives event" "touch" is "pressed"

Those conditions will ensure that you can only move the weight when the metronome is off.

Drag and drop two Constrain Attribute behaviors into the rule and change:

- Weight.Position.X to 160
- Weight.Position.Y to max(120,min(340, game.mouse.position.Y))

The last constrain will ensure that the weight is positioned where your finger touched the screen within the limit of 120 to 340.

Drag and drop a Constrain Attribute behaviors into the rule and change:

- Weight.InitY to Weight.Position.Y

This will ensure that InitX and InitY always contain the last position of the weight before pressing the On button. You will use this information to calculate the movement and to return the weight to its position when you press the Off button.

Last but not least, use the position of the weight to determine the speed of the metronome. The higher the weight is, the faster the pendulum will go. Use the formula precision(120/Weight.Position.Y),2). Precision function will help you to keep only two digits below the second.

Drag and drop another Constrain Attribute into the rule and change:

- game.speed to precision(120/Weight.Position.Y),2)

Your Weight Setting rule is shown in Figure 10-21.

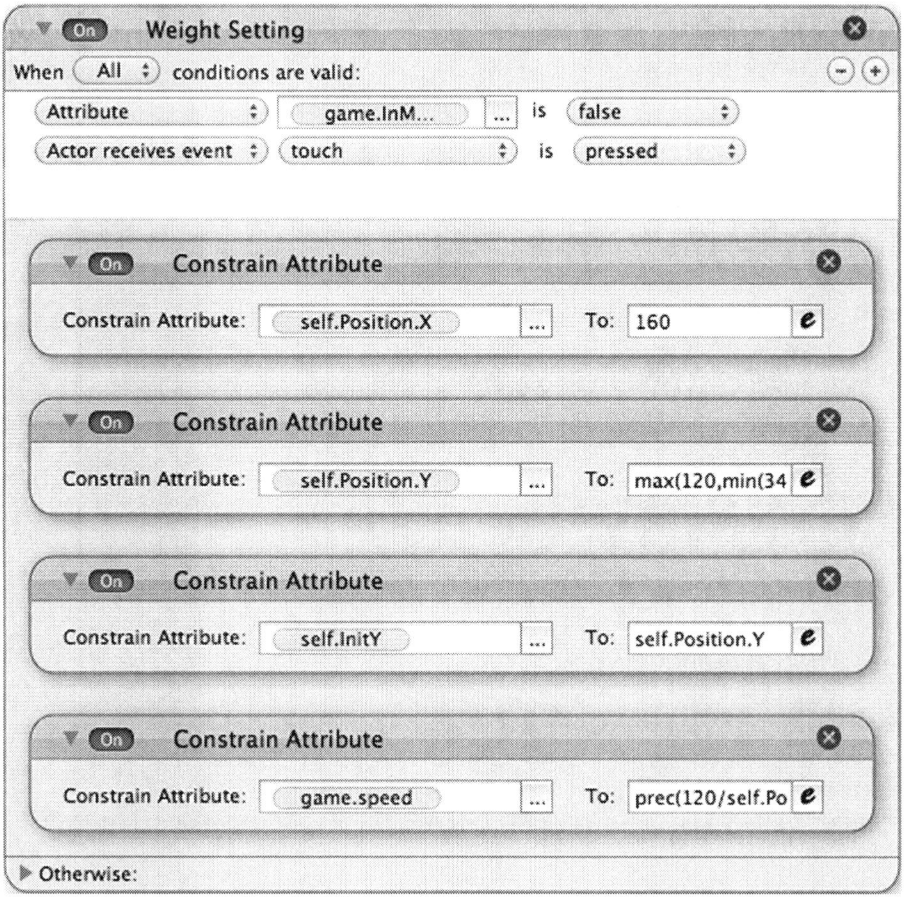

Figure 10-21. *Weight Setting rule*

Next, you will create a rule that will detect when the InMovement attribute changes to false in order to reset the weight to its starting position.

Create a new rule named "Go to starting position." The condition of this rule is "Attribute" "game.InMovement" is "false."Drag and drop three Change Attribute behaviors into the rule and change:

- Weight.Position.X to Weight.InitX
- Weight.Position.Y to Weight.InitY
- Weight.Rotation to 0

The rule is shown in Figure 10-22.

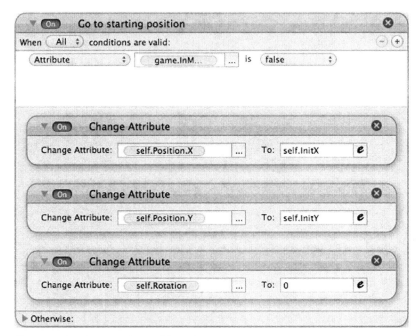

Figure 10-22. *Go to starting position rule*

Finally, you need to set up the most complex rule. You need to have the weight move at the same time as the pendulum but across an arc and rotating at the same time. There is a little bit of trigonometry involved here. I always recommend that you use a piece of paper and draw your equations. My sketch is in Figure 10-23.

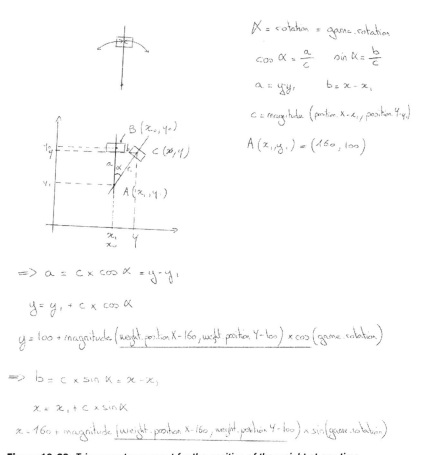

Figure 10-23. *Trigonometry concept for the position of the weight at any time*

By using the cosinus and sinus of the angle (α in Figure 10-23), you can derive the value of x and y at point C. You use the magnitude function to calculate the distance between two points.

Create a new rule and name it "Sync the movement." The condition is "Attribute""game.InMovement" is "true." Then drag and drop three Constrain Attribute behaviors into the rule and change:

- Weight.Rotation to game.Rotation-90

- Weight.Position.X to160+magnitude(Weight.Position.X-160, Weight.Position.Y-100) * sin (-(game.rotation-90))

- Weight.Position.Yto 100+magnitude(Weight.Position.X-160, Weight.Position.Y-100) * cos (game.rotation-90)

Your rule should match Figure 10-24.

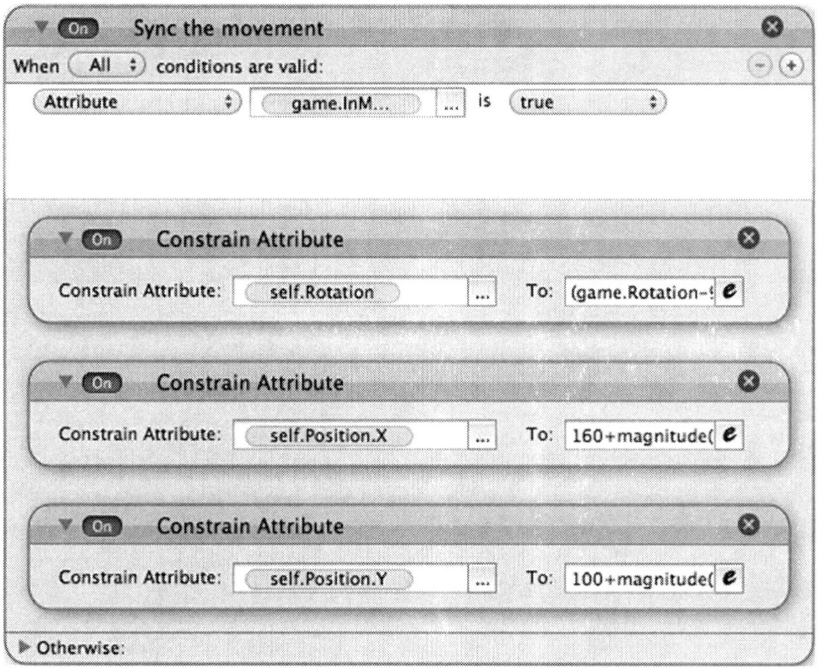

Figure 10-24. *Sync the movement rule*

Building the Metronome: Laying out the Scene

The layout of the scene is quite easy, as you have positioned your actors using behaviors. But the order in which you position the actors is important for the visual aspect.

Position the actors in the center of the scene in the following order, as per Figure 10-25:

- Pendulum
- Weight
- Metronome
- On
- Off

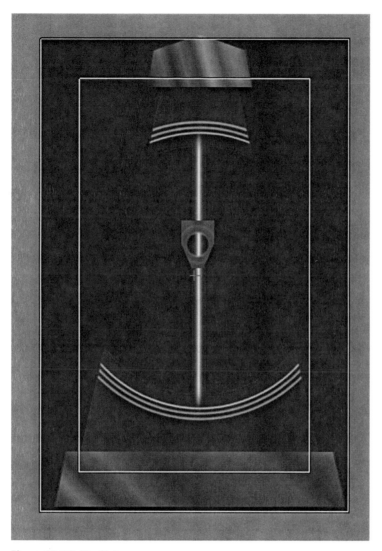

Figure 10-25. *The Metronome scene*

Preview the project on your iPhone or in the Preview window.

Summary

This chapter concludes the GameSalad development of this book. You have seen that GameSalad can be used to create apps other than games with just a little bit of creativity.

In this chapter, you have learned how to:

- Create apps other than games in GameSalad.
- Use the device internal clock features.
- Create cyclic movement in GameSalad.

Submitting Your Game to the App Store

This is the moment. Yes, the big moment. You have spent countless hours working on your game and it is now time for everybody to see it. But one more critical step lies ahead. You need to publish your game to the App Store.

> **REMINDER:** You need to be a registered iOS developer. Please refer to Chapter 1 for more information.

In this chapter, you will go through all the steps to publish a game in the App Store:

- You will create your App ID.
- You will get a Distribution Certificate and create a Distribution Provisioning Profile.
- You will create the iTunes Connect Application Profile.
- You will enable Game Center and iAd for your game.
- You will generate the binary file and upload it to Apple.
- You will make the game available in the App Store.

Getting the AppID, Certificate, and Distribution Provisioning Profile on the Provisioning Portal

This section covers all the necessary actions on the Provisioning Portal. You will create the App ID that will be the unique ID of your game. You will also use your Distribution Certificate (created in Chapter 1) to sign your app. Lastly, you will create the Distribution Provisioning Profile that will be used to publish the game in GameSalad.

Creating Your App ID

First, you need to create an ID for your game. This is the AppID.

Go to the Provisioning Portal (`developer.apple.com`, then Member Centre ➤ iOS Provisioning Portal).

Click the App IDs option located on the left side on the screen and then click the New App ID button to land on the Create AppID page, as shown in Figure 11-1.

You will need to provide:

- Description: This should be a way to find your App ID rapidly. I suggest using the name of your game.

- Bundle Seed ID: You can leave it as "Use Team ID" unless you want to select a Bundle Seed ID. The Bundle Seed ID is used when you have several games that will share the same Keychain access (to share data such as usernames and passwords).

- Bundle Identifier: Enter something that will be unique for this app in the whole world. Apple recommends using a reverse domain name, but you may not have a domain name. In such a case, use something that will be unique to you and that nobody else would pick.

Then click the Submit button.

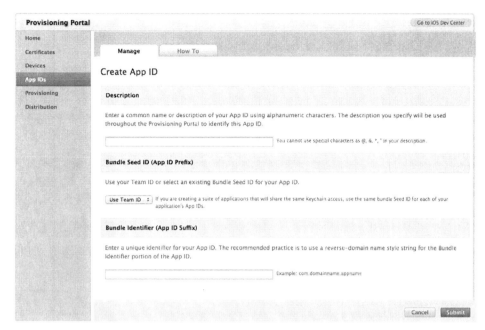

Figure 11-1. *Creating an App ID*

Your Distribution Certificate

In Chapter 1, the "Installing the Developer Certificate in Your Keychain" section covered the steps of creating your Distribution Certificate. This file is named iOS_distribution.cer.

You can verify its presence in the KeyChain utilities under Certificate. If the certificate is not present, refer back to the aforementioned section of Chapter 1.

Creating the Distribution Provisioning Profile

The next step is to create an App Store Distribution Provisioning Profile for your game.

Click the Provisioning link below App IDs located on the left side. Select the Distribution tab and click the New Profile button to get to the Create iOS Distribution Provisioning Profile page shown in Figure 11-2.

Provide the following information:

- Distribution Method: Select App Store.

- Profile Name: Enter a name for your profile. I recommend using the name of the application followed by "AppStore" so that you know this is the profile for the store.

- App ID: Select the game App ID that you created in the previous step.

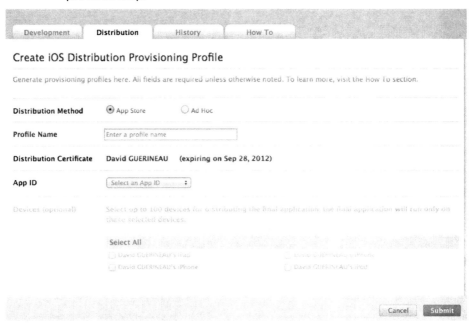

Figure 11-2. *Creating the Distribution Profile*

Click the Submit button to generate the Distribution Profile. You may need to hit refresh on your web browser if the status is still pending. It should take from a few seconds to two minutes.

Click the Download button shown in Figure 11-3 to download the Distribution Profile onto your computer.

Figure 11-3. *Your newly created Distribution Profile*

Next, you need to install the profile by double-clicking it or by opening Xcode and dragging it into the Organizer. It will automatically open the Organizer tool from Xcode, as per Figure 11-4.

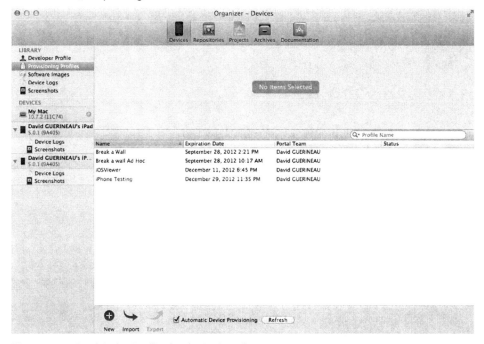

Figure 11-4. *Provisioning Profile view in the Organizer*

Creating the Game on iTunes Connect

Before starting the publishing process with the newly created Distribution Profile, you need create the game on iTunes Connect. This will enable you to activate GameCenter, iAD, or iApp if you use these functionalities in your game.

Step 1: Logging into iTunes Connect

Connect to iTunes Connect at `itunesconnect.apple.com`. Click the Manage Your Applications link shown in Figure 11-5.

Manage Your Applications
Add, view, and manage your applications in the iTunes Store.

Figure 11-5. *Managing your applications in iTunes Connect*

Step 2: Creating a New App

Click the Add New App button shown in Figure 11-6.

Figure 11-6. *Adding a new app*

Step 3: Providing Basic Information

Next, you need to provide the following information as per Figure 11-7:

- Default language of your application: This is the default language of your game.

- App Name: Your game name.

- SKU Number: This is a tracking number. It is used in-house to track uniquely the version of their software. I recommend using a date in the format YYYYMMDD, but you can use any random number.

- Bundle ID: Select the App ID that you created previously.

App Information

Enter the following information about your app.

Default Language	English ⌄ ⑦
App Name	⑦
SKU Number	⑦
Bundle ID	Select ⌄ ⑦
	You can register a new Bundle ID here.

Does your app have specific device requirements? Learn more

Cancel   Continue

Figure 11-7. *Game name*

Step 4: Release Date and Pricing Information

Next you need to provide a targeted release date and pricing information as per Figure 11-8.

- Availability Date: Keep in mind that if you pick a date before getting the store approval, your game will be release on the day you obtain the approval.

- Price Tier: There are many different strategies regarding pricing. Just keep in mind that Apple keeps 30% of each sale.

- Discount for Educational Institutions: Indicate if you are willing to provide a discount for education institutions if they buy large numbers of your game.

- Custom B2B App: Check if you have developed a game for a company for its own use.

Figure 11-8. *Release date and pricing information*

Step 5: Providing Version and Category Information

Next you need to provide information about the game as per Figure 11-9.

- Version Number: I recommend using conventions like major.minor.maintenance with maintenance for bug correction only, minor for minor features, and major for major changes in the game.

- Copyright: Put your copyright information here.

- Primary Category: Select Game or any other appropriate category according to the purpose of your development. Select two sub-categories (only if you selected Game as your category).

- Second Category: This is optional. However, it's recommended to reach a larger audience.

- Review Notes: If you want to give specific instruction to the reviewers.

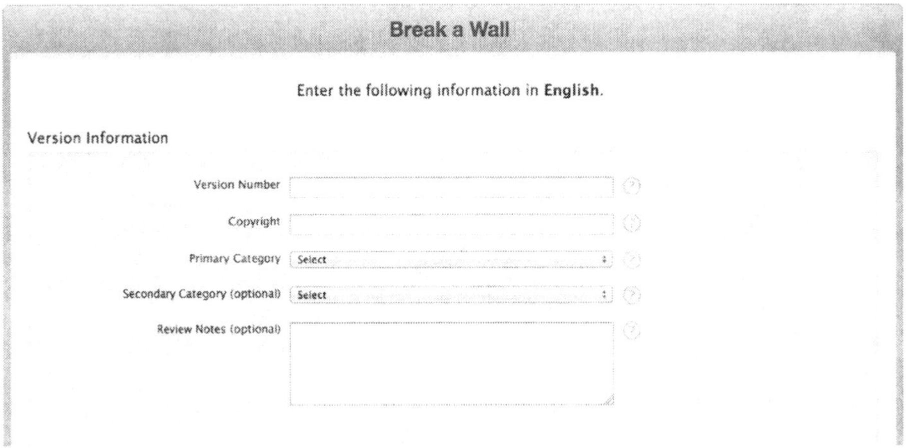

Figure 11-9. *Version information*

Step 6: Defining Your Application Rating

The next screen is the rating of your application. The questions are self-explanatory, as per Figure 11-10.

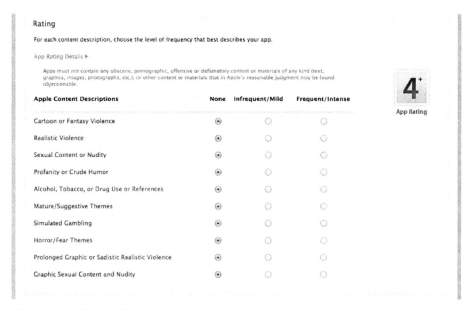

Figure 11-10. *Game rating*

Step 7: Providing Metadata Information

Then you provide the metadata for the game as per Figure 11-11.

- Description: Put on the salesman suit and use your best pitch for the game. I recommend that you prepare in advance.

- Keywords: The keywords are very important, as they will be searchable in the App Store. You can use Google Keywords to optimize your keyword selection.

- Email address: For contacting you.

- Support URL: You need to provide a web site for game support (you own web site or your blog page).

- Marketing URL: This is optional but it's a good idea to have one.

- Privacy policy URL: Also optional.

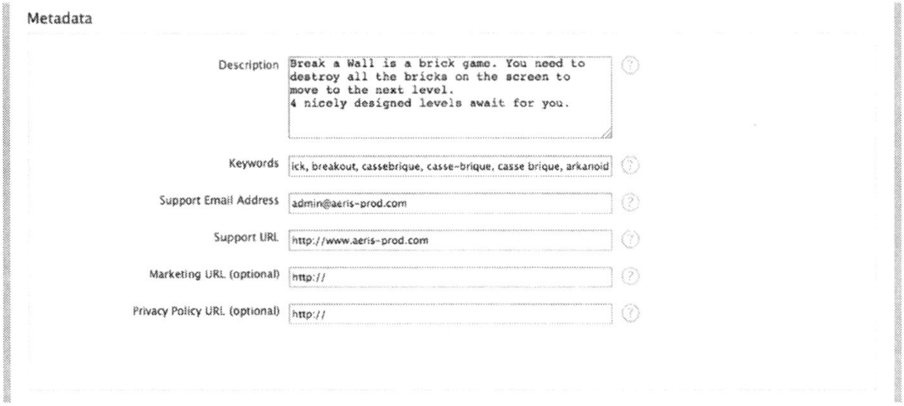

Figure 11-11. *Metadata*

Step 8: Reading and Accepting the EULA Agreement

Now you need to read and accept the default End User License Agreement (EULA) or provide your own, as shown in Figure 11-12.

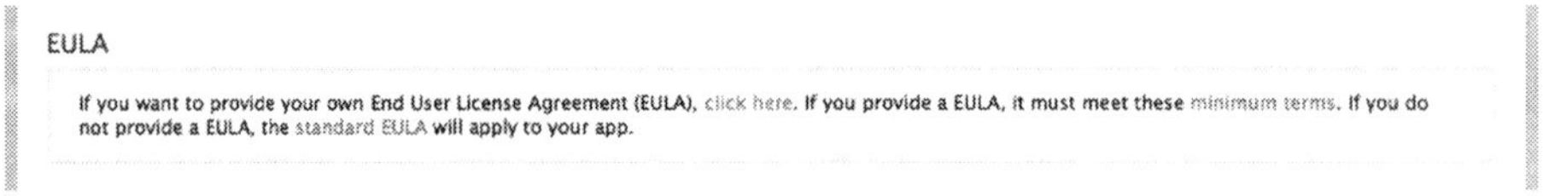

Figure 11-12. *End User License Agreement*

Step 9: Providing the Game Artwork

And finally, you need to upload your art (Figure 11-13). You must provide:

- 512 x 512 icon for iTunes art: 72 dpi and I recommend png format.

- Up to five screens captures for either iPhone or iPad.

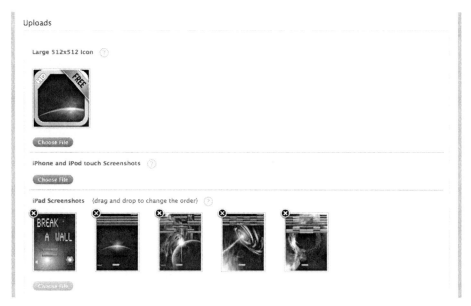

Figure 11-13. *Uploading your art*

Once you have provided all of the above information, you will be directed to a summary page (Figure 11-14).

Figure 11-14. *New application summary*

At this stage you new app has a status of Prepare for Upload.

You can now enable Game Center and iAd for your game.

Enabling Game Center for Your App

If you are using Game Center in your game, you need to enable Game Center in order to get the required information to finish the configuration of your game. Click the Manage Game Center button in the new application summary page. You will be directed to a page to enable Game Centre as per Figure 11-15. Click the Enable button.

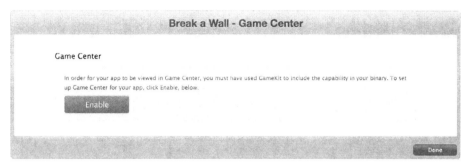

Figure 11-15. *Enabling Game Center*

Once you have clicked the Enable button, the page will update with options to set up Leaderboards and Achievements, as per Figure 11-16.

Figure 11-16. *Leaderboards and Achievements setup page*

Game Salad only supports Leaderboards. Achievements are on the roadmap but not yet delivered at the time of writing.

Click the Setup button in the Leaderboard section. You will be directed to the Leaderboards management page as per Figure 11-17.

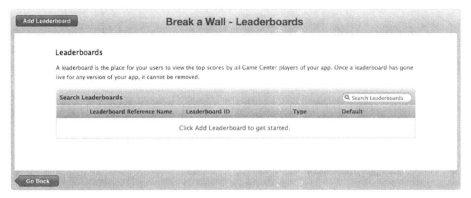

Figure 11-17. *Leaderboards management page*

Click the Add Leaderboard button to create a new leaderboard. First you will be asked to choose between a single leaderboard or a combined leaderboard, as per Figure 11-18.

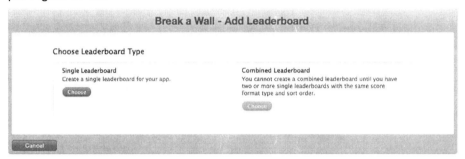

Figure 11-18. *Single or combined leaderboard*

Choose single leaderboard. Combined leaderboards are simply combinations of several single leaderboards.

Next, you need to provide the following information for your leaderboard (Figure 11-19):

- Leaderboard Reference Name: This is your leaderboard name (Highest score, Fastest race, etc.). Although this is an internal name, make it explicit. This will make your life easier later.

- Leaderboard ID: This one is key as you will need to implement this number into the GameSalad Creator for your game. This ID is alphanumeric.

- Score Format Type: Integer, time, etc.

- Sort Order: Low-to-High or High-to-Low.

- Score Range: Display scores only in the range. This is optional.

- Localization: You need to add a minimum of one language for your leaderboard. Click the Add Language button to provide the name to display on the leaderboard, the formatting of the score, the words to follow this score in both singular and plural, and an image (optional), as per Figure 11-20.

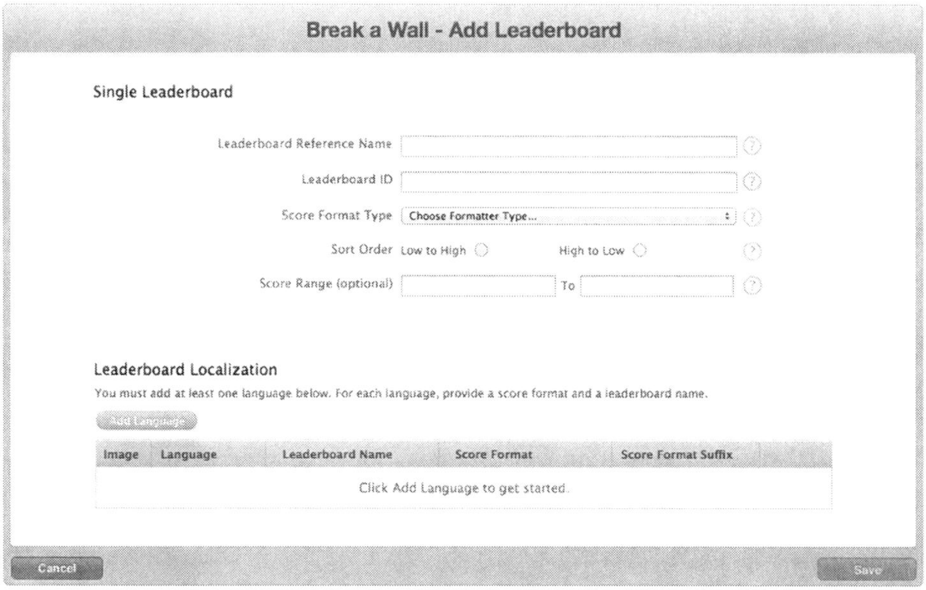

Figure 11-19. *New leaderboard*

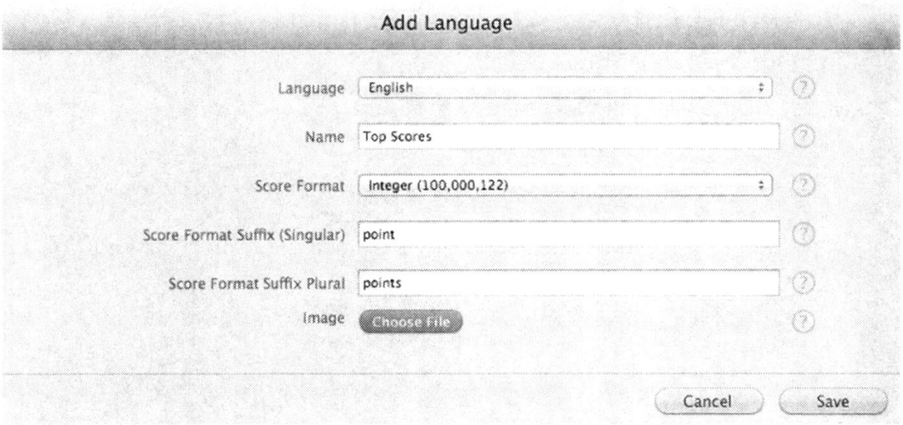

Figure 11-20. *Localization of your leaderboard*

Enabling iAd

If you are using iAd, you also need to enable it in iTunes Connect for your game. In your game overview page (Figure 11-14), you need to click the Enable iAd network option.

The Enable iAd page appears as per Figure 11-21.

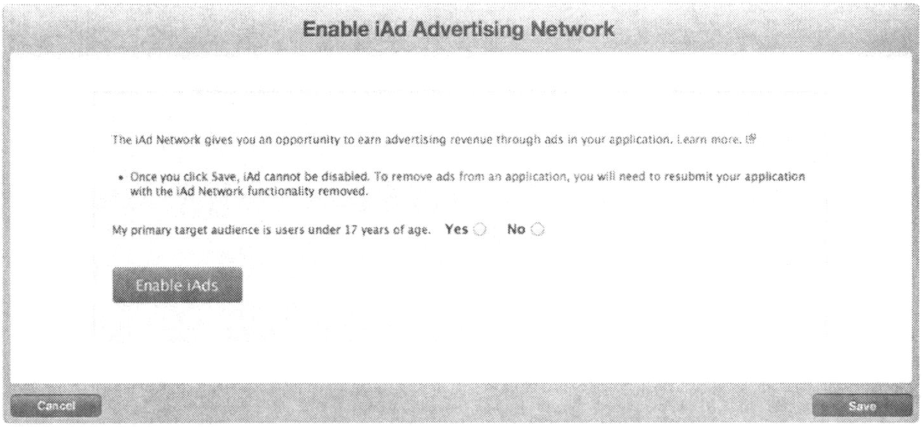

Figure 11-21. *Enabling iAd*

Just click the Enable iAd and Save buttons.

You are all set up in iTunes Connect for the moment. The next step is to prepare the binary file to upload.

Updating Game Center in GameSalad

Open your game in GameSalad Creator.

For every action with GameCenter that you may have used in your game you need to update the Post Score and Show Leaderboards behaviors with the appropriate Leaderboard ID that you just created, as per Figures 11-22 and 11-23.

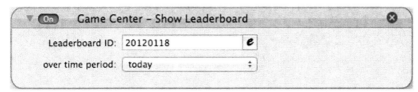

Figure 11-22. *Show Leaderboard behavior*

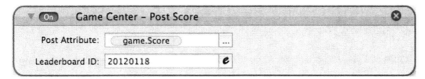

Figure 11-23. *Post Score behavior*

Publishing the Game Inside GameSalad

You now need to create the binaries for uploading to the iTunes store. This step is called *publishing* in GameSalad Creator. During this step, your game will be signed with the appropriate certificate and provisioning profiles, enabling you to send it to Apple.

Step 1: Selecting the Targeted Platform

With the game you want to publish opened, click the Publish button in the GameSalad Creator.

The following screen will ask you on which platform you want to publish your game (Figure 11-24). Select the appropriate platform.

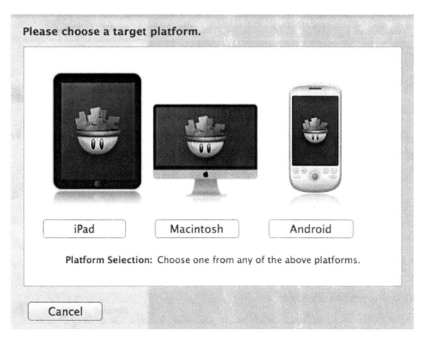

Figure 11-24. *Choosing the target platform*

Step 2: Providing Overview Information

The next step is to provide the overview information about your game as per Figure 11-25.

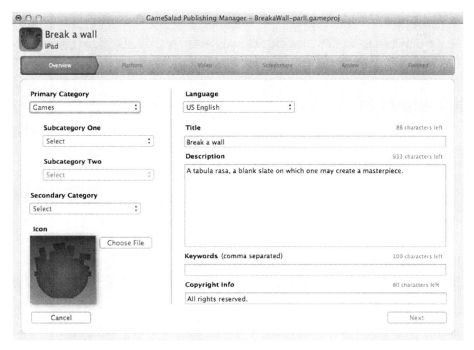

Figure 11-25. *Overview information*

You need to provide:

- Primary Category: Most of the time you should pick Games but you have seen that you may do things other than games in GameSalad.

- Subcategory: Select two subcategories in your primary category according to your game type (only for Game category).

- Secondary category: Select a second category in which your game will appear.

- Icon: Upload the game icon (512 x 512)

- Language: Select the language of your game.

- Title: This is the name of your game.

- Description: Provide the description of your game.

- Keywords: Provide a selection of keywords for your game separated by a comma.

▒   Copyright info: Provide your copyright information here.

A lot of this information was provided already when you created your game in iTunes Connect. Make it match!

Step 3: Selecting Your Provisioning Profile

The next screen asks you to select your Provisioning Profile. You must select the profile that you created for distribution on the App Store. You will also be asked for the display name of your game as well as its version.

> **NOTE:** The version in GameSalad MUST match the version you input in iTunes Connect.

Notice the advanced options on this screen. They allow you to customize the orientation as well as the splash screen (for Pro members) as per Figure 11-26.

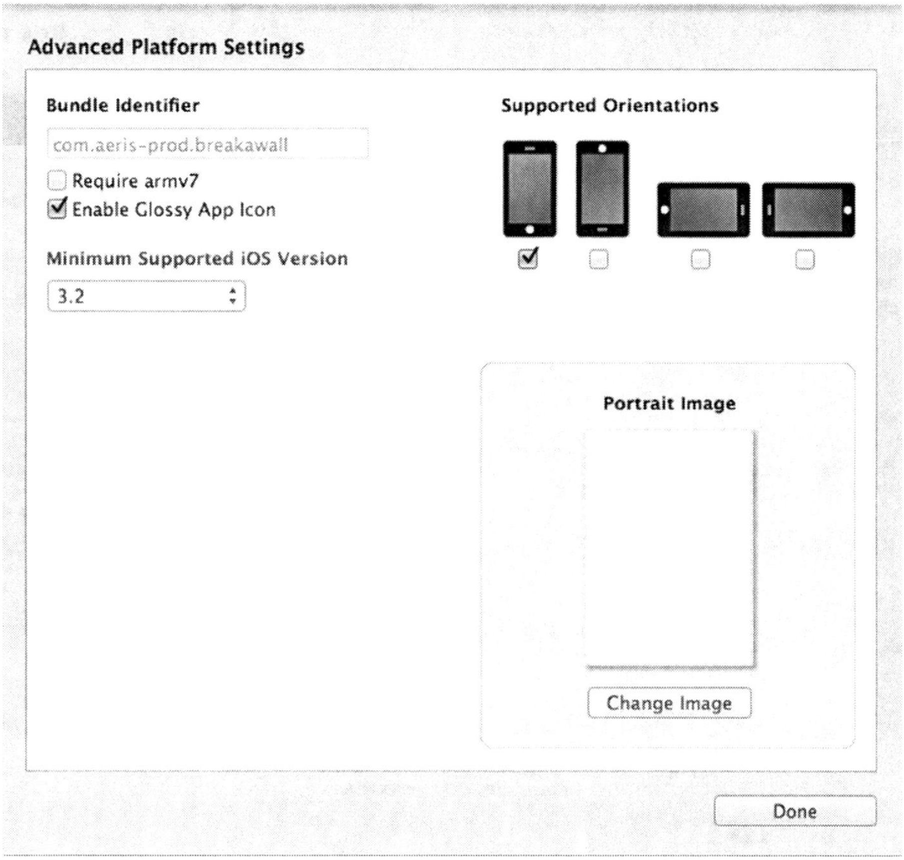

Figure 11-26. *Advanced platform settings*

The splash screen must be the size of the resolution of your target device. You will also have the opportunity to select armv7 or enable the Glossy App icon.

About armv7:

Armv7 is the processor instruction set standard. It is used from iPhone 3GS, iPad 1st Gen, iPod Touch 3rd Gen, and all following generations. If you check armv7, your game will only work on devices that support armv7.

Step 4: Providing a Link to a Promotional YouTube Video

This step is optional and enables you to provide a link to a promotional video on YouTube.

Step 5: Uploading Your Screenshots

This step requires you to upload up to five screenshots of your game as per Figure 11-27.

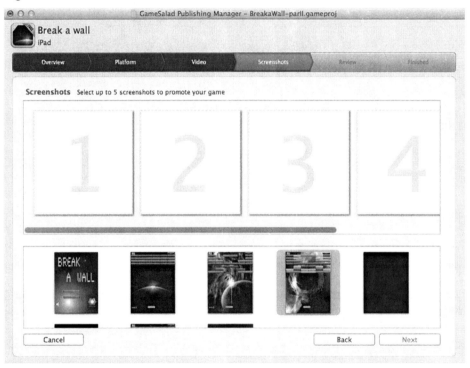

Figure 11-27. *Screenshots*

Step 6: Reading and Accepting the Agreement

Next, you can review all the information that you just provided. When you are happy with the data, click Publish.

Read and accept the GameSalad Submission Terms and Agreement as per Figure 11-28.

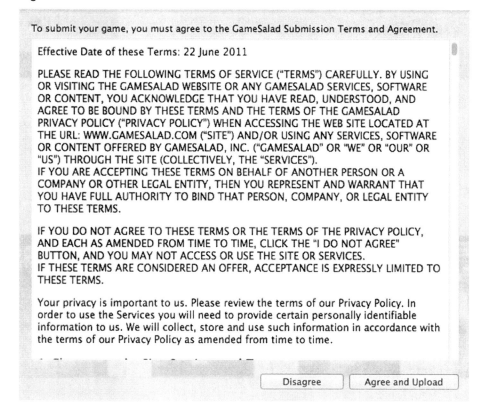

Figure 11-28. *GameSalad Submission Terms and Agreement*

Once you agree, the uploading of your game to the GameSalad servers will start. After a short while (depending on your game size), you will be asked to save your signed binary on your computer. The final screen will confirm that you successfully published you game in GameSalad, meaning you received your binary file (Figure 11-29).

Figure 11-29. *Congrats*

Step 7: Compressing Your File

The last step is to compress the file you just received by right-clicking and choosing Compress. You are now ready to upload your game.

Uploading the Game to iTunes

Go back to iTunes Connect and select your game in the Manage your Application section. The summary page should be similar to Figure 11-30 with a status of Prepare for Upload.

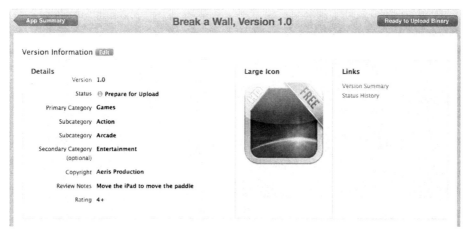

Figure 11-30. *Prepare for Upload status*

Click the Ready to Upload button. You will be directed to the Export Compliance page as per Figure 11-31.

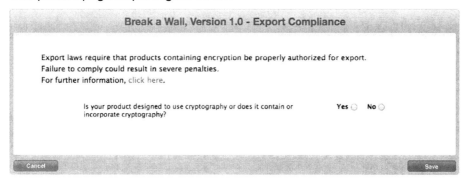

Figure 11-31. *Export Compliance*

The next screen indicates where to find the Application Loader that will be used to upload the game. You will find the Application Loader at the following path: /Developer/Application/Utilities/Application Loader.app.

Open the Application Loader. If this is the first time you've used it, you will be asked to accept the Software License Agreement as per Figure 11-32.

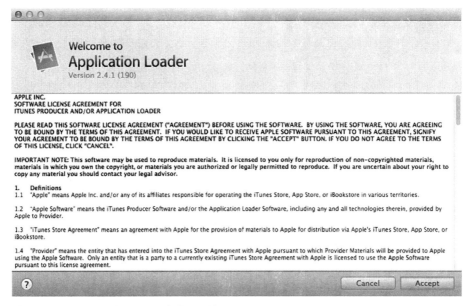

Figure 11-32. *Application Loader Software License Agreement*

Next you need to provide your Developer Apple ID and password as the Application Loader will use them to connect to your account and upload your game.

In the Application Loader main screen, select Deliver Your App as per Figure 11-33.

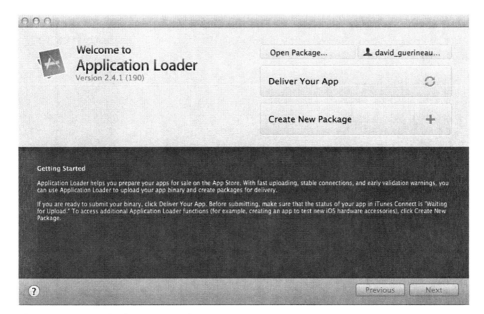

Figure 11-33. *Application Loader main screen*

Next, select your application by clicking "Choose your application." Click Next. Then, click the Choose button as per Figure 11-34 to select the binary file to upload.

Figure 11-34. *App info before upload*

A file-browsing window will open. Select the binary file to upload and confirm by clicking Send. You can follow the progress of the upload on the screen as per Figure 11-35.

Figure 11-35. *Uploading your file*

Once the upload is completed, a Thank You screen will appear. You can close the window and the Application Loader.

The status of your game will change to Upload Received as per Figure 11-36.

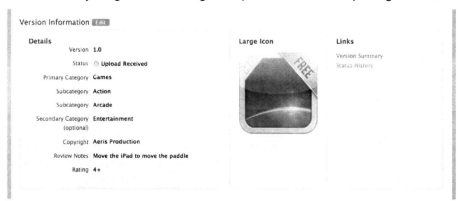

Figure 11-36. *Upload Received status*

After a very short while, your game status will automatically update to Waiting for Review (Figure 11-37).

Figure 11-37. *Waiting for Review status*

Wait and Wait and Wait

Now you have to wait… and wait… and wait until Apple reviews your application. At this stage, there is nothing more that you can do on the game submission. I recommend that you plan to work either on other project or on your game promotion if not done yet.

Once the Apple team starts to review your game, you will receive an e-mail notification (Figure 11-38) and your level of stress will increase because you know you will get your approval/rejection in a few hours.

The status for the following app has changed to **In Review**.
App Name: Break a Wall
App Version Number: 1.0
App SKU: 20120118
App Apple ID:496154190
To make changes to this app, sign in to iTunes Connect and open the Manage Your Applications module.
If you have any questions regarding your app, click Contact Us in iTunes Connect.
Regards,
The iTunes Store Team

Figure 11-38. *E-mail notification of In Review status*

At the time of writing, the review is about three to four days, but it changes depending on the number of new apps added.

What if you get rejected? Don't get discouraged. This happens very often, especially for your first game. Apple will provide you with the reason of the rejection. Let their feedback guide you in improving your game and then resubmit it. You can contact them if you don't understand the feedback and they will provide you with more insight.

My first app got rejected three times before I got it right!

Your Game is Ready for Sale

Congratulations!!!! You have received an e-mail indicating that your app is now ready for sale (Figure 11-39).

The following app has been approved. The status has changed to **Ready for Sale**.
If your contracts are not in effect at this time, however, your app status will be Pending Contract. You may track the progress of your contracts in the Contracts, Tax, and Banking module in iTunes Connect.
Note that it may take up to 24 hours before your app is live on the App Store. This delay is dependent upon any app availability issues.
App Name: Break a Wall ⊕
App Version Number: 1.0
App SKU: 20120118
App Apple ID:496154190
To make changes to this app, sign in to iTunes Connect and open the Manage Your Applications module.
If you have any questions regarding your app, click Contact Us in iTunes Connect.
Regards,
The iTunes Store Team

Are you looking for opportunities to generate additional revenue and market your apps to millions of iPhone and iPod touch users around the world? Learn more about the iAd Network and iAd for Developers.

Figure 11-39. *Ready for Sale status notification*

Good luck with your sales!

Summary

I hope that your game is selling quickly now! In this chapter, you learned how to:

- Create your AppID and your Distribution Provisioning Profile.
- Create your game description on iTunes Connect.
- Publish your game in GameSalad.
- Upload your game to Apple.

Still think that your sales figures are too low? Then jump to the next chapter where you will get a quick introduction to promotional tactics.

Chapter 12

Introduction to Game Promotion

The purpose of this chapter is not to provide you with a complete and exhaustive course on game marketing but rather a quick introduction to some important concepts that may help you to increase your sales.

You have developed a wonderful game and you want people to know about it. Even more, you want people to purchase it! So you have to tell the world, but going around yelling "I have the best game" is just not enough!

Before jumping into operational tactics, you need to prepare yourself with a little bit of introspective work: Who are your possible customers? Who are your competitors? What is unique about your game?

In this chapter, I will cover:

- The definition of your target customers.
- The investigation into your competition.
- The draft of your unique value definition.
- Basic operational tactics like press releases and their distribution.
- Getting reviews from influencers.
- Promoting your game with Facebook.

Pre-Development Phase

The preparation phase is in fact the most important task for an efficient promotion. By crafting the appropriate message you may increase your download rate significantly. The preparation phase is mostly composed of three areas of investigation: your targeted customers, your competition, and your unique value proposition.

Defining Your Targeted Customers

In order to craft a relevant message to your potential customers, you need to study them. You could spend years and years studying social psychology and getting deep insight into customer purchasing behavior, but this is not the purpose of this book. Instead I will provide you with a few questions that will help you to qualify your potential targets.

The very first step is to identify if your targeted customers buy games at the App Store. If they don't, you need to ask yourselves why. You may end up with the conclusion that they don't buy games at the App Store because they don't use iOS devices. Or they are not authorized to make the purchase (minors, young kids, people under management of another adult). In that case, you will need to qualify both populations: the player and the purchaser.

Population Profiling

To qualify a population, you will need to provide the following information about your population:

- Age
- Sex
- Income
- Education
- Marital status
- Geographical location
- Profession

Let's practice with an illustration. Let's imagine that you intend create a kindergarten game targeted to the United States. Let's fill in the appropriate information in Table 12-1.

Table 12-1. *Targeted Customers Profiling*

	Target Player	Purchaser
Age	2 to 6	20 to 50
Sex	Not relevant	Mother concerned with toddler development and learning activities
Income	None	UMC and above (Upper Middle Class)
Education	None	Diploma and above
Marital Status	None	Not relevant
Geographical location	US	US
Profession	Kindergarten	Executives with a busy lifestyle; this game will have the kid performing independent activities

Remember that the profiling does not aim at being exhaustive but at targeting 80% of your potential customers with minimal effort.

Source of Information

The next step is to identify where your targeted audience collects information to make their purchasing decisions. Once these sources of information are identified, you will communicate through them about your game. For example, Internet forums on parenthood are a great source of information for parents. A Google search on "Toddler parent US forum" will provide you with a list of forums where you can talk about your game. Also, there are web sites that cover apps for toddlers. Identifying them and getting them to review your game will bring you great exposure.

Understanding the Purchasing Decision

The last step in the qualification of your targeted customers is to identify the way your potential customers make purchase decisions for your type of game. Will the purchase decision be impulsive, analyzed, referred, or influenced? Again, getting this information is essential in the way your will define the content of your messaging.

In this example, it's critical for parents to have other parents recommend the app. So your operational tactic is to get positive recommendations from other parents and then communicate these recommendations. How do you get positive recommendations? One way is to distribute free download codes in exchange of answering a survey andthen creating a database of reliable reviewers.

Identifying and Qualifying Your Competition

For iOS games, locating your competition is both easy and tricky. Locating the games that you will compete against is simple as finding the App Store. But with more than 500,000 apps in the store, finding the games that you will fight against for market share may be tricky.

You can use the Search feature of iTunes (shown in Figure 12-1).

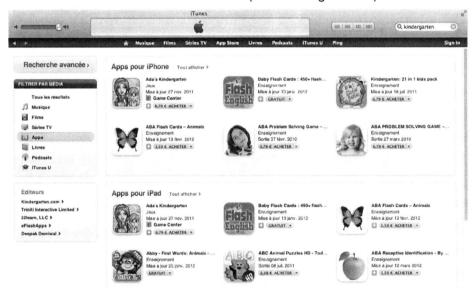

Figure 12-1. *The result of "Kindergarten" search in iTunes*

Another approach is to use Google with keywords like iPhone, iOS, or iPad. Then you can use all the power of Google to get results. The result of search "kindergarten ios games" is shown in Figure 12-2.

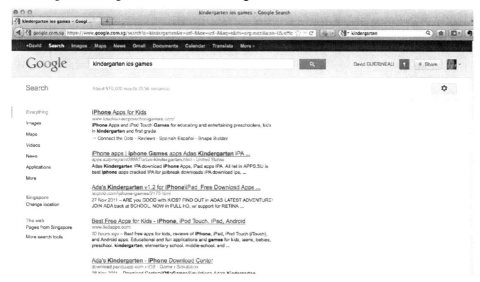

Figure 12-2. *Google "kindergarten ios game" results*

Once you have identified the list of potential competitors, create a table with one competitor per line and the information shown in Table 12-2 as columns.

Table 12-2. *Competition Information*

Name of the game	Name of the game as it appears in the App Store
Game description on the store	Description of the game as it is in the App Store - remove useless information
Screenshots	Copy the most important screen captures
Reviews on the store	Select the most relevant part of the reviews. This will be the positive and negative comments. They will provide you with the features that customers of your competitors appreciate and the features that they are missing
Price Tier	Indicate the price in the App Store
Rating	Indicate the number of stars
Released data	Date the game was released
Website	Website of the game or the developer
Key features	List the main important features of your competitor
Key messages	From the info that you have collected, analyze the messaging that is pushed by your competitor
Targeted audience	List the audience targeted by your competitors. It may differ from yours.
Strengths	List what you identify as key strengths of your competitor
Weaknesses	List what you identify as key weaknesses of your competitor

You can use the Excel template named `Competitive Review template.xls` located in the Chapter12_Files folder.

Creating Your Unique Value Proposition

The last step is to create your unique value proposition. This is the main reason why your customers will buy your game. The main generic reasons for a customer to buy your game is the entertainment value, the educational value, and the addiction value that your game provides for a specified price. By listing the features and the benefits of these features you will create values in these three categories and this will generate your unique value proposition.

Finding the Perfect Name

As the name is one of the most important criteria for search in the store, you should spend a relatively long amount of time finding the right name. It will need to be descriptive enough so that your game has a good match when potential buyers look for a game.

Among the checks to be performed on the name selection, you need to ensure that there is no offensive meaning in another country or culture that you are targeted. Also, you must respect copyright and trademark rules. A good tip is to do a Google search using the name you may want to use.

Last but not least, you may want to check what domain names are available in relation to the game name. Figure 12-3 shows the results of a domain check on "kindergarten."

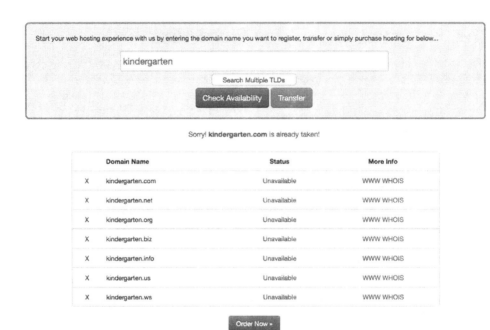

Figure 12-3. *Domain check on "kindergarten"*

Working on Your Icon

Your icon is your friend! Your icon is your best ally. A potential target customer performing a search will see two things on the App Store search result page: your title and your icon.

Thus your icon is extremely important. You must spend the necessary time to correctly design your icon. It must be descriptive with a catchy visual.

Table 12-3 shows the various requirements for icon sizes.

Table 12-3. *Icon Sizes*

	Size for iPhone (until 3GS)	Size for iPhone retina (4 and 4S)	Size for iPad (1st and 2nd Gen)	Size for iPad retina (3rd Gen)
Application icon	57 x 57	114 x 114	72 x 72	144 x 144
App icon for the App Store	512 x 512	1024 x 1024	512 x 512	1024 x 1024
Small icon	29 x 29	58 x 58	50 x 50	100 x 100

Here is the link to the Apple developer documentation regarding game icons:

`http://developer.apple.com/library/ios/#documentation/userexperience/con`
`ceptual/mobilehig/IconsImages/IconsImages.html`

In addition, here is the link to the Apple developer documentation on icon guidelines:

`http://developer.apple.com/library/ios/#documentation/userexperience/con`
`ceptual/mobilehig/IconsImages/IconsImages.html#//apple_ref/doc/uid/TP400`
`06556-CH14-SW2`

Writing the App Store Description

The description of your game in the App Store needs to follow some golden rules. Let's face it: most potential buyers will only read the first lines and then jump to the screen captures. At this point, there are three possibilities: they buy it, they go away, or they read further to make up their mind. I am not sure that the third option will be the most common. What does this mean? It means that you need to focus your key messages in the top of your description.

In addition, your content should not be static over the time. For example, if you decide to have a new-school-year sale, then advertise it on the top for the limited period of the sale.

Here are my golden rules for game description:

- State positive feedback from customers or recognized reviewers.
- Be direct and short in your game description.

- Explain why the player will have a good time playing your game.

- Be simple, direct, and honest.

- When publishing a new release, include a What's New section.

- List your main features and benefits with a strong highlight on the ones that are unique to your game.

No bla-bla, just the essential!

Operational Tactics

This section focuses on a few tools that you may want to use in order to get your game some visibility in the outside world, such as press releases, product web pages, game reviews, and Facebook pages.

Writing a Press Release

A press release is an official statement that is issued to the media. This is a formal way of communicating and informing news organizations (press, TV, Internet news sites).

You have several opportunities to issue a press release regarding game promotion:

- Your new game announcement.

- A major update of your game that provides more value to the customers.

- You have reached a significant number of downloads of your game.

- Your game has won some recognition of any sort: awards, game of the month, best game reviews, App Store special placement.

Writing a good press release is difficult as it requires very good written communication skills. For those who can afford it, I strongly recommend hiring a professional copywriter. Freelance copywriters will probably cost you a few hundred dollars. A Google search returns plenty of contacts to choose from. Based on the market research that you have already done, he/she will be able to write a very powerful press release that you will then broadcast.

If you choose (or have no other choice) to write it yourself, you need to respect a recognized formatted structure:

- Headline
- Summary (optional if the headline is explicit)
- Body
- Contact info

In today's digital communication age, you will distribute your press release electronically. Take advantage of this distribution mode to include a link to a video of your game. A good 30-second video will convince people to try the game.

To distribute your press release, you may send it directly to a database of key contacts that you created based on your market research. Alternatively, you may want to use some Internet services that will distribute your press releases to the media. Some may do it for free; some other may require a fee. Here are just a few names of such services:

- PRMac (www.prmac.com)
- PRWeb (www.prweb.com)
- Get2press (www.get2press.sg)

Creating a Web Page

Creating a simple product webpage is also a good and cheap promotional tool. You can easily find some service to host your page as well as a tool to design your page from a graphical interface.

Personally, I use a WordPress site, which is hosted for a few dollars per year. Then I dedicate a page of the site per game. In order to have an efficient message, here are some simple guidelines:

- Keep it clean and simple.
- Quickly describe your game at the top of the page.
- Make the graphical support niceby using an icon on the main page and the name of your game in big letters.
- Make use of all media possibilities: video, picture gallery, etc.

- Relay the content of your App Store page and add additional sections like Q&As, tips, user guides.

- As the purpose is to sell your game, make sure to have a Buy button easily visible that will link to the App Store page for your game.

Getting Your Game Reviewed on App Review WebSites

A strong purchase enabler is a referral. This is why it is critical for your game to gain reviews from prominent App review sites.

A good approach is to send a personalized message to them with a free download code of your game and the press release as an attachment.

Here are a few sites that I use:

- www.148apps.com

- www.slidetoplay.com

- www.appspy.com

- http://toucharcade.com

- www.metacritic.com/games/ios

Also, this page (http://maniacdev.com/2011/08/ios-app-review-sites/) lists 116 sites that review Apps.

Creating a Facebook Page

Although social networking is not limited to Facebook, let's face it: Facebook is a powerful tool.

With a Facebook account you can create Facebook pages. A Facebook page is an excellent vehicle for community communication. You can provide a description of your game using the description you prepared for the App Store. To create a Facebook page, go to www.facebook.com/FacebookPages (Figure 12-4).

Figure 12-4. *Facebook Pages page*

Click the Create a Page button at the top right corner of the page (you must be logged in to create a page). Select one of the following:

- Local Business or Place

- Company, Organization, or Institution

- Brand or Product

- Artist, Band, or Public Figure

- Entertainment

- Cause or Community

Games for iOS devices fall under "Brand or Product." Then, select the category called "App." Type the name of your game. Read the Facebook Pages terms (www.facebook.com/page_guidelines.php) and check the box to signify your acceptance of these terms. Last, click the "Get Started" button shown in Figure 12-5.

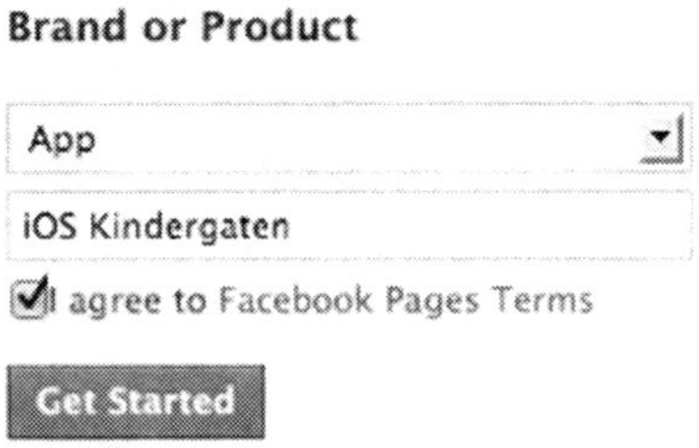

Brand or Product

App ▾

iOS Kindergaten

☑ I agree to Facebook Pages Terms

Get Started

Figure 12-5. *Creating a Facebook page for iOS Kindergarten*

You can provide a profile picture, as shown in Figure 12-6. Use the icon that you prepared for your App Store page.

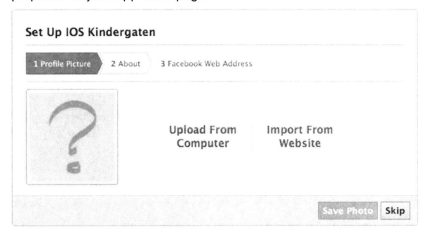

Figure 12-6. *Uploading the profile picture*

Next is the description of your game (Figure 12-7). Again, use the work you did for the App Store description.

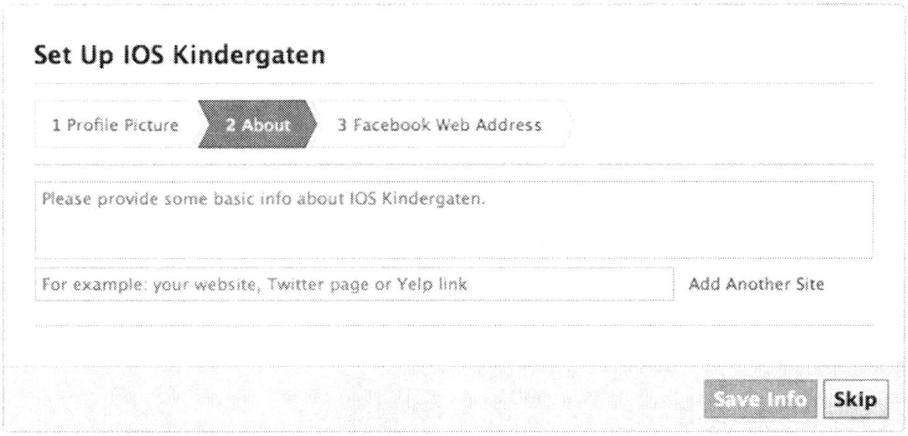

Figure 12-7. *Provide information about your game*

The last step in the page creation is to choose the web address of your page. If will be something like `http://www.facebook.com/yourpage`, as shown in Figure 12-8.

Figure 12-8. *Set up your web address*

Your page is created! You will automatically be directed to the admin area of your page, as shown in Figure 12-9.

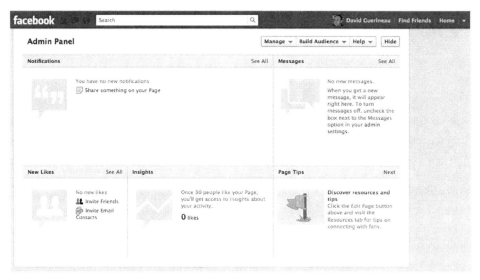

Figure 12-9. *Your Facebook page admin panel*

Use this page to create a community around your game and use it to communicate with the community. Once people "Like" the page, they will receive in their news feed any post on your page wall.

Summary

This ends the introduction to game promotion. It was a very basic approach to marketing concepts. If you wish to explore more about games marketing and promotion, I recommend *The Business of iPhone and iPad App Development* by Dave Wooldridge and Michael Schneider.

In this chapter you learned how to:

- Define your target customers.
- Research your competition.
- Draft your unique value definition.
- Write press releases and distribute them.
- Approach app review web sites.
- Create a Facebook page.

Index

CPSIA information can be obtained at www.ICGtesting.com
Printed in the USA
LVOW111915010712

288415LV00005B/5/P